Praise for *In Defence of History*

'History needs defending and, in Richard Evans, it has found a well-tempered contemporary champion. He writes clearly and calmly, treating fools with scholarly courtesy . . . [It] needs defending both against the complacent arrogance of many of the old school and the postmodernists to whom it is a tale told by idiots, signifying nothing but an academic job' Bernard Crick, *Independent*

'In this lucid, rumbustious book, Richard Evans responds to the postmodernist challenge . . . and amply satisfies the Horatian requirement that an author should give us pleasure and instruction combined' A.C. Grayling, *Financial Times*

'Richard Evans has entered the bull ring with *In Defence of History* . . . a defence of his craft at a time when there are serious doubts as to whether anything can be learnt from the past or whether it is possible to recapture any serious sense of past cultures. Evans performs a powerful demolition of the postmodern philosophical rejection of objectivity as epitomized by G.R. Elton and E.H. Carr' *History Today*

'Evans is a master of the one-line put down' Richard Gott, *New Statesman & Society*

'Richard Evans offers a spirited and elegant defence of the discipline . . . he deals with a wide range of issues germane to the practice of history in a manner that is blessedly free of jargon, making the book of interest to a wide readership' Steve Smith, *Times Higher Education Supplement*

'Richard Evans gave me much pleasure from the beginning, including the declared aim of the title. The book is also brilliantly readable – as all history should be' Antonia Fraser, *Guardian*

'He takes us on a fascinating journey during which we observe a top-class professional labouring to make sense out of the past . . . With this book Evans deserves to reach the widest possible audience. If you want to know what it is modern historians think they are doing, and how they go about it, you will find no finer guide' John Charmley, *Daily Telegraph*

'A robust and shrewd analysis of some of the games historians play' Linda Colley, *New Statesman & Society*

'Outstanding . . . magisterial' Boyd Tonkin, *Independent*

'A model of lucid and intelligent historiographical analysis' Stefan Collini, *Guardian*

'Essential reading for anyone interested in history or looking for a short, lucid introduction to current theoretical debate' James Eve, *The Times*

'Richard Evans's *In Defence of History* is a more subtle, more engaged, brilliantly barbed and often amusing case for historical truth' Kevin Sharpe, *Sunday Times*

'Excellent reporting on the news, the views and the hues and cries that postmodernism has occasioned' *Times Literary Supplement*

IN DEFENCE OF HISTORY

Richard J. Evans is Professor of Modern History at Cambridge University, and a Fellow of Gonville and Caius College, Cambridge. He has previously taught at the University of East Anglia, where he was Professor of European History from 1983 to 1989, and Birkbeck College, University of London, where he was Professor of History and Vice-Master and served as Acting Master in 1997. Among his many books are the landmark studies *Death in Hamburg*, which won the Wolfson Literary Award for History and the William H. Welch Medal of the American Association for the History of Medicine, and *Rituals of Retribution*, which was awarded the Fraenkel Prize in Contemporary History. His other books include *In Hitler's Shadow*, *Rereading German History* and the widely-acclaimed *Tales from the German Underworld*. His most recent publications are *The Coming of the Third Reich* and *The Third Reich in Power*. He is a Fellow of the British Academy and a frequent contributor to radio and television programmes, including *In Our Time*, *Start the Week* and *Nightwaves*.

Also by Richard J. Evans

IN
DEFENCE
OF
HISTORY

Richard J. Evans

Granta Books
London

Granta Publications, 2/3 Hanover Yard, London N1 8BE

First published in Great Britain by Granta Books 1997

A CIP catalogue record for this book is
available from the British Library.

The Random House Group Limited supports The Forest
Stewardship Council (FSC), the leading international forest
certification organisation. All our titles that are printed on
Greenpeace approved FSC certified paper carry the FSC logo.
Our paper procurement policy can be found at:
www.rbooks.co.uk/environment

11

ISBN 978 1 86207 395 1

Typeset by M Rules
Printed in Great Britain by CPI Bookmarque, Croydon, CR0 4TD

Mixed Sources
Product group from well-managed
forests and other controlled sources
www.fsc.org Cert no. TT-COC-002227
© 1996 Forest Stewardship Council
FSC

ACKNOWLEDGEMENTS

My first debt is to the students at Birkbeck with whom I have spent many fruitful evenings discussing historical knowledge, truth and objectivity, and to the colleagues in the History Department who encouraged me to turn my rough ideas on history and its current predicament into a book. During the many rewritings and reworkings of the text since then I have had the benefit of constructive criticism from many people, but I would especially like to thank David Cannadine for his wise criticisms and Neil Belton, at Granta Books, for his detailed and helpful comments. Ros Tatham helped me find out what happened at the Stalybridge Wakes. Christine Corton, as always, has provided support and encouragement. Becky Hardie and the production and design teams at Granta have done a superb job on the finished text. My thanks to all of them.

RICHARD J. EVANS
London, March 1997

For Christine, with love

CONTENTS

INTRODUCTION

I

This book is about how we study history, how we research and write about it, and how we read it. In the postmodern age, historians are being compelled to address these questions afresh. Of course, there have been many attempts to tackle them in the past. But whatever the intellectual climate, they need to be confronted by every new generation of historians in turn. Currently the field is held by two books published thirty or more years ago, by the British historians Edward Hallett Carr and Sir Geoffrey Elton. E. H. Carr's *What is History?* has been widely used as an introduction to historical study by teachers and students since its first publication in 1961, and it is easy to see why. Carr was a practising historian of vast experience, who had the ability to think clearly about difficult philosophical issues and to communicate his thought in a concise, witty and thoroughly readable manner. *What is History?* does not talk down to the student in the manner of conventional history primers or introductions to the study of history. It addresses the reader as an equal. Carr engages in lively arguments with many other historians about the nature of history. He challenges and undermines the belief, brought to university by too many students on leaving school, that history is simply a matter of objective fact. He introduces the idea that history books, like the people who write them, are products of their own times, and that their authors bring particular ideas and ideologies to bear on the past.

Against Carr's relativistic approach to historical study, it is a common tactic to pit G. R. Elton's *The Practice of History*, published in 1967. Elton's book mounts a trenchant defence of the belief that history is a search for the objective truth about the past. It concludes optimistically that historians' efforts in this enterprise more often than not meet with success. Elton, too, was a historian of enormous erudition, and in the course of dispensing a good deal of sensible advice on how history should be studied, written and taught, his book also had a lot to say about particular historians and the ways in which they either lived up to or (more commonly) fell short of the ideals he proclaimed. While Carr championed a sociological approach to the past, Elton declared that any serious historical work should have a backbone narrative of political events. Those which lacked such a spine, he dismissed as not really being proper history at all. And while Carr enjoined his readers to study the historian before they studied his 'facts', Elton told his audience to focus above all on the documentary record, the ultimate arbiter of historical accuracy and truth, and to leave historians and their motives to themselves.

While Elton and Carr are both still very much worth reading, there is, however, something rather strange about two books written more than thirty years ago still serving as basic introductions to a scholarly discipline.[1] Yet in many universities they undoubtedly still do.[2] Although some historians seem to think that Elton continues to represent 'conventional wisdom in the historical profession',[3] or (more pretentiously) the '*doxa* amongst professional academic historians',[4] in practice this has long ceased to be the case. Few historians would now defend the hard-line concept of historical objectivity espoused by Elton. The prevalence of historical controversy, endemic in the profession for decades, has long since disabused historians of the idea that the truth lies buried in the documents, and that once the historian has unearthed it, no one ever need perform the same operation again.

Nothing has outdated the views not only of Elton, but even of Carr, more obviously than the arrival in the 1980s of postmodernist theory, which has called into question most of the arguments put forward by both of them.[5] Instead of causes, which Carr regarded as central to historical scholarship, the 'linguistic turn' has given us discourses. And history is widely argued to be only one discourse among many. The notion of scientific history, based on the rigorous investigation of primary sources, has been vehemently attacked. Increasing numbers of writers on the subject deny that there is any such thing as historical truth or objectivity – both concepts defended, in different ways, by Carr as well as Elton. The question is now not so much 'What is History?', as 'Is It Possible to Do History at All?' In place of the optimistic belief in the progress of the discipline held by both Carr, who saw it in the expansion of historical scholarship, and Elton, who saw it in the accumulation of historical knowledge, historians at the end of the twentieth century are haunted by a sense of gloom. The intellectual historian David Harlan, writing in 1989, for example, thought that historical studies were undergoing 'an extended epistemological crisis'.[6] Writing in the mid-1990s, the American historians Joyce Appleby, Lynn Hunt and Margaret Jacob echoed this view: 'History has been shaken right down to its scientific and cultural foundations.'[7] The postmodernist view that language could not relate to anything except itself must, as another alarmed historian observed, 'entail the dissolution of history' and 'necessarily jeopardizes historical study as normally understood.'[8] The postmodernist challenge, warns the distinguished Princeton historian Lawrence Stone, has thrown the historical profession 'into a crisis of self-confidence about what it is doing and how it is doing it'.[9] 'Historians,' declares another writer on the subject, 'have suffered a major theoretical challenge to the validity of their subject.'[10] Some indeed see this challenge as more than merely theoretical: 'poststructuralism,' in one historian's opinion, even 'threatens to throw historians out of work' by robbing their discipline of its traditional legitimacy and *raison d'être*.[11] Such has been the power and influence of the postmodernist critique of history that growing numbers of historians themselves are abandoning the search for truth, the belief in objectivity, and the quest for a scientific approach to the past. No wonder so many historians are worried about the future of their discipline.

II

Yet this sense of crisis is far from universal. Many commentators have discerned a widespread sense of complacency among practising historians in the 1980s and 1990s. While the American intellectual historian Allan Megill indicted the historical profession in 1989 for what he called its 'sclerotic self-satisfaction'[12] in the face of the postmodernist challenge, the American medievalist Nancy F. Partner, writing in 1995, thought this same attitude was 'entirely commendable', adding:

> The theoretical destabilizing of history achieved by language-based modes of criticism has had no practical effect on academic practice because academics have had nothing to gain and everything to lose by dismantling their special visible code of evidence-grounded reasoning and opening themselves to the inevitable charges of fraud, dishonesty and shoddiness.[13]

The British historian James Vernon similarly complained in 1994 about his colleagues' 'general air of complacency' about postmodernism. 'While elsewhere,' he noted, 'historians are at least discussing the problems of writing social history in the 1990s, indeed the possibility of writing "history" at all in these postmodern times, the editorial of *Social History*'s fiftieth issue boldly declared that "social history is emphatically not in crisis."'[14] 'Far from the historian being beleaguered,' another British historian, Patrick Joyce, observed in 1991, 'the commanding heights of academy history seem secure against the skirmishing bands outside, though some notable walls have fallen, chiefly in the United States.' In Britain, Joyce's view is that 'rank indifference rather than outright hostility' is the 'dominant response'.[15] Much of 'the historical profession at large,' he has complained, has tended to 'fail to register the intellectual history of their own time, above all the now decades-long challenge to received ways of historical thinking represented by what may loosely be termed post-modernism.'[16] In 1995 he repeated his charge in an article published in *Past and Present*, a leading journal of social history. 'The journal *Past and*

Present,' he commented, somewhat ungratefully abusing the publication which was acting as a vehicle for his arguments, 'is a good example . . . of the poacher turned gamekeeper. The elders of social history remain in station still, supported by a younger generation of scholars largely immune to the intellectual history of our own times.'[17]

Of course, by 'the intellectual history of our own times', what Joyce really meant was his own ideas. The fact that they were being debated in the journal itself amounted to an implicit rebuttal of his complaint. Thanks not least to Joyce's interventions, the debate in Britain has become steadily more heated, and has been gathering pace in an increasing number of scholarly journals. Already by 1993, two American specialists in British history could describe postmodernism as 'a now all-pervasive academic discourse'.[18] In 1995, even the much-maligned editor of *Social History* was forced to admit that as a result of the emergence of postmodernism, the optimism with which he had founded the journal in the late 1970s was now 'in shreds'.[19] By the late 1990s, therefore, there can be little doubt that the debate over history, truth and objectivity unleashed by postmodernism has become too widespread for all but the most obscurantist to ignore. The critics' complaints of complacency and self-satisfaction in the historical profession are now little more than a rhetorical means of goading those whom they are criticizing into making a reply.

No less a traditionalist than Sir Geoffrey Elton himself charged into the lists not long before he died, to underline the growing sense among historians that their enterprise was under severe and unprecedented attack. Elton roundly denounced postmodernist ideas on history as 'menacing', 'destructive', 'absurd' and 'meaningless'. 'Total relativism', he declared, was 'the ultimate heresy', a 'virus' of 'frivolous nihilism' that was infecting a disturbing number of young historians, above all in the United States. 'In battling against people who would subject historical studies to the dictates of literary critics,' he pronounced, 'we historians are, in a way, fighting for our lives. Certainly, we are fighting for the lives of innocent young people beset by devilish tempters who claim to offer higher forms of thought and deeper truths and insights – the intellectual equivalent of crack.'[20] It is not only for conservatives like Elton that alarm bells have been set ringing. The left-liberal historian Lawrence Stone has called upon historians to arm themselves to repel the new intellectual barbarians at the disciplinary gates. If postmodernists gained any more influence, he warned, 'history might be on the way to becoming an endangered species.'[21] On the socialist left, the radical historian Raphael Samuel, progenitor of *History Workshop*, warned in one of his last publications that 'the deconstructive turn in contemporary thought' invited everyone to 'see history not as a record of the past, more or less faithful to the facts', but 'as an invention, or fiction, of historians themselves'.[22] He made it clear that this was something which he found completely unacceptable. Arthur Marwick, founding professor of history at Britain's Open University, voiced his fears that history students would find the postmodernists' 'presumptuous and ill-informed criticisms' of history 'disorienting', and might 'even be persuaded that the history of the historians is worthless'.[23] Postmodernist ideas, he declared, were a 'menace to serious historical study'.[24] Theories which 'suggest that historians are in the business of creating – not discovering or interpreting – historical meaning', added two historians from the University of Pennsylvania, 'undermine our authority, the mystique of our enterprise, the very purpose of our work.'[25]

Where so many historians are issuing such dire warnings couched in such colourful and alarmist language, something important is clearly going on. No one should doubt that the postmodernist challenge to historical study as conceived in different ways by Carr and Elton is a serious one. Some of the intellectual barbarians at the disciplinary gates are loitering there with distinctly hostile intent. 'Autumn,' declared the Dutch postmodernist Frank Ankersmit triumphantly in 1990, 'has come to Western historiography.'[26] Similarly, Keith Jenkins, author of two recent postmodernist critiques of history, announced approvingly in a reconsideration of Carr's work published in 1995: 'We have reached the end of modernist versions of what history is.'[27] Patrick Joyce has declared that 'contemporary history', meaning history as practised today, 'is itself in fact the offspring of modernity,' and therefore part of the intellectual world which postmodernity is now displacing.[28] As Geoff Eley and Keith Nield, two British historians who have tried to moderate the debate, have remarked of the two opposing sides: 'A theoretical *hauteur* instructs a redoubt of methodological conservatism, and the latter shouts defiantly back. Between the two lies a silence, a barrier that in these tones cannot be crossed.'[29]

Yet drawing up the disciplinary drawbridge has never been a good idea for historians. For centuries they have profited immeasurably from the invasions of neighbouring disciplines, starting with philology, the foundation of the methods of source-criticism associated with the name of the great German historian Leopold von Ranke in the nineteenth century, and moving on through economics, sociology, anthropology, statistics, geography, psychology and other alien forces as time has gone on. Lawrence Stone himself has in the past been one of the main advocates – and practitioners – of the opening-up of history to influences from the social sciences. Why not influences from literary criticism and linguistic analysis as well? Historians should approach the invading hordes of semioticians, post-structuralists, New Historicists, Foucauldians, Lacanians and the rest with more discrimination. Some of them might prove more friendly, or more useful, than they seem at first sight.

Moreover, the questions they raise – about the possibility or impossibility of attaining objective knowledge, the elusive and relative nature of truth, the difficulties involved in distinguishing between fact and fiction – do not merely challenge historians to re-examine the theory and practice of their own discipline, they also have wider implications that go far beyond the boundaries of academic and university life. In this sense, the problem of how historians approach the acquisition of knowledge about the past, and whether they can ever wholly succeed in this enterprise, symbolizes the much bigger problem of how far society can ever attain the kind of objective certainty about the great issues of our time that can serve as a reliable basis for taking vital decisions for our future in the twenty-first century.

III

In many ways it makes sense to approach such wider questions by looking at how we acquire knowledge about the past. Many of the problems involved in finding out about contemporary society and politics are very similar to those historians have to face. Yet the past presents more difficulties because it is no longer with us. Moreover, the theory and history of history have become an entirely separate branch of learning since Carr and Elton wrote. In the process this subject has developed its own concepts and its own jargon which have made it often rather impenetrable to outsiders. Some have indeed argued that the nature of historical explanation is a topic best left to the philosophers. How we know about the past, what historical causation is, how we define a historical fact, whether there is such a thing as historical truth or objectivity – these are questions that most historians have happily left to one side as unnecessary distractions from their essential work in the archives.[30] 'Many historians,' one observer has correctly noted, 'are by instinctive inclination hostile to philosophical and methodological criticism of their work, often wishing to rely instead on "common sense".'[31] Nor have the few historians who have actually ventured to write about their discipline necessarily earned the plaudits of their colleagues. 'Historians,' the Oxford specialist on French history Theodore Zeldin has observed, '. . . are probably no more reliable as guides to their own work than politicians are to their policies.'[32] Or, to use the analogy preferred by his former colleague Norman Stone: 'It is probably as much a mistake to ask a working historian to discuss this theme as to ask a painter to give his views on aesthetics.'[33]

Of course, very few historians in practice have possessed the necessary expertise to discuss the theory of history at a level that a trained philosopher would consider acceptable. On the other hand, the level of abstraction at which most studies of historical epistemology operate is so theoretical, so far removed from actual problems experienced by working historians, that the subject in general is of little practical relevance to what historians actually do.[34] One of the few twentieth-century scholars who was equally at home in the two fields of history and philosophy, R.G. Collingwood, was the author of both the *Oxford History of*

Roman Britain and a celebrated philosophical treatise on *The Idea of History*. But there is no indication at all that the two books stood in any relation to one another; they might have been written by two different people. Indeed, one philosopher of history has declared rather loftily that 'philosophers interest themselves in history for their own purposes: the instrumental value, or disvalue, of their investigations to history is wholly accidental.'[35] Thus we have what has often seemed to be a dialogue of the deaf.

Some historians have even disputed the right of non-historians to write about the nature of historical knowledge and explanation at all. It should come as no surprise that Sir Geoffrey Elton was among them. Drawing up the disciplinary drawbridge once again, he declared: 'There is no reason why great historians (or indeed lesser ones) should not have their manner of thinking and operating investigated, but such studies are pointless unless the investigator can demonstrate that he knows at first hand what working on the materials left to us by the past actually means.'[36] In other words, only historians are qualified to talk about history; a view echoed in only slightly less stentorian tones by others, such as Arthur Marwick. Even the great French historian Fernand Braudel once pronounced that history as a discipline 'cannot be understood without practising it.'[37] Yet Hayden White, the influential American writer on the theory of history, has made the obvious retort that the 'insistence that only historians know what historians really do is similar to modern scientists' objections to being studied by sociologists, ethnographers, philosophers and *historians*.'[38] Historians are therefore denying to other disciplines a right they claim for their own.

White is surely correct to insist that historians – teachers as well as students – have a lot to learn from what others outside the discipline tell them. Moreover, as Raymond Martin has put it: 'When it comes to understanding *the past*, historians are the acknowledged experts. But when it comes to understanding *how we understand the past*, there are no experts.'[39] The American apostle of quantitative history Robert Fogel declares somewhat gloomily in the light of all this, that historians have a choice: 'Either they ignore the philosophers and get on with what they are doing, but that might mean that they will continue to work without understanding how they are doing it. Or they down tools to listen to the philosophers, but this will most likely mean that tools will stay permanently downed.'[40] But this counsel of despair is belied by the numerous examples of practising historians who have managed to do both. Increasing numbers of scholars, provoked perhaps by the challenge of postmodernism, are finding it necessary to reflect on the nature of the project in which they are engaged. The more this happens, the better. As a group of three American historians announced in a recent book: 'It is time we historians took responsibility for explaining what we do, how we do it, and why it is worth doing.'[41]

To be sure, postmodernist critics of history and the historical profession have sometimes dismissed the views of practising historians as not worth listening to anyway (unless of course they simply accept without criticism the ideas the postmodernists themselves are propounding). 'Those who announce the advent of postmodernism,' as Perez Zagorin, an eminent American specialist on seventeenth-century England, has observed, frequently claim that it 'cannot be withstood.'[42] This is true. 'Times have moved on,' Patrick Joyce has declared, 'and historians simply have to learn to keep up with them.'[43] Keith Jenkins asserted roundly that 'Today we live within the general condition of *postmodernity*.

We do not have a choice about this. For postmodernity is not an "ideology" or a position we can choose to subscribe to or not; postmodernity is precisely our condition: it is our fate.'[44] Thus debating whether or not we should accept it is a futile exercise. But, *postmodernity* is only a word we use to describe something whose presence in the human condition some have diagnosed but others still dispute. Given the stress laid upon the shifting nature of concepts by postmodernists, and the emphasis given to the indirect, contingent or even arbitrary or non-existent correspondence of words to reality, the dogmatic and apodictic tone of Jenkins's declaration that postmodernity is an indisputable fact of life seems strangely out of place, coming as it does from a self-confessed proponent of such ideas.

Moreover, just because an intellectual trend seems irresistible is no reason for not resisting it. Lest this seem a legacy of my own education in Oxford, that proverbial home of lost causes, let me refer to a case of an intellectual trend that swept all before it slightly further afield. In the 1920s and 1930s, German historians overwhelmingly believed in the primacy of foreign policy in shaping a nation's history, and linked this to a political drive to provide historical arguments for revising the Treaty of Versailles and recovering the territories lost by their country at the end of the First World War. The German historical profession blocked the careers of those who thought otherwise, and except for a small handful of its members, collaborated willingly in the Nazi seizure of power and the Nazification of university education. Was this, however, any reason for not resisting it? And did this irresistible trend not damage the quality and reputation of German historical scholarship for a whole generation? It would of course be going too far to draw a parallel between postmodernism and fascist ideology. The real conclusion to be drawn from this example is surely that arguments and theories, however dominant in the intellectual life of their day, have to be assessed on their own merits, not accepted uncritically simply because they are espoused by a majority. In similar vein, some apologists for postmodernism have a tendency to proclaim that they have already won the argument and that there is no further point in historians trying to refute them.[45] But the fact is that historians' replies to at least some postmodernist critiques of history have caused some postmodernist theorists to shift their ground in crucial respects, just as historians themselves have been forced to shift their ground by these critiques. What we have, in other words, is no longer a dialogue of the deaf, but a genuine debate. Historians themselves have an important contribution to make to this discussion. The theory of history is too important a matter to be left to the theoreticians. Practising historians may not have a God-given monopoly of pronouncing sensibly on such matters, but they surely have as much right to try to think and write about them as anybody else; and the experience of actually doing historical research ought to mean that they have something to contribute which those who have not shared this experience cannot offer.

I

THE HISTORY OF HISTORY

I

However much they might have agreed on the need for accuracy and truthfulness, historians down the ages have held widely differing views on the purposes to which these things were to be put, and the way in which the facts they presented were to be explained. In medieval and early modern times, many historians saw their function as chronicling the working-out of God's purposes in the world. Things happened, ultimately, because God willed them to happen; human history was the playground of supernatural forces of Good and Evil. The rationalist historians of the Enlightenment substituted for this a mode of historical explanation which rested on human forces, but they still thought of their work as a species of moral illustration. In the greatest of the Enlightenment histories, for example, Edward Gibbon's *Decline and Fall of the Roman Empire*, the actors are moral qualities rather than human beings, and the ultimate lesson is that superstition, fanaticism and religious belief, all of which were of course anathema to Enlightenment rationalists, were dangerous forces that had brought down one great and benign empire and could well wreak further havoc in the future if they were not eradicated. History was 'philosophy teaching by example'; human nature was universal, unchanging and unhistorical.[1]

In the Romantic era, historians repudiated this kind of thinking. Under the influence of writers like Sir Walter Scott, they came to see the past as exciting because it was different. Under the influence of political theorists like Edmund Burke, they began to argue that it provided the only possible basis for the kind of political stability that had been so rudely shattered by the French Revolution of 1789. The purpose of history was seen not in providing examples for some abstract philosophical doctrine or principle, but simply in finding out about the past as something to cherish and preserve, as the only proper foundation for a true understanding and appreciation of the institutions of state and society in the present. The lead in this change of direction was provided by the German historian Leopold von Ranke, a scholar whose exceptionally long life and extraordinary productivity made him something of a legend. The author of over sixty works, including multi-volume histories of the Popes, of Germany in the time of the Reformation, and of the Latin and Germanic nations, he began a history of the world when he was eighty-three years of age and had completed seventeen volumes by the time of his death in 1886 at the age of ninety-one. He was converted to history by the shock of discovering that Scott's novel *Quentin Durward* was historically inaccurate. He determined therefore that he would apply the methods he had learned as a philologist to the study of historical texts in order to make such inaccuracy impossible in the future.

Ranke's contribution to historical scholarship was

threefold. First, he helped establish history as a separate discipline, independent from philosophy or literature. 'To history,' he wrote in the preface to one of his works, 'has been assigned the office of judging the past, of instructing the present for the benefit of future ages. To such high offices this work does not aspire: it wants only to show what actually happened.'[2] This last phrase is perhaps Ranke's most famous, and it has been widely misunderstood. The German phrase which Ranke used – '*Wie es eigentlich gewesen*' – is better translated as 'how it essentially was', for Ranke meant not that he just wanted to collect facts, but that he sought to understand the inner being of the past.[3]

In pursuit of this task, said Ranke, the historian had to recognize that 'every epoch is immediate to God.'[4] That is, God in His eternity made no distinction between periods of history; all were the same in His eyes. In other words, the past could not be judged by the standards of the present. It had to be seen in its own terms. This was the second major contribution which Ranke made to historical scholarship: the determination to strip away the veneer of posthumous condescension applied to the past by philosophizing historians such as Voltaire and to reveal it in its original colours; to try to understand the past as the people who lived in it understood it, even while deciphering hieroglyphs of interconnectedness of which they had been largely unaware. One conclusion that followed from this doctrine was that at any given time, including the present, whatever existed had to be accepted as divinely ordained. Ranke was a profoundly conservative figure, who equated the actual and the ideal and regarded the European states of his day as 'spiritual substances . . . thoughts of God'.[5] This distanced him from the Prussian school of German historians, from nationalists such as Treitschke, who condemned his impartiality and regretted his universalism. The fact that he regarded all states, not just Prussia, as supreme examples of God's purposes working themselves out on earth, gave him on the other hand a reputation for impartiality that greatly helped the spread of his influence abroad.[6]

Thirdly, and perhaps most importantly, Ranke introduced into the study of modern history the methods that had recently been developed by philologists in the study of ancient and medieval literature to determine whether a text, say of a Shakespeare play or of a medieval legend like the *Nibelungenlied*, was true or corrupted by later interpolations, whether it was written by the author it was supposed to be written by, and which of the available versions was the most reliable. Historians, argued Ranke, had to root out forgeries and falsifications from the record. They had to test documents on the basis of their internal consistency, and their consistency with other documents originating at the same period. They had to stick to 'primary sources', eyewitness reports and what Ranke called the 'purest, most immediate documents' which could be shown to have originated at the time under investigation, and avoid reliance on 'secondary sources' such as memoirs or histories generated after the event. Moreover, they had to investigate and subject to the critical method *all* the sources relating to the events in which they were interested. They should not be content, as for example Gibbon had been, to rely on printed documents and chronicles generally available in libraries. They had instead to sally forth, as Ranke did, into the archives, to work their way through the vast unpublished hoards of original manuscripts stored up by the state chancelleries of Europe. Only then, by gathering, criticizing and verifying all the available sources, could they put themselves in a position to reconstruct the past accurately.

The application of philological techniques to historical sources was a major breakthrough. Ranke's principles still form the basis for much historical research and teaching today. History Special Subjects in many British universities, for example, offer a basic training in source-criticism; students are examined on extracts or 'gobbets' from set documents and are expected to comment on them in terms of their internal consistency, their relationship to other documents on the same subject, their reliability and their usefulness as a source. Questions of authenticity and attribution continue to be vitally important in historical research. Forgeries, as the lamentable case of the 'Hitler Diaries' showed over a decade ago, are still regrettably common; outright falsification and doctoring of the evidence abound in printed collections of documents and other publications relating to subjects such as the origins of the First World War and the Third Reich. They are even more common in medieval history. Technological innovation has added substantially to the Rankean armoury; the 'Hitler Diaries' were easily exposed as forgeries by simple testing of the age of the paper on which they were written, which dated from the 1950s; perhaps Hugh Trevor-Roper (Lord Dacre), who originally 'authenticated' them for the London *Times* newspaper, should not have rested content with the fact that the name 'Adolf Hitler' was signed at the bottom of every page.[7] Whatever the means they use, historians still have to engage in the basic Rankean spadework of investigating the provenance of documents, of enquiring about the motives of those who wrote them, the circumstances in which they were written, and the ways in which they relate to other documents on the same subject. The perils which await them should they fail to do this are only too obvious.

All these things have belonged to the basic training of historians since the nineteenth century, and rightly so. However many forgeries and falsifications there have been, they seldom escape undetected for long. Sceptics who point to the fact that all sources are 'biased', and conclude from this that historians are bound to be misled by them, are as wide of the mark as politicians who imagine that future historians will take their memoirs on trust. Nor is there anything unusual in the fact that a modern discipline places such heavy reliance on principles developed over a century and a half before: chemistry, for example, still uses the periodic table of elements, while medical research continues to employ the mid-nineteenth-century device of 'Koch's postulates' to prove that a micro-organism is the carrier of a particular disease. These analogies with scientific method point up the fact that when source-criticism was introduced into historical study, it too was regarded as a 'scientific' technique. Its use legitimated history as an independent profession, and those historians in other countries who wanted to establish themselves on a professional basis soon began to flock to Germany to undergo training at the feet of its leading exponents in Göttingen and Berlin.

In the course of this Rankean revolution, the university-based historical seminar in which members of the profession were trained, wrote the American historian Herbert Baxter Adams, had 'evolved from a nursery of dogma into a laboratory of scientific truth.'[8] The French historian Fustel de Coulanges, of Strasbourg University, declared in 1862: 'History is, and should be, a science.'[9] The understanding of science which these claims implied was rigorously inductive. Out there, in the documents, lay the facts, waiting to be discovered by historians, just as the stars shone out there in the heavens, waiting to be discovered by astronomers; all the historian had to do was apply the proper scientific method, eliminate his own personality from the investigation, and the facts would come to light. The object of research was thus to 'fill in the gaps' in knowledge – a rationale that is still given as the basis for the vast majority of PhD theses in history today. As the most widely-used primer in historical method at the time, by the French historians Langlois and Seignobos, remarked, 'When all the documents are known, and have gone through the operations which fit them for use, the work of critical scholarship will be finished. In the case of some ancient periods, for which documents are rare, we can now see that in a generation or two it will be time to stop.' Similar beliefs were indeed common in the natural sciences: when the German physicist Max Planck took up his studies in the 1870s, for example, he was warned by his professor that it would be a waste of time, since there was nothing left to discover in the field.[10]

But these views rested on a series of misapprehensions. The belief that all the evidence left to posterity by the past *could* actually be surveyed and evaluated was already beginning to look less plausible even before the end of the nineteenth century, as new techniques and discoveries in archaeology began to open up whole new areas of knowledge even about the most distant periods in time. From early on in the twentieth century, too, historians began to look away from the narrow confines of the history and antecedents of the nation-state towards economic history, social history, cultural history and, subsequently, other new branches of historical enquiry as well. New questions, it seemed, could render previously neglected areas of evidence freshly meaningful. And as the passing of time continued to consign new ages to history, historians also began to recognize the almost exponential growth that was taking place in the quantity of source material available to them. Late-nineteenth-century American and European society was not only vastly more populous than before, it not only produced many more doc-uments, reflecting both the increase of literacy and the rapidly increasing functions of the state, it also generated new kinds of sources, from mass newspapers to photographs and films. 'The history of the Victorian age will never be written,' declared Lytton Strachey in a fit of ironic despair: 'we know too much about it.'[11]

Not only the idea of the final discovery of all the facts that could be known, but also the notion of a truly scientific history, began to seem more than a little shaky by the turn of the century too. Many of the advocates of a scientific approach to history failed to practise what they preached. A. F. Pollard, founder of the Institute of Historical Research at London University, established to introduce professional scientific training for history postgraduates, made little use of manuscript sources in his own work on Tudor history, preferring instead to use the transcripts and summaries provided in the *Calendars of State Papers*, which of course were shot through with inevitable mistakes and *lacunae*, seri-ously reducing the reliability of his writings.[12] Even the great Ranke was open to criticism according to the criteria which he himself did so much to establish. His writing, far from being 'colourless', as some thought, was suffused with metaphor.[13] His belief that he was writing objective history derived to a great extent from the fact that he based a great deal of his work on the dispatches of Venetian ambassadors to various European states, documents which themselves gave a deliberate impression of neutrality and value-free reporting. As the British historian John Pemble has pointed out, 'To the next generation Ranke was not Rankean enough.' His Venetian sources were partial, selective and narrow, and he made too little use of other archival material; only in this way, indeed, was he able to write so much. 'Flaubert once commented,' as Pemble remarks, 'that writing history was like drinking an ocean and pissing a cupful. Ranke it seemed was doing the opposite.'[14]

The realization that the founders of scientific history had all too often failed to follow their own precepts did not stop historians before the First World War from proclaiming the virtues of the scientific approach: on the contrary, it merely spurred them to greater efforts. In 1903, in a famous inaugural lecture as Regius Professor of Modern History in Cambridge, J.B. Bury declared: 'History is a science, no less and no more . . . History is not a branch of literature. The facts of history, like the facts of geology or astronomy, can supply material for literary art . . . but to clothe the story of human society in a literary dress is no more the part of a historian as a historian, than it is the part of an astronomer to present in an artistic shape the story of the stars.' Bury pointed up the contrast between history as literature and history as science by referring to the example of the man he called the 'greatest living historian', the German, Theodor Mommsen. Mommsen's stature as a historian lay, Bury declared, not in his authorship of a widely-read Roman history, which merely gave him a reputation as a 'man of letters' (indeed, it won him the Nobel Prize for literature), but in his detailed critical compilation of Roman inscriptions and his specialized studies on Roman law. Here was the realm in which he had applied the scientific method; here was his true claim, therefore, to greatness as a historian. It was this example, Bury implied, that others should follow.[15]

II

One member of the audience at that lecture in Cambridge in 1903 was the twenty-six-year-old George Macaulay Trevelyan, who was to be appointed to the Regius Chair when Bury died in 1927. Trevelyan took the lecture as a deliberate personal insult to his great-uncle, the Whig historian Lord Macaulay, whose *History of England* had been one of the greatest literary sensations of the early Victorian era. He rushed into print with an uncharacteristically savage denunciation, in his essay 'Clio: A Muse' – referring in this title to the muse of history in Ancient Greek mythology.[16] The 'crusade' which Bury and others were waging against the 'artistic and emotional treatment of the whole past of mankind', said Trevelyan, had become so successful that it now threatened 'the complete annihilation of the few remaining individuals' who still thought history was an art. If history was merely a 'chronicle of bare facts arranged on scientific principles', then 'literature, emotion and speculative thought' would be 'banished' from the human race's contemplation of its own past.[17] In his long career, Trevelyan did much to bridge the gap between the historian and the public in such widely popular works as his *English Social History*. Contrary to what many of his detractors have alleged, he was thoroughly professional both in his university career and in his research, which he based, especially in the case of his *magnum opus*, a magnificent three-volume history of *England under Queen Anne*, on scholarship that was as rigorous as it was extensive.[18] But although he paid due regard to the 'scientific' aspects of his subject, he thought that 'the idea that the facts of history are of value as part of an exact science confined to specialists is due to a misapplication of the analogy of physical science.' The natural sciences, he thought, were valuable in terms of practical utility and in the deduction of laws of cause and effect, whether or not the general public understood them. But history had no practical value unless it was widely disseminated, and nobody had ever succeeded in deriving general laws of cause and effect from history in such a way that they stood the essential test of such laws in the physical sciences, namely by enabling people to predict the future. Trevelyan conceded that 'the collection of facts, the weighing of evidence as to what events happened, are in some sense scientific; but not so the discovery of the causes and effects of these events.'

In reaching this judgment, he was echoing the original principles of Ranke, who had distinguished in his day between the rigorous principles of source-criticism needed for an accurate representation of events in the past, and the intuitive method needed to establish the 'interconnectedness' of these events and penetrate to the 'essence' of an epoch. It was this latter operation, which Ranke conceived of in Romantic and religious terms, and Trevelyan in literary and aesthetic terms, that made the difference, in the view of both of them, between the chronicler and the historian. History, said Trevelyan, was a mixture of the scientific (research), the imaginative or speculative (interpretation) and the literary (presentation). What the historian required was not 'more knowledge of facts', which in any case would always be incomplete. Nobody was ever going to unravel scientifically the mental processes of twenty million Frenchmen during the Revolution of 1789. Nor could interpretations of this event be arrived at by a mere process of induction. The causes and effects of the Revolution could never be known scientifically like the causes and effects of some chemical reaction, nor could they be grounded in discoverable laws like the law of gravity or the second law of thermodynamics. The historian who would give the best interpretation of the Revolution was the one who, 'having discovered and weighed all the important evidence available, has the largest grasp of intellect, the warmest human sympathy, the highest imaginative power.'

Trevelyan was essentially a *nationalist* historian; his major works were histories of England, and his objection to the 'scientific' conception of history was based not least on the fact that it was German. 'Who is the mother country to Anglo-Saxon historians?' he asked in his essay. 'Some reply "Germany", but others of us prefer to answer "England". The methods and limitations of German learning presumably suit the Germans, but are certain to prove a strait waistcoat to English limbs and faculties. We ought,' he declared, 'to look to the free, popular, literary traditions of history in our own land.' And he lamented the fact that 'the historians of to-day were trained by the Germanizing hierarchy to regard history not as . . . a "story", but as a "science".' The Germanizing tendencies of the period, he thought, were authoritarian and hierarchical, and unsuited to the liberal intellectual traditions of his own country.[19]

Just as Trevelyan looked to English traditions and circumstances as the source of historical inspiration, so in other European countries, too, historians rejected the universalizing tendencies of both Enlightenment writers such as Voltaire and Gibbon and Romantics such as Ranke. Popular, nationalist history had reached its apogee in Britain with Macaulay, in France with Michelet, in Germany with Treitschke; and it was not without its influence even on the most 'scientific' of scholars in the late nineteenth century. Virtually all historians, for example, assumed that the nation-state was the primary object of historical study. The emerging historical profession was dominated by the view that the historian's task lay principally in the study of the origins and development of states and in their relations with one another. Even the most narrow and rigorous of learned articles were usually written within this framework; while huge resources of scientific scholarship were lavished on the publication of vast documentary collections designed to provide the basic materials for national histories, such as the *Monumenta Germaniae Historica* or the *Calendars of State Papers*.

The Prussian school of historians, led by figures such as Droysen, were happy to proclaim that 'the German nation has outstripped all others' in its application of the critical method to historical sources; but they were just as critical as Trevelyan was of the notion that this was sufficient to constitute history in itself. 'History,' stated Droysen, 'is the only science enjoying the ambiguous fortune of being required to be at the same time an art.' He complained that because the German middle classes had for so long regarded 'the German method in history [as] pedantic, exclusive, unenjoyable', they all read Macaulay instead, or turned to the great French historian and statesman Thiers, so that 'German historical judgment' and even 'German political judgment' was 'formed and guided . . . by the rhetorical superiority of other nations.' The German middle classes did indeed look to the examples of English liberalism and the principles of the French Revolution for much of the nineteenth century. The Prussian school of historians set themselves the task of demonstrating through a mixture of scientific method, historical intuition and literary skill the superiority of Prussian values and their inevitable triumph in the unification of Germany in 1871. They could claim at least some credit for the drift of middle-class opinion in Germany from a liberal to a more authoritarian form of nationalism in the three decades leading up to the First World War.[20]

Already before 1914, therefore, the ability of the scientific method to deliver a neutral and value-free history was under some doubt. Its credibility was even more severely shaken by the events of 1914–18 and their aftermath. Professional historians in every country rushed into print with elaborate defences of the war aims of their own governments and denunciations of other great powers for having begun the conflict. Substantial collections of documents on the origins of the war were produced with all the usual scholarly paraphernalia and edited by reputable professionals, but on principles of selection that seemed manifestly biased to colleagues in other countries. The rigorous scientific training which they had undergone seemed to have had no effect at all in inculcating a properly neutral and 'objective' attitude to the recent past; a view that was underlined as the 1920s progressed by the continuing violent controversies between learned historians of different nations about the origins of the war.[21] Moreover, among British, French and American historians, the support for the war of the overwhelming majority of the 'scientific' German colleagues whose work they so admired came as a further blow.[22] Many historians who had studied in Germany now rushed to denounce German scholarship as pedantic and anti-democratic. 'The age of German footnotes,' as one of them said in 1915, 'is on the wane.'[23] And for G. M. Trevelyan, the defeat of the Germans also represented the defeat of 'German "scientific history"', a mirage which had 'led the nation that looked to it for political prophesy and guidance' about as far astray as it was possible to go.[24]

The war also revealed previous, apparently neutral

scholarly histories of, for example, Germany, or nineteenth-century Europe, to have been deeply flawed in their interpretations. Events such as the Russian Revolution, the Treaty of Versailles, the triumph of modernism in art, music and literature, increased this sense of disorientation among historians. Reflective historians of the older generation realized that their faith in objectivity had accompanied their sense of living in an ordered and predictable world. One senior American historian, Clarence Alvord, confessed after the war that he had always 'conformed to the canons of my science . . . walked along the straight and narrow road of approved scholarship . . . learned to babble the words of von Ranke . . . prided [myself] on telling the story *wie es eigentlich gewesen* . . .' This had all been very fine, he said, while the world was a safe place to live in and people had been able to believe in ordered, rational and inevitable progress. But now, he said, 'all the spawn of hell roamed at will over the world and made of it a shambles . . . The pretty edifice of . . . history which had been designed and built by my contemporaries was rent asunder . . . The meaning we historians had read into events was false, cruelly false.' If unpredictable and uncontrollable forces were shaping the present, it seemed, then the previous belief of historians that they could understand by a simple process of induction the forces that shaped the past now seemed dangerously naïve.[25]

Some historians even despaired of finding any pattern or meaning in the past at all. As the English liberal historian H. A. L. Fisher remarked in the preface to his widely-read *History of Europe*, published in 1934:

Men wiser and more learned than I have discerned in history a plot, a rhythm, a predetermined pattern. These harmonies are concealed from me. I can see only one emergency following upon another as wave follows upon wave, only one great fact with respect to which, since it is unique, there can be no generalizations, only one safe rule for the historian: that he should recognize in the development of human destinies the play of the contingent and the unforseen. . . . The ground gained by one generation may be lost by the next.[26]

History, in this bewildered view, was just 'one damned thing after another', devoid of meaning, and beyond interpretation.

Such views were reinforced at a more theoretical level by the changing nature of the natural sciences in this period. Einstein's General Theory of Relativity (1913), widely popularized after it was confirmed by astronomical observation in 1919, helped create an intellectual climate in which it was thought that the 'aspect of things' changed with the position of the observer. The idea of the relativity of observer and fact was applied to history by a number of inter-war philosophers as well, in particular by the liberal Italian thinker Benedetto Croce and his English counterpart R. G. Collingwood. In doing so, they were echoing pre-war German philosophers such as Wilhelm Dilthey, who had begun to take a sceptical view of the possibility of objective knowledge about the past. And they paralleled the much more far-reaching doubts of cultural pessimists in Germany under the Weimar Republic, for whom Germany's defeat in the First World War had rendered history largely meaningless. Croce argued that historians were guided in their judgment as to what documents and events were important in the past, and what were unimportant, by their present concerns. All history was thus written, consciously or unconsciously, from the perspective of the present. 'All history,' in Croce's famous phrase, 'is con-temporary history.'[27] Collingwood went even further by arguing that 'all history is the history of thought,' because the documents left to the historian by the past were meaningless unless the historian reconstituted the thought that they expressed. 'History,' Collingwood concluded, 'is the re-enactment in the historian's mind of the thought whose history he is studying.'[28]

Leaving aside for the moment the merits and defects of such arguments, what all this did in broad terms was to blur the distinction commonly made by pre-war historians, even those of a literary bent such as G. M. Trevelyan, between fact and interpretation. It was not a case, in their view, of the historian observing, collecting and verifying the facts and then 'interpreting' them. The very act of observing and col-lecting them was itself governed by the historian's *a priori* beliefs about the past. Such views gained currency not least because, as E. H. Carr wrote, 'after the First World War, the facts seemed to smile on us less propitiously than in the years before 1914, and we were therefore more accessible to a philosophy which sought to diminish their prestige.'[29] The crisis-ridden decades of the 1920s, 1930s and 1940s, with their economic privations, international conflicts, revolu-tionary upheavals, and perhaps above all their revelations, in Italy, Spain, Russia and Germany, of violence and inhuman-ity on a scale, and to a degree, previously thought barely possible, severely undermined the belief in progress that had sustained the historians of the pre-war era. The new scientific discoveries and concepts destroyed the belief that history-writing would one day come to an end when everything had been discovered. If 'discovery' depended not least on the intentions and assumptions of historians influenced by the context of their own age, then it became clear that every fresh age would have to research and write the history of all past ages from scratch, all over again.

III

All these developments reflected the fact that the chaotic and disturbed inter-war period was not, on the whole, a great age of historical scholarship. Economic dislocation in Europe and America meant that historians' income declined, relatively few new historians were trained, and in the many European countries – the majority, in fact – which fell victim to dictatorships, free historical enquiry ceased. It was only after the Second World War, as economic recovery began, and the mass armies of the 1930s and 1940s were finally demobilized, that a new generation of historians entered the profession. They were immediately confronted with the task of overcoming the scepticism and disorientation of their predecessors in the inter-war years. Many historians tried to reassert what they regarded as the traditional values of historical scholarship which they thought had been perverted by the political and intellectual pressures and upheavals of the previous few decades. Their mentor and example in England was the Polish-born historian Sir Lewis Namier, whose scholarship was famously painstaking and exact. As one of his pupils noted, he thought that 'If history was not to be a catalogue of suppositions . . . it had to be solidly based on minute facts.' Namier thought that Freud rather than Ranke had established the scientific principles on which the study of the past could be more solidly based than before, and to this extent he was prepared to update the notion of 'scientific' history. But the consequences he drew from this belief were far removed from those of the speculative American psychohistorians of later decades. Namier always eschewed speculation, so he never thought that he could find out enough about an individual in the past to subject his character to psychoanalysis. However, he did think, as a result of his Freudian views, that what drove people to do the things they did were essentially personal motives and forces rather than ideologies or beliefs.

Namier used this approach, combined with formidably thorough and exhaustive research, to devastating effect in his most famous book, *The Structure of Politics at the Accession of George III*. The book was launched as a frontal assault on the 'Whig interpretation' of British history, which saw eighteenth-century politics in terms of a struggle between the forces of liberty and constitutionalism, led by the Whigs, and absolutism and royal power, represented by the Tories. In the Whig view, the latter cause was eventually taken up by George III and his pet minister Lord Bute. The new King's tendencies towards absolutism lost England the American colonies under the Premiership of Lord North. Namier looked beyond these ideologies to the personal relationships of the politicians involved. Investigating them minutely, he suggested that 'party' was irrelevant, ideology unimportant; what mattered was the struggle of individuals through patronage and kinship networks for power, money and influence. Seen from this perspective, what led to the political crisis was the disruption to these networks caused by the accession of a new King, not any particular beliefs which he might have held, or political principles with which he might have clashed. In this way, Namier's rapier-like scholarship deflated and destroyed the Whig interpretation of British history by puncturing it at its most vulnerable point.

There was no doubting that this was a major and significant scholarly achievement. When I was an undergraduate in the 1960s, Namier's *Structure of Politics* was considered by history tutors to have been the greatest work ever penned about English history, and Namier was a god. 'Namier,' one historian said, 'perhaps, has found the ultimate way of doing history.' 'If Namier had his way,' another remarked, 'all controversies would cease, and we would know as much historical truth as is humanly possible.' 'Fifty years from now,' one of his disciples declared at the beginning of the 1960s, '*all* history will be done as Sir Lewis does it.' Namier, as even E. H. Carr admitted, was 'the greatest British historian to emerge on the academic scene since the First World War.'[30] Seen from the perspective of the 1990s, however, these claims appear ludicrously inflated.[31] Typically, what British empiricists admired in Namier was the thoroughness of his scholarship; they more or less ignored his Freudianism as an embarrassing but excusable continental heresy. Many historians since Namier have matched his painstakingly high standards of archival scholarship. They have long since re-established the centrality of party labels and party ideology to the politics of the majority of the eighteenth century and made the 1760s, Namier's chosen decade, seem rather exceptional by comparison. Nobody nowadays would maintain that George III's constitutional practice was the same as that of his predecessors, and assiduous historians have made the inevitable discovery that Namier, in his anxiety to exculpate the King, was highly selective in his use of evidence and not above 'pruning' his quotations from the sources to serve his argument.[32] The belief that Namier had found a new method of writing history was misplaced. Already in the 1950s, there were those who complained that he had 'taken the mind out of history' in his reduction of political action to the operation of individual self-interest.[33] In the hands of his pupils and emulators, and indeed eventually in his own, his method degenerated into mindless prosopography, ending up with a series of narrow and arid studies of eighteenth-century cabinets, and producing that great white elephant of twentieth-century British historical scholarship, the huge (and hugely expensive) multi-volume *History of Parliament*, a compilation which amounts in the end to little more than a minutely researched biographical dictionary of MPs through the ages; flattering to MPs, which is no doubt why they subsidize it, but of little influence in advancing historical understanding in a larger sense.[34]

Like H. A. L. Fisher, Namier saw no pattern in history, and distrusted ideas and ideologies, an approach which was reassuring to the pragmatism of British intellectuals. He despised and distrusted the masses whose emergence on to the social and political scene in the wake of the post-war Labour government was so threatening to conservative university dons. Insofar as he raised the standards of English historical scholarship with his meticulous, indeed obsessive pursuit of unpublished manuscript materials, he undoubtedly performed a useful service. But English historians were excessively intimidated by this, and thought that Namier had replaced Whig myth with true objectivity. He had not. Namier's work did not attract much attention when it first appeared in 1927. He really came into his own after the war. His views held sway among British historians in the 1950s and 1960s not least because they were well suited to the atmosphere of the Cold War, in which the Communist advocacy of the interests of the masses, belief in the 'laws' of history and progress, and enthronement of ideology and belief at the centre of the historical process and historical interpretation, were thought of by liberals and conservatives as principles to be combatted in the interests of the freedom of the individual.[35] Soviet historians, it was believed, had betrayed the ideals of factual accuracy, neutrality and detachment in the same way as Nazi historians had. History had become a means of indoctrination, pressed into the service of the state, and of the spread of Communism. Western history, on the contrary, was now held to represent the virtues of accuracy, objectivity and truthfulness.

The Cold War reassertion of objectivity which underpinned Namier's overwhelming influence in Britain in the 1950s and early 1960s also took place in the philosophy of science, where Sir Karl Popper, a philosopher of Viennese origin who dedicated much of his life to disputing the claims of Marxism to be a scientific doctrine, reasserted the objective nature of scientific knowledge in two highly influential works, *The Poverty of Historicism* and *The Open Society and Its Enemies*. Popper argued that objective knowledge could best be approached through propositions for which one could specify the conditions under which they might be falsified. Theories − such as Marxism − which accounted for everything, and which could be adapted to any circumstances, were merely metaphysical; only theories which did not claim to explain everything, and yet which resisted attempts to prove them false, were truly scientific. Popper excoriated the Marxist view that history had a discernible direction, and was subject to laws; objective knowledge of history, he said, could only be obtained in respect of short- or medium-term developments, where it was clear what evidence was needed to falsify the interpretations put forward. No historical evidence could 'disprove' the idea that history was moving through stages towards the goal of a communist society, because every conceivable kind of evidence could be adapted to fit the theory if so desired. On the other hand, the idea that (for example) the First World War was caused by German aggression *could* be falsified (in theory at least), because it was possible to specify the kind of evidence that would be needed to prove or disprove it.[36]

IV

This reassertion of historical objectivity came at a time in the 1950s and 1960s when the historical profession was re-establishing itself, undergoing slow but steady growth, and recapturing the social and financial position it had enjoyed in the late nineteenth century. Not only Britain and the USA, but other countries too experienced similar developments. In West Germany, the growing prosperity brought about by the post-war 'economic miracle' allowed historians, like other university professors, to regain much of the power and status they had had before the upheavals of Weimar and the anti-intellectual assaults of Nazism. A determination to distance themselves from the outrageous lies and distortions of Nazi historiography gave them a belief in the value of an 'objective' approach to history that has never entirely deserted them since. The German historians of the post-1968 generation, the first to have reached professional maturity in the post-war era, eagerly imported the theories and methods of American and above all neo-Weberian sociology into their work, in an attempt to escape from the perils of subjectivity which had engulfed the old tradition of liberal-nationalist historiography in their country in the 1930s and 1940s. So pervasive was the influence of the social sciences on German historiography that there were proposals to dissolve history as a separate subject in the secondary school curriculum and incorporate it into social studies, citizenship education, political science and the like; while university undergraduates were now taught, as indeed they still are in Germany, to present their work not in the traditional form of literary essays but after the manner of social-scientific research reports instead. The rhetorical style of the social sciences still pervades the work of professional historians in Germany too, with a passive, anonymous written style dominant, all reference to the author as an individual eliminated, and the word 'I' banished even from the preface and acknowledgements of the typical German research monograph or work of historical synthesis. The cult of the individual under Nazism provoked a similar negative reaction among German historians. They avoided biography and concentrated on writing the history of people in the past mainly as a history of averages, groups and global trends. [37]

The same decade saw the invasion of the social sciences into history in Britain as well, launched by a famous issue of the *Times Literary Supplement* in 1966, in which a series of young historians heralded the transformation of their discipline by imported theories and methods from anthropology, social theory, and statistics. Beginning with E. H. Carr himself, historians queued up to urge history and the social sciences to move closer together. [38] Writing in 1976, Lawrence Stone claimed that the influence of the social sciences was refining the historian's conceptual apparatus and research strategies, while rigorous quantification was destroying many cherished historical myths. The social sciences were posing new questions for the historian to answer, new hypotheses to test, and transforming the discipline beyond recognition as a result. [39] In France, too, a 'scientific' and 'objective' approach to the past gained in prestige and influence in the post-war years. It was exemplified above all in the group of historians associated with the journal *Annales*, who had begun their work before the war but only really gained significant influence after it. By incorporating the methods of economics, sociology and especially geography and statistics into their approach to the past, the *Annales* historians thought that it would be possible to make history far more objective and scientific than ever before. The traditional methods and objects of enquiry no longer sufficed. History should be the central, synthesizing discipline of the social sciences. It had to quantify. 'History that is not quantifiable,' remarked Emmanuel Le Roy Ladurie, one of the school's leading exponents, in 1979, 'cannot claim to be scientific.' 'Tomorrow's historian,' he added, 'will have to be able to programme a computer in order to survive.'[40]

These beliefs reached their most extreme form, perhaps, in the United States in the late 1960s and 1970s, with the rise of 'social science history'. One of its principal exponents, the econometric historian Robert Fogel, drew a sharp distinction between 'scientific' and 'traditional' history.[41] Scientific history, made possible above all by the computer, rested not on vague, incomplete, implicit and inconsistent sets of assumptions about human behaviour in the way that traditional history did, but on explicitly elaborated, sometimes mathematical models that could be rigorously tested by quantitative means. It applied not to individuals but to groups, and sought to develop not particular explanations but general hypotheses which could be statistically tested. It assumed that there were systematic relationships between events, structures and processes in history. It was neutral and non-ideological. It tended to be carried out by teams of scholars, just as experimental programmes in the natural sciences did, rather than by the individual scholars who were the norm for the researcher in traditional history. And it addressed itself not to a wider public but to a specialist readership of fellow-scientists, just as the natural sciences did.

Scientific methods used in this way, argued Fogel, were overturning the received wisdom of traditional history on many points and thus proving their superiority. Peter Laslett and the Cambridge Group of demographic historians, for instance, had demonstrated the statistical prevalence of the nuclear family in pre-industrial society and established a relatively high age at marriage, confounding traditional historians' belief in the dominance of extended family forms and the normality of marriage at a very early age. Similar, major advances in knowledge had come in many branches of economic history through the application of scientific, statistical methods.[42] Convinced that not only demographic and economic history, but also social and political history, indeed all forms of history, had to be put on to this new scientific basis, the 'cliometricians' of the 1970s unrolled a vastly ambitious programme of disciplinary transformation which was intended to spell the end of traditional history altogether.[43] There was a widespread feeling in the 1970s that 'traditional' history had proved vulnerable to the criticisms of relativists like Carr because it had not been scientific enough. By the end of the decade, there was a general consensus among observers of the historical profession that, as Georg G. Iggers put it, historical scholarship over the decades had become 'scientifically ever more rigorous', and 'historians have become more committed than ever to the scientific ideal of history.'[44]

But were the differences between 'scientific' and 'traditional' history in fact so very great? Not surprisingly, Sir Geoffrey Elton did not think so. He pointed to the fact that what he had described as 'traditional' history was itself widely regarded by its defenders as 'scientific' well into the second half of the twentieth century. Teamwork was common in some areas in 'traditional' history too, from the editing of documents to the compilation of prosopographies. Cliometrics had delivered only on a very limited number of generally rather narrow questions. When it came to the really big issues in history, it had to remain silent, because they could not be solved by quantitative methods.[45] A glance at *Social Science History*, the flagship journal of the cliometricians, will easily support Elton's claim. Moreover, it quickly became clear that the ability of Fogel's scientific methods to settle beyond dispute even the questions they did address was highly questionable. In 1974, Fogel and his collaborator Stanley L. Engerman published a formidable two-volume study of slavery in the old American South. Full of elaborate statistical charts, tables and equations, it claimed to represent a new level of scientific rigour in testing well-worn hypotheses. The result was a set of conclusions which overturned existing, 'traditional' historical orthodoxy. Slavery was not, as had previously been thought, unprofitable, economically inefficient, and bad for the slaves. Fogel and Engerman argued that the economic efficiency of slavery was so high that slaves benefited from standards of living at least as high as those of free workers at the time. In defending themselves against accusations of political incorrectness for espousing such a view, the two authors suggested that this showed how proud the slaves could be of their achievements, and how dubious, even racist, were claims that their labour had been unproductive.[46]

Fogel and Engerman were immediately attacked by their fellow-historians for flawed statistical procedures, misuse and over-interpretation of sources, vague hypotheses, and plain inaccuracy. One group of critics concluded, at the end of a lengthy re-examination of the data:

> *Time on the Cross* is full of errors. The book embraces errors
> of mathematics, disregards standard principles of statistical
> inference, mis-cites sources, takes quotations out of con-
> text, distorts the views and findings of other historians and
> economists, and relies upon dubious and largely unex-
> plained models of market behavior, economic dynamics,
> socialization, sexual behavior, fertility determination, and
> genetics (to name some).

Moreover, all the errors apparently had a 'consistent tendency' to work in favour of Fogel and Engerman's overall
argument. When the faults were corrected and the evidence
was re-examined, the two authors' entire argument simply
fell apart. Quantification and statistics had thus signally failed
to deliver the 'scientific' certainties which their advocates
had proclaimed.[47]

Moreover, the cliometricians' claim to be achieving a
higher, indeed virtually unassailable level of objectivity and
certainty through the use of properly scientific methods was
also being undermined by new developments in the philosophy of science. After the broadly empiricist position of
Popper had held sway in the 1950s, Thomas Kuhn's post-
empiricist view of science, expounded in 1962 in his
enormously influential book *The Structure of Scientific
Revolutions*, took over as the dominant explanatory model. In
place of the existing view of science as continuous progress,
Kuhn argued that most scientists worked, often unconsciously, within a 'paradigm' or set of theories, assumptions,
research agendas and so on, which guided their experiments
and ensured that their observations matched the theories
they held. Paradigms could thus not be falsified, and anomalies, where the data did not fit the paradigm, were usually
ignored or worked around. Only when the anomalies had

accumulated to a point where they caused a general sense of unease in the scientific community did the search for a new paradigm begin. The disadvantage of a new paradigm was often, however, that it failed to account for some phenomena that the old one succeeded in explaining. And different paradigms constituted different mental worlds, which were not comparable with one another. Thus science was not necessarily progressive, and falsifiable scientific theories were not established by experimental confirmation, but maintained by intellectual consensus. This view was widely attacked by scientists as irrationalist and relativist, portraying their disciplines as guided by 'mob rule'. But by the 1970s it had become the dominant view among philosophers of science and was being applied to other forms of knowledge as well. To be sure, Kuhn believed that the natural sciences progressed entirely free of any external influences and insisted that his ideas were not applicable to other fields. Nor is the Kuhnian notion of a paradigm really applicable to history; historians in general do not work within rigid and constricting paradigms.[48] But substitute the words 'historical interpretation' for 'scientific paradigm' and one can see that those historians who did take Kuhn's ideas on board found their implications to be strongly relativist, as well as corrosive of the idea that the 'scientific' credentials of history could be established by methods which guaranteed the production of 'objective' knowledge about the past.

By the 1980s, therefore, the long search for a scientific method of history had failed to yield any definitive results. The period in which the social sciences, encouraged by historians like E. H. Carr, had been exerting their influence over the practice of historical research and in the most extreme cases such as that of Fogel threatening to displace 'traditional' methods of history altogether, seemed to be coming to an end. The argument that history is, or should be, a science, in principle no different from quantum mechanics or crystallography, began to come under renewed and sustained attack, more radical than ever before. In the next chapter, we will see to what extent the belief that history is a science has managed to weather this fresh storm.

2

HISTORY, SCIENCE AND
MORALITY

I

Attempts to turn history into a science have been going on
for the best part of two centuries now, and show no signs of
letting up. Yet, as E. H. Carr correctly observed, the question of whether or not history is a science has been discussed
in Anglo-American circles largely because of 'an eccentric-
ity of the English language'.[1] The problem lies in the fact that
the German term *Wissenschaft* simply means a discipline or
body of organized knowledge. Germans have never had any
difficulty in applying it to a whole range of subjects, including not only *Naturwissenschaft* but also *Sozialwissenschaft*,
Geschichtswissenschaft and *Literaturwissenschaft*. The mere
attempt to translate these terms into English indicates the
problem: 'natural science' and even 'social science' sound
fine;[2] but 'historical science' and 'literary science' do not.
We can use the term 'sociology' or 'geology', but 'histori-
ology', somehow, has never entered general usage. In
German, the discipline of history, *Geschichtswissenschaft*, has
been classified from the outset as a *Geisteswissenschaft*, an

45

aspect of the organized study of the human spirit, and so the debate about the scientific or non-scientific nature of history has never arisen.[3]

Modern philosophies of science, said Carr, argued plausibly that the natural scientist was anything but a neutral observer of autonomous processes in the laboratory. In history and the social sciences, to be sure, human beings were studying other human beings, or in other words humanity was studying itself, while in the natural sciences the object of study in most cases was not human but something else. But even this distinction breaks down in fact in disciplines such as medicine, biology, biochemistry, experimental psychology and the like.[4] Carr would have been more correct simply to say that in no subject could there be an entirely clear separation between the researcher and the object of research. As Sir Geoffrey Elton observed: 'The post-Newtonian view of the physical world, denying the absolute, allowing for the unpredictably contingent, and accepting the effect of the observer upon the matter observed, might not be a bad analogy for good history.'[5] In this sense, the difference between the views of Carr and Elton on this matter did not seem so great, though Elton thought that history in the end was neither an art nor a science. 'History,' he declared proudly, 'is a study different from any other and governed by rules peculiar to itself.'[6] In truth, far from being irrelevant or unimportant or based on a mere terminological misunderstanding, the debate over whether history is an art or science has been central to historians' self-understanding for more than a century. Even in Germany, there has been intensive discussion over whether or not the methods and approaches of natural science can be applied to history in its guise as a 'human science', or whether it can or should be classified as a 'social science'; so the debate in effect goes beyond the Anglo-Saxon linguistic boundary after all.

Many writers have argued that history is not a science because while scientific knowledge is cumulative, historical knowledge is not. Clearly, our knowledge of physics or chemistry today rests on the foundations built by the scientific discoveries of the past, from Newton and Faraday to Einstein and Rutherford, even if some of the theories propounded by those who laid those foundations have now been superseded. But because each historian, by and large, advances a different interpretation from that of previous historians studying the same subject, many commentators have concluded that historical knowledge does not accumulate in the way that scientific knowledge does; historians are usually more concerned to dispute the findings of their predecessors than to build on them. Such conclusions were vigorously disputed by Sir Geoffrey Elton, who declared optimistically that through the steady accumulation of empirical knowledge, professional historians were advancing 'ever nearer to the fortress of truth', even if they would never be able to capture it completely. Of course, he conceded, historical research was subject to review and revision, but if it was good, its reconstruction of the past would mostly stand up to future tests.[7] Writing a definitive history of something, so definitive that it would never need to be written again, was an ambition that was not only laudable in his eyes but also eminently achievable. Predictably enough, perhaps, such views have not gone unchallenged in their turn. Thus according to Keith Jenkins for example, Elton's claim that historical knowledge did grow over time, and that we know in the present vastly more about, for example, the Tudor Age than we did twenty or thirty years ago, means that he 'sees himself as standing at the end of a process' of the accumulation of historical knowledge, in which the historians of the past are judged according to what they have contributed to this Eltonian teleology. This smacks of an arrogance that historians would do better to avoid.[8]

Anyone who has carried out historical research quickly becomes aware that their knowledge is more complete than that of others: this is an experience common even to the humblest of PhD students within a few months of starting on their project. The reason for this is that the materials left to us by the past are so extensive that all the historians who have ever worked have done little more than scratch the surface of the deposits which have accumulated, and continue to accumulate, over time. Of course, the further back we go in time, the less evidence there is, and the more thoroughly what there is has been worked over by previous generations of historians. Even in medieval or ancient history, however, there are still many new things to discover, which do not necessarily depend on a reworking of old material. And indeed, despite the emphasis of university teaching on controversy, debate and interpretation, the majority of working historians probably consider that adding to our knowledge of the past – 'filling in a gap' – is just as important as transforming our understanding of what is already known, if not more so. It is in this sense, to begin with, that historical knowledge is cumulative. The researcher identifies gaps in knowledge with reference to what is already known. Far from this meaning that we rate previous historians according to what they have contributed to our own work, we are usually concerned above all to escape from them by doing something different. Moreover, distance not only adds to our knowledge, it also adds to our understanding. Even E. H. Carr conceded that the further in time historians got from, say, Bismarck, the closer they were likely to get to an objective judgment of his work.[9] And the fact that historical knowledge is constantly being added to often enables historians to advance new interpretations in the fields which they are studying, whatever the theoretical impulses behind these interpretations might be.

Another reason for distinguishing between history and science is the argument that the former must necessarily involve an element of moral judgment, while the latter does not. E. H. Carr met this assertion with a flat denial. Historians, according to Carr, should not judge the past in moral terms; their purpose was rather to understand how the past had contributed to human progress. It was pointless, for example, to condemn slavery in the ancient world as immoral; the point was to understand how it came about, how it functioned, and why it declined, opening the way to another form of social organization. This general view was put most trenchantly by Professor David Knowles, the great British medievalist, who rejected moral judgment as an aspect of history, observing 'The historian is not a judge, still less a hanging judge'.[10] Since Knowles was not only an eminent historian but also a Benedictine monk of saintly character and ascetic appearance, his views on this matter are certainly deserving of respect. It is, moreover, easy to discover moral judgments by historians that reveal themselves in retrospect to be little more than articulations of the prejudices of their own day. The Victorians were particularly apt to condemn figures in the past for sexual behaviour that would scarcely raise an eyebrow in the present, a tendency whose relentless lampooning in that classic satire on history textbooks, Sellar and Yeatman's *1066 and All That*, should by now have laid to rest for ever.[11] But while historians would scarcely judge a medieval monarch as 'a bad man, but a good king' or 'a good man, but a bad king' any more, the issue is rather different when it comes to twentieth-century dictators such as Hitler and Stalin. Carr suggested that moral denunciations of such figures often served to deflect attention from the responsibility of the wider society that produced them, and considered that moral judgment was perfectly acceptable when applied to the latter.[12] But this too was problematical, since he went on to suggest that moral standards were relative, and that historians should judge past societies not in relation to some absolute standard but in relation to each other.[13] Since Carr ridiculed the application of Victorian moral standards to the Middle Ages, however, the validity of this principle would seem in practice to be rather doubtful.

No doubt Knowles was right to argue that historians should not engage in explicit moral judgments on the past – an argument which was convenient indeed for him as a Catholic monk dealing with English monasticism in the fifteenth and early sixteenth centuries, when monks and nuns alike had been widely condemned by Protestant historians for all kinds of supposedly immoral behaviour. In practice, however, Knowles certainly did engage in moral judgment, relating the behaviour of all the subjects of his work to the eternal and divinely commanded rule of St Benedict, the founder of monasticism. No human historian, he implied, but God Himself had the role of passing judgment here. The lesson of the story he told, Knowles wrote on the final page of his vast work, was that 'when once a religious house or a religious order ceases to direct its sons to the abandonment of all that is not God . . . it sinks to the level of a purely human institution.'[14] Hence his comment on William More, Prior of Worcester, whose 'life was in great part that of a country squire,' that 'he followed . . . the way of the world' has to be read as moral criticism.[15] In Knowles's view, the decline of the monasteries in the late Middle Ages was real;

and indeed, judged by such high religious standards, it certainly was. Measuring medieval monks and nuns against these standards – a task which he carried out with great subtlety and scrupulosity – was what Knowles's four-volume history was principally about; and this rather simplistic approach arguably prevented him from gaining the kind of sophisticated and differentiated interpretative perspective on the behaviour of the regular clergy that might have been possible had he, for example, approached their belief-systems and their changing social roles and mores in secular terms, using the kind of anthropological theories employed by subsequent historians of other belief-systems such as witchcraft.

Yet despite his failure to follow it in practice, the principle Knowles laid down, of avoiding explicit moral judgments on the past and the people who lived in it, is surely a good one for the historian to follow. A historian who uses terms like 'wicked' or 'evil' about a person or persons in the past will only succeed in looking ridiculous. It is perfectly legitimate, however, to point out in factual terms when people in the past, such as monks and nuns, behaved in private in a manner quite different to that which they advocated for other people, and boasted of themselves, in public. On a larger scale, one may argue, as Carr did, that, for example, collectivization in Russia was necessary in order to support industrialization, and that the brutalities and abuses, to say nothing of mass murder, to which the Russian peasantry were subjected were a necessary price to pay for progress; but if one wishes to refute this point of view, whatever one's feelings about the morality of the Stalinist regime, the way to do it *as a historian* is not to propound moral arguments about the iniquities of 'dekulakization' (the expropriation, imprisonment, beating and killing of the most prosperous section of the peasantry), nor to put the moral argument that no process of economic change such as this can justify deliberate cruelty and murder on this or any other scale. The *historian's* way of undermining the moral validity of Carr's argument is surely to undermine its *historical* validity, and let the reader draw the moral conclusion; to show, for instance, that the growth rates achieved by Russian industry in the 1930s were no higher than those achieved by the semi-capitalist 'New Economic Policy' in the 1920s, or to demonstrate that the 'liquidation' of the kulaks was carried out according to arbitrary quotas imposed from Moscow, which bore no relation at all to the nature or scale of the task of collectivization carried out in the localities.[16] Overloading the historian's text with expressions of moral outrage will add little to the argument.

In making moral judgments on the past, historians have far more powerful rhetorical and stylistic weapons at their disposal than mere denunciation: sarcasm, irony, the juxtaposition of rhetoric and reality, the factual exposure of hypocrisy, self-interest, and greed, the uncommented recounting of courageous acts of rebellion and defiance. All of this can be achieved without the direct application of the transient moral vocabulary of the society the historian is living in.[17] Particularly in periods of mass destruction such as the years 1914–45, it is difficult for the historian not to take a moral stance; but that moral stance is still best articulated historically. In a similar way, there is surely a moral element involved in all kinds of research in the natural sciences, from embryology to nuclear physics. Moral concerns may drive scientific research, or they may emerge from it; the key point surely is that, just as in history, the element of moral judgment, insofar as it is exercised at all, is in the end extraneous to the research rather than being embedded in the theory or methodology of it.

If some have adduced the moral dimension as an argument against the scientific nature of history, another reason often given for supposing that history is not a science is the fact that historians' conclusions cannot be experimentally replicated. But of course important aspects of a number of sciences are based, like history, on observation rather than experimentation – such as, for example, astronomy. Such observation may not be directly visual; it may be indirect, for instance, as when the existence of the planet Pluto was postulated through the observation of irregularities in the orbital path of the next-outermost planet in the solar system, Neptune, which could only have been caused by the exertion of a gravitational pull from a large but as yet unseen object further out. We can return to this evidence, or to other forms of traces, such as radio waves, from which the existence of certain objects in outer space can be inferred, just as we can return to historical documents, but we cannot somehow create them in experiments, like we can a chemical reaction. Yet nobody has ventured to claim that astronomy is not a science. It is not necessary, therefore, to mount elaborate defences of the scientific nature of history of the sort Sir Geoffrey Elton engaged in when he claimed that historical fact, because it could not be manufactured by the historian, was actually more independent of the observer than scientific fact was.[18] In non-experimental sciences the distinction simply breaks down.

II

Perhaps the most serious challenge to history's claim to be scientific rests on the belief that a true science can only exist if it is able to posit general laws. This argument has a long pedigree, going back at least as far as a notorious remark made by the English Rankean James Anthony Froude in 1864: 'It often seems to me as if history is like a child's box of letters, with which we can spell any word we please. We have only to pick out such letters as we want, arrange them as we like, and say nothing about those which do not suit our purpose.'[19] Froude's enemies seized on this statement as an admission that the procedures he himself adopted were arbitrary and unscientific. But he meant it in fact as a criticism of philosophies of history such as that of his contemporary Henry Thomas Buckle, who believed that the movement of history could be scientifically reduced to a series of mathematical formulae. In Froude's view history had to confine itself to a presentation of the facts, and not be used to 'spell out' theories of a 'scientific' nature. Indeed, in every case where historians have tried to prove generally applicable laws of history, they have been easily refuted by critics who have demonstrated instances in which they do not apply – most notoriously, perhaps, in the case of Arnold Toynbee's once-popular *A Study of History*. Published in thirteen volumes between 1934 and 1947, this vast work ranged across twenty-one human 'civilizations' and six thousand years of human history, drawing from them a series of general laws according to which civilizations rose, developed and collapsed.

Toynbee's laws were detailed and exact. He posited for example four methods by which great men appeared in history to save civilizations in danger of imminent collapse, and he presented the stages in which new institutions emerged from the body of a disintegrating civilization in the form of a table. The work was hailed by the press as 'an immortal masterpiece', and 'the greatest work of our time'. Yet professional historians, foremost among them Pieter Geyl, a thoughtful writer on modern historiography as well as a leading specialist on the history of The Netherlands, were deeply sceptical. Geyl charged that Toynbee simply selected the evidence he wanted and picked out a few arbitrary strands from the tangled skein of historical fact. In arguing that 'ease' was inimical to the growth of civilization, Toynbee for example pointed to the triumph of the hardy New Englanders in seventeenth- and eighteenth-century North America over the effete French in Louisiana or the idle Spaniards in Florida. 'The greater the difficulty, the greater the stimulus'; thus American civilization was born, and triumphed, out of hardship and adversity in combating the challenge of a hostile environment. Yet Toynbee ignored the fact that the conquest of New Amsterdam which turned it into New England was carried out in 1664 by the luxurious court of Charles II, and he suppressed other explanations for the eventual hegemony of the New Englanders, from the decline of Spain as an imperial power to the superiority of British sea might at a time when the French were embroiled in wars on the European continent. The explanation in other words had to be sought in the relative positions of the colonial powers, not in the relationship of the settlers of New England to their environment. 'Challenge and response' was completely irrelevant here.

Geyl charged that this example was typical of the 'innumerable fallacious arguments and spurious demonstrations of which the whole book is made up'. Toynbee was a prophet, not a historian:

It is not only – not even in the first place – the looking for laws, the generalizations, even the faulty reasonings, that offend; it is the vision itself in which every age and every civilization is judged by a standard foreign to it and its importance restricted to what it contributed to the progress of an arbitrarily chosen principle. The historian believes that history can enrich the civilization of his own age especially by trying to enter into the habits of thought and the relationships of past generations and that only thus can these be understood . . . To see a self-styled historian reducing the whole of the wonderful and mysterious movement of history to one single motif, rejecting whole centuries as uninteresting, forcing it all into the scheme of a presumptuous construction, strikes him as going against all that history stands for.

Geyl also lambasted the 'spate of moral judgments' which gushed from Toynbee's pen, above all in the final volume of *A Study of History*, in which the author launched a violent attack on 'neo-paganism' and defended Christianity as the only defence of civilization against barbarity of the sort that had overwhelmed Germany and Europe during the Second World War. All this was deeply unhistorical, utterly alien to the spirit of the historian's enterprise.[20]

Toynbee's huge and pretentious work enjoyed only a brief vogue before disappearing into the obscurity in which it has languished, along with similar tracts such as Buckle's *History of Civilizations*, ever since.[21] Most historians have always felt the establishment of general laws to be alien to the enterprise in which they are engaged. This clearly differentiates them very sharply from natural scientists. Yet there have been some exceptions, most notably in recent times E. H. Carr. In trying to refute the argument that history was not a science because it posited no general laws, Carr pointed out that while no two historical events were identical, no two atoms were either, no two stars, no two living organisms, nor any other two things that any scientist studied. Yet this did not stop scientists from framing their laws. Similarly, 'the very use of language', he said, 'commits the historian, like the scientist, to generalization.'[22] He pointed out that history was as concerned with generalization as any science; it was not merely confined to the establishment of particular, isolated facts. It taught lessons, as for example the constant reference made by delegates at the Versailles Conference in 1919 to the Vienna Congress of 1815, and countless other examples; in this sense, it could be used to predict the future, based on a knowledge of given conditions, and thus to shape it. Carr poured scorn on the argument that history was not a science because it could not predict the future. The law of gravity, he observed, could not predict that a particular apple would fall at some particular time and in some particular place. Scientific laws operated only under certain specific conditions; and Carr sought to rescue the predictive capabilities of history by making the claim that historians could, for instance, say that a revolution was going to occur in some country or other if conditions there were the same as in similar countries where revolutions had already taken place.[23] Thus, he concluded, history was just like any other science in its generation of laws and its predictive capacities.

Those who have attempted to assimilate history into the social sciences have often tried to take account of this point. Social-scientific history concerns itself overwhelmingly with averages and means, not with discrete individuals. The *Annales* school interested itself in collective behaviour and mentalities, not in individuals, while the cliometricians only worked on statistically significant numbers of people, if they worked on people at all. Yet history clearly includes the study of individual people, events and structures as well as groups and collectivities. The differences that exist between two human beings, even when they live in the same time and place, are vastly more complex than the differences between two atoms or two molecules. Human individuality is far greater than microbial individuality. This makes the framing of general laws to cover it correspondingly far more difficult.

Moreover, Carr was blurring important distinctions in his discussion of the matter. For laws are not the same as generalizations. As the English historian John Vincent puts it: 'Where science asserts, say, the Second Law of Thermodynamics, it is asserting something more than a pattern with inevitable exceptions.'[24] The latter, however, is all that history, even Marxist history, can hope to aspire to. In addition, even the most inexperienced history student can dispute interpretations put forward by even the grandest of professors, while no chemistry or biology student is going to dispute the scientific laws taught in the classroom by the most junior instructor. The American intellectual historian Allan Megill has made the distinction between laws and generalizations particularly clear:

> In historians' language, the following invented statement counts as a generalization . . .: "As a result of the growth of towns and trade, feudalism gave way to incipient capitalism in late medieval and early modern Europe." The "problem of generalization" as historians conceive of it, is usually the problem of how to get from fragmentary and confusing data to such larger assertions. But such assertions are not what the logical positivists, or Windelband before them, had in mind when they spoke of general laws. In "nomothetic" science, the desired generalizations *transcend* particular times and places, as in, for instance, this invented statement: "*Wherever*, within a feudal system, towns and trade begin to grow . . . *then* feudalism gives way to capitalism."[25]

In this latter case, a single exception would be enough to invalidate the law. In the former case, it would not undermine the generalization, but on the contrary prove an interesting exception to it that would itself require explanation.

While many people, especially politicians, try to learn lessons from history, history itself shows that in retrospect very few of these lessons have been the right ones. Time and again, history has proved a very bad predictor of future events. This is because history never repeats itself; nothing in human society, the main concern of the historian, ever happens twice under exactly the same conditions or in exactly the same way. And when people try to use history they often do so not in order to accommodate themselves to the inevitable, but in order to avoid it. For example, British politicians in the post-war era based much of their conduct of foreign policy on the belief that the 'appeasement' of dictators, such as was carried out by Prime Minister Neville Chamberlain in his relations with Hitler in 1938–39, could only lead to disaster. In practice, however, this very belief only too often led to disaster itself, most notoriously in 1956, when the British Prime Minister Sir Anthony Eden, obsessed with the desire to avoid the 'appeasement' of dictators which he had himself criticized in the later 1930s, launched an ill-advised and unsuccessful military strike against the Egyptian government under Colonel Nasser when it nationalized the Anglo-French-owned Suez Canal.

Again, many of the Russian Bolsheviks thought that because the events of 1917 constituted Russia's bourgeois revolution, they would have to wait a long time before they were followed by the proletarian revolution that was their ultimate goal. It was Lenin and Trotsky who argued that unlike previous bourgeois revolutions, in England in 1640 for example or France in 1789, the Russian revolution could be given a permanency which would enable it to lead on immediately to the dictatorship of the proletariat. Having surmounted this problem, however, they were then faced with the fact that the two historical revolutions to which they looked back, in seventeenth-century England and eighteenth-century France, had both ended in military dictatorships, run respectively by Oliver Cromwell and Napoleon Bonaparte. After Lenin's death in 1924, fear of this happening again was a material influence in causing the leading Bolsheviks to gang up on Trotsky, the head of the Red Army and the man everyone thought most likely to become the Russian Bonaparte. Thus in practice the historical law of revolutions broke down because people in one revolution used the memory of previous ones to change the way they occurred.

Nor does history enable one to predict revolutions, however they are defined. Historians notoriously failed to predict, for instance, the fall of the Berlin Wall and the collapse of the Soviet Union in 1989–91.[26] And in any case, although Carr argued repeatedly that the historian's role was to use an understanding of the past in order to gain control of the future, very few historians indeed have shared this concept of their function in the sense of using the past as the basis for concrete predictions. The fact is that while a chemist, for instance, knows in advance the result of mixing two elements in a crucible, the historian has no such advance knowledge of anything, nor is trying to gain such knowledge really central to the business historians are engaged in.

History, then, can produce generalizations, though the broader they are, the more exceptions there are likely to be and the further removed they will become from hard evidence which can be cited in their support. Its objects of study are in no sense confined to discrete individuals or events. It can identify, or posit with a high degree of plausibility, patterns, trends and structures in the human past. In these respects it can legitimately be regarded as scientific. But history cannot create laws with predictive power. An understanding of the past might help in the present insofar as it broadens our knowledge of human nature, provides us with an inspiration – or a warning – or suggests plausible, though always fallible arguments about the likely possibilities of certain things happening under certain conditions. None of this, however, comes anywhere near the immutable predictive certainty of a scientific law. All those who thought, or claimed, that they had discovered laws in history, from Marx and Engels to Toynbee and Buckle, were wrong; indeed, as we have seen, as soon as Marxists in Russia thought they recognized a historical law, they proceeded to do their level best to break it.

An instructive recent example has been that of the British historian Paul Kennedy, whose profoundly researched and carefully argued study of *The Rise and Fall of the Great Powers*, argued that there was a pattern in modern history according to which wealthy states created empires but eventually overstretched their resources and declined. Illustrated with a wealth of historical detail, the book attracted attention not because of its learned demonstration of the reasons for the failure of the Habsburg Empire to achieve European domination in the sixteenth and seventeenth centuries, but because of its conclusion that the United States would be unable to sustain its global hegemony far into the twenty-first century. At a time when US President Ronald Reagan was about to ride off into the sunset, this gloomy prophecy struck a deep vein of anxiety in the American public. The book became a bestseller overnight. Written in 1987, the book also made a point of arguing that the Soviet Union was not close to collapse, so that the situation seemed to many American readers to be ominous indeed.[27] Within a few years these prophecies had been confounded. The Soviet Union had indeed collapsed, not in the international war which Kennedy had argued was the invariable and inevitable trigger for such processes, but through internal transformation and disintegration. The world hegemony of the United States seemed more assured than ever, and in the economic boom of the 1990s showed few signs of suffering from the 'imperial overstretch' which Kennedy had prophesied. In the first seven chapters of his book, in other words, Kennedy, writing as a historian, had produced some instructive and workable generalizations about the rise and fall of international superpowers and the relationship of economic and military strength. These chapters also incidentally demonstrated the continuing vitality and viability of 'grand narrative' in history. Had Kennedy stopped here, his book would not have attracted the attention it did, and would not have sold so many copies. But it would also have been better history. As soon as he turned his generalizations into laws, and used them, in his final chapter, to prophesy the future, he ran into trouble. It is always a mistake for a historian to try to predict the future. Life, unlike science, is simply too full of surprises.

III

If history is not a science, then are historians any different in essence from novelists or poets? Historians have often attempted to distinguish what they do from what artists do by arguing that their discipline does indeed require a rigorous professional or scientific training, while if art and music also need technical expertise that can only be acquired through education, writing novels or poems, for all the proliferation of creative writing courses in recent years, demonstrably does not. Sir Geoffrey Elton was particularly insistent on this point. The series of examples of readings of source-material with which Elton illustrated his claim suggests that by training he meant that historians had to learn about the technical details of the documents they used, or in other words, the meaning for contemporaries of the language they employed, and the nature and customs of the institutions in which the documents were produced. Thus it was necessary to know, for instance, that when a medieval English king differentiated in his correspondence between recipients he addressed as 'trusty and well-beloved' and 'right trusty and well-beloved', this did not indicate the difference between a distant political ally and a close one, but rather reflected the social status of the addressee. Or that when noble families in early modern Europe had pictures painted in which their children were dressed in adult clothes, this did not mean, as the amateur historian Philippe Ariès had supposed, that they had no notion of childhood as a separate stage of human existence. Other sources indicate that in everyday life children were indeed dressed differently from adults; they were just put in grown-up clothes to have their portraits painted.[28]

All this may be both admirable and true, but what does it have to do with scientific training? The basic point Elton seemed to want to make is that in order to understand a source, historians had to ask how it came into existence, what purposes it served to those who created it, and how they proceeded in bringing it into being. But how much training do they need for this, and in what does it consist? Traditionally, historians have been trained by being put through an undergraduate degree, culminating in the documentary-based Special Subject, and then by doing a PhD. This has involved a kind of trial-and-error technique, with the student handing the tutor or supervisor essays, drafts or chapters of a thesis, and getting them back with critical comments. Augmenting all this has been the research seminar, in which the professor and others have led critical discussion of students' work; but this too essentially operates by the same principle. Even so rigorous a historian as the English medievalist T. F. Tout, a champion of the importation of German research methods into British universities in the early part of the twentieth century, observed that students were trained to be professional historians 'by observation, osmosis and occasional words of advice'.[29] In saying this, he was echoing the great German historian of Ancient Rome, Theodor Mommsen, who declared in 1874 that it was a 'dangerous and harmful illusion for the professor of history to believe that historians can be trained at the university in the same way as philologists or mathematicians most assuredly can be'. The true historian, he said, was 'not trained but born'.[30] Modern historians frequently agree with this point. While there is plenty of training, and there are plenty of rules for assessing the factual reliability of the traces left by the past, as two American historians have observed, 'there is no training and there are no rules for the process of constructing a story out of the disparate pieces of evidence . . . When it comes to creating a coherent account out of these evidential fragments, the historical method consists only of appealing to the muse.'[31]

Mommsen's scepticism about the necessity of even a very modest degree of training in the making of a good historian was echoed a century later by the Oxford specialist in modern French history, Theodore Zeldin, who argued in

1976 that 'the ideals or models that historians have set before their pupils have always been rapidly forgotten'. 'Personally,' he went on,

> I have no wish to urge anyone to write history in any particular way. I believe that the history you write is the expression of your individuality; I agree with Mommsen that one cannot teach people to write history; I believe that much more can be gained by encouraging young historians to develop their own personality, their own vision, their own eccentricities, than by setting them examples to follow. Original history is the reflection of an original mind, and there is no prescription which will produce that.[32]

There was something very English, perhaps, in the view of this particular Oxford don that the best way to become a good historian was to become a good eccentric. Eccentric people, one might argue, produce eccentric history. Certainly – assuming he has obeyed his own maxim – that has been the case with Zeldin himself, whose most recent books, *Happiness* and the bestselling *Intimate History of Humanity*, have concentrated, respectively, on the imaginary adventures of a girl called 'Sumdy' and on the real personal life-histories of a handful of individuals, mainly French, in the present, as the starting-point for a series of ruminations on the possible ways individuals in the West might shape their personal lives in the coming century.

Most historians, in practice, would agree that at least some degree of training and supervision is necessary to equip young scholars for a career in the profession, and that the PhD is probably the best way of doing this. The historian's training through the PhD is necessarily mostly training on the job, learning through practice. But historians also have to learn theories and techniques before they are let loose on their materials; they must absorb not only the Rankean principles of source-criticism and citation but also relevant skills such as languages, palaeography, statistics and so on. Moreover they also have to read and digest a large amount of contextual material and master the secondary literature relating to their subject. This kind of training, it has been argued, is more characteristic of a craft than a science. History, the American historical theorist Hayden White has observed, is not a 'science that utilizes technical languages, hypothetico-deductive arguments controlled by experimental methods, and laboratory procedures relatively well canonized and agreed on by practitioners of the discipline in question', but 'rather a craftlike discipline, which means that it tends to be governed by convention and custom rather than by methodology and theory and to utilize ordinary or natural language.'[33] But is science actually defined by any of the things which White says history is not? We have already seen that experimental methods and laboratory procedures are not necessary to constitute a basically observational science such as astronomy. Much if not most training in many of the sciences consists of learning the material (properties of elements and the like), and mastering ancillary techniques such as mathematics, spectroscopy, computer imaging and so on. Much the same could be said of history. Moreover, historical research also has its agreed procedures. The differences in the end are not as great as one might initially suppose.

IV

As White suggests, history *per se* does not have a specialized technical language of its own in the way that, say, microbiology or climatology does. Like many historians, Sir Geoffrey Elton for example argued that all historians should try to write clearly and comprehensibly, and there is nothing wrong with that; but he also declared that no historical problem was 'incapable of being explained with full clarity to any person of reasonable intelligence', and that in practice is a very debatable claim.[34] There are many historical works, for example in econometric history or demographic history, which clearly do require a good deal of technical knowledge in order to be understood. Technical language is also used by many historians in specialized areas of research. Discussions of topics such as the medieval manorial economy, the structure of landholding and serfdom in eighteenth-century central Europe, the legal basis of the slaveholding system in the old American South, or the debate on stamp duty and other aspects of taxation policy in pre-revolutionary America, can be highly technical, and comprehensible only to the initiated. But does this make it scientific, and historical work written in non-technical language non-scientific? The distinction seems entirely artificial. Of course, in practice, when dealing with an area of the past where obsolete technical terms were involved, it is frequently impossible to avoid using specialized terminology. But this surely does not abrogate the historian's general responsibility to write as clearly and unpretentiously as is possible under the circumstances. Lamenting the tendency in recent years to move away from this habit, Lawrence Stone says that he was taught 'that one should always try to write plain English, avoiding jargon and obfuscation, and making one's meaning as clear as possible to the reader.'[35] It is hard to disagree with him. Clarity of presentation, after all, is a necessary part of intellectual precision: there is nothing necessarily 'unscientific' or sloppy about it, quite the reverse.

Yet historians, as White points out, customarily use the medium of literary prose, involving all kinds of images and figures of speech which are not present in the sources they employ. This means that they are doing far more than merely reporting or reflecting the sources. Indeed, far from wanting them to expunge literary artifice from their work, White positively encourages historians to write in a colourful way, since telling the story plain and unvarnished in his view does not deliver anything more 'scientific', merely an impoverished and unimaginative historical text.[36] Similarly, another American intellectual historian, Dominick LaCapra, also points to the way in which 'the "voice" of the historian . . . employs self-critical reflection about its own protocols of enquiry, and makes use of modes such as irony, parody, self-parody and humour, that is, double- or multiple-voiced uses of language.'[37] And he goes on to call for historians to be still more self-conscious about their use of language. 'The anti-rhetoric of plain style, or, more elaborately, of "scientificity",' he points out, implies a quest for a mathematically precise language that is illusory.[38] It would not be going too far to say that it was itself a form of rhetoric.

White's exhortation surely has a good deal to recommend it, as does LaCapra's. Metaphor and imagery can illuminate the past just as much as statistics and social theory. Yet this should add to rather than detract from the clarity and precision of the historian's prose. In unpractised hands, the return of history to a literary mode can have unfortunate consequences. The American historian Marjorie Becker, author of a monograph on the Mexican revolution of 1910, claims for example that she uses metaphors 'with great liberality' in her book because 'the separation between history and poetry is a false and dangerous one.' The publisher's advertising copy for her book claims that this results in a 'beautifully written work'. Yet the reviewer for the *Times Literary Supplement*, a leading expert in the field, considered the book's style to be 'rambling, opaque and affected'.[39] Perhaps, in the end, it is better for historians to stick to a plain style unless they are very sure of what they are doing, and to make sure that literary artifice, when they employ it, is used consciously, and in the service of clarification rather than obfuscation.

While most historians trundle on with a style that is either plain or literary, give or take a handful of quantifiers who prefer to express themselves in mathematical formulae, literary theorists who write about history adopt a very different tactic. Hayden White, as Russell Jacoby, one of his most acute critics, has noted, 'assumes the idiom of the cool scientist scoffing at the emotionalism of the artist.' An inspection of White's own rhetoric, Jacoby comments, reveals 'the language – and cadence – of aggressive science'. Similarly, Dominick LaCapra in his view shows a 'palpable disdain' for 'less than technical prose'. The *ne plus ultra*, or perhaps the *reductio ad absurdum*, of this tendency occurs in Sande Cohen's book *Historical Culture*, which is written in such technical language that it is supplied with a glossary so that the ordinary reader can understand the words it commonly uses, such as 'actantial', 'psychologeme' and 'distransitivity'.[40] Now of course there is nothing wrong in itself with the invention of new terms to denote newly discovered or newly posited phenomena. But this goes far beyond such necessary technicality. As Jacoby notes, moreover: 'The concentration on language and texts by the new intellectual historians ignores language and texts – their own.'[41] He is puzzled that scholars who advocate history's return to literature should write so badly themselves; but he is missing the essential point here, which is that they do not think of themselves as historians any more, least of all in the sense they are advocating, but as literary scientists.

As three American historians have recently pointed out in their reflections on the current state of the debate: 'History is much more than a branch of letters to be judged only in terms of its literary merit.'[42] If it were so judged, of course, it would generally be found wanting. Few historians write competently; fewer still display any real mastery of the language in which they publish their work. Most history books are hopelessly unreadable. For this situation, the dominance in the past thirty years of social-science models bears a heavy responsibility. Professional historians publish works that no sane person would attempt to read from beginning to end; works that are designed explicitly for reference rather than for reading. They usually lack the kind of literary ability that would make their work rival that of minor poets or novelists. If they had it, no doubt most of them would be writing poetry or fiction.

There is no reason why historians' works should not be subjected to literary and linguistic analysis. It can sharpen up our perceptions of their thought. Historical writings are so diverse that the styles in which they are written runs from the rebarbatively technical and formula-laden work of econometric or demographic historians at one extreme to the literary gems of practised communicators at the other. Ultimately, however illuminating it may be in itself, the study of historians' writings as linguistic texts is almost bound to be of secondary importance to their critical scrutiny as pieces of historical scholarship. The historians who can be read for literary pleasure are few indeed, and most of them, such as Gibbon, Michelet, Tocqueville or Carlyle, wrote in the eighteenth or nineteenth century, which is no doubt why literary analysts have concentrated their attentions on this period rather than applying their techniques to historians of the twentieth, when the desire to be scientific has increasingly driven literary qualities out of their texts. Thus we have a paradoxical situation in which arguments are overwhelmingly advanced – by Hayden White, Stephen Bann, Linda Orr and many others – about the nature of the historian's enterprise as a whole, on the basis of a reading of the subject's practitioners writing a cen-tury or more ago.[43] Given the extent to which historical research has moved on in purely empirical terms since then – we now know a lot more about the French Revolution than any of these nineteenth-century authors did – it is not surprising that such an approach feels justified in largely neglecting the empirical content of what Michelet, Tocqueville and their contemporaries wrote. For modern and contemporary historians, however, the scrutiny of their work as historical scholarship generally remains more important than criticism of their status as literary texts.

V

Given the vast range of styles and modes in which history is written and researched today, defending it as necessarily or even preferably scientific can be a dangerous game. Yet many historians persist in claiming that their discipline as a whole, whenever and however it is practised by university-based professionals, is characterized precisely by its superiority to linguistic and literary forms of analysis. 'The techniques of deconstruction or discourse analysis,' declares Professor Arthur Marwick of Britain's Open University, for example, 'have little value compared with the sophisticated methods historians have been developing over the years.'[44] In view of

his stout championing of the historian's superior sophistication, it seems legitimate to ask how Marwick has deployed
these sophisticated methods in his own work. Here is one
sample, taken from Marwick's discussion of the popular
novels of Jeffrey Archer in his book *Culture in Britain since
1945*:

> I have read only one of these novels: I found my attention
> firmly held while reading, but, the book finished, I had only
> the feeling of deepest nullity: no perceptions broadened,
> nothing to think about, just nothing – the classic outcome of
> empty entertainment, the opposite pole from serious art.[45]

Does this kind of judgment really reflect the 'sophisticated
methods historians have been developing over the years'? In
another book, on *Beauty in History*, Marwick waxes lyrical
about 'the most beautiful black woman I personally have
ever seen, an absolutely beautifully proportioned and
intensely appealing face, surmounted by close-cropped fuzzy
hair'. Further examples of his 'sophisticated methods' can be
found in the same work, when he states that 'most people
tend to look better full face than in profile' and that: 'What
we find most desirable is most beautiful, what is beautiful we
wish to possess.'[46] Such personal opinions and gems of
homespun wisdom permeate a book which argues in the
face of a mass of historical evidence that human beauty has
never varied according to the eye of the age or the society in
which it has been assessed. According to Marwick, it has
always been judged throughout history by absolute and
unvarying standards. These turn out, of course, to be
Marwick's own – those of a middle-class white male living in
late-twentieth-century Britain. Apart from indulging in such
obviously arrogant and unreflective subjectivity, Marwick's

'sophisticated methods' also include innumerable opaque and half-thought-out metaphors, as in: 'Politicians liked to speak of the "mosaic" of the welfare state; in reality it was more of a crazy paving.' Or: 'These austerity years were a threshold to the whole first post-war era: rock-hard and grey, whitened maybe by dedication and labour, but opening on the warmer times within.'[47] The main characteristic of the Marwickian metaphor seems to be its complete absence of identifiable meaning. This kind of thing would not have been easily accepted by the more austere exponents of the scientific view of history, such as J. B. Bury or Fustel de Coulanges.

As Isaiah Berlin observed many years ago, in history 'there plainly exists a far greater variety of methods and procedures than is usually provided for in textbooks on logic or scientific method.'[48] History, in the end, may for the most part be seen as a science in the weak sense of the German term *Wissenschaft*, an organized body of knowledge acquired through research carried out according to generally agreed methods, presented in published reports, and subject to peer review. It is not a science in the strong sense that it can frame general laws or predict the future. But there are sciences such as geology which cannot predict the future either. The fact seems to be that the differences between what in English are known as the 'sciences' are at least as great as the differences between these disciplines taken together and a humane discipline such as history. 'Science' here is only a convenient label, so no wonder its application varies from one language to another. To search for a truly 'scientific' history is to pursue a mirage. Insofar as it has succeeded in generating new methods and techniques, this quest has of course been enormously beneficial. But every time a new wave of historians comes along and declares its method – whether it is philology, as in the nineteenth century, or economics, sociology, anthropology, psychology, statistics, linguistics or literary theory, as in the twentieth – to be the one true 'scientific' way of studying the past, rendering all previous historical methods outmoded at a stroke and consigning all previous historical writing to the realm of myth, anyone who is on the receiving end of this kind of rhetoric is entitled to a healthy degree of scepticism. For such claims have never been able to establish themselves for very long. History is not only a science in the weak sense of the word, it is, or can be, an art, in the sense that in skilful hands it can be presented in a literary form and language that achieves comparability with other literary works of art and is widely recognized as such. And it is a craft, as the great French historian Marc Bloch insisted, because its practitioners learn on the job how to handle their materials and wield the tools of their trade.[49] It is all of these things not least because it is a varied and protean discipline, and historians approach what they do in many different ways. Claims that history in general is more 'professional' or 'scientific' than literary or linguistic analysis are as misplaced as counter-claims for the superiority of the latter. In this, as in other areas of the debate, it is surely time for a little mutual tolerance.

3

HISTORIANS AND THEIR FACTS

I

What is a historical fact? Sir Geoffrey Elton, for one, had no doubts about the matter (there were indeed few things about which he had doubts). A historical fact was something that happened in the past, which had left traces in documents which could be used by the historian to reconstruct it in the present. In order to perform this operation successfully, the historian had in the first place to shed all prejudices and preconceptions and approach the documents with a completely open mind. 'Ideological theory,' Elton declared, 'threatens the work of the historian by subjecting him to predetermined explanatory schemes and thus forcing him to tailor his evidence so that it fits the so-called paradigm imposed from outside.' He argued instead that the material left to us in the past must be read 'in the context of the day that produced it . . . The present must be kept out of the past if the search for the truth of that past is to move towards such success as in the circumstances is possible.'[1] Thus the historian's questions should be formulated not by some present theory but from the historical sources themselves.[2]

In putting forward this view, Elton was disagreeing strongly with E. H. Carr's definition of a historical fact. Carr argued that a past event did not become a historical fact until it was accepted as such by historians. His example was the fact that a gingerbread-seller was kicked to death by a crowd at Stalybridge Wakes in 1850; until mentioned by George Kitson Clark in a book on Victorian England, this was not, Carr says, a historical fact. Historical facts were therefore constituted by theory and interpretation. They did not exist independently.[3] There is a semantic confusion here which has caused endless trouble ever since Carr fell into it and which needs clearing up before the discussion can proceed. A historical fact is something that happened in history and can be verified as such through the traces history has left behind. Whether or not a historian has actually carried out the act of verification is irrelevant to its factuality: it really is there entirely independently of the historian. This is why historians commonly speak of 'discovering' facts about the past, for instance, in coming across a source which tells them of this previously unknown incident at the Stalybridge Wakes. Where theory and interpretation come in is where facts are converted into evidence (that is, facts used in support of an argument); and here theory and interpretation do indeed play a constitutive role. For historians are seldom if ever interested in discrete facts entirely for their own sake; they have almost always been concerned with what Ranke called the 'interconnectedness' of these facts. Thus the fact of the gingerbread salesman's death can be used as evidence in a number of different ways, according to the historian's purpose: as an aspect of crowd behaviour in this period; as part of a study of food supplies; as an example of festivals and leisure pursuits; as an element in a history of the Manchester area; and so on. Nevertheless, while it is multifaceted as evidence, the gingerbread salesman's death is singular as fact. Facts thus precede interpretation conceptually, while interpretation precedes evidence.

The likelihood of the gingerbread salesman's unfortunate death being a historical fact in this sense is moderately but not overwhelmingly high, because the reference Kitson Clark used for it was not a contemporary one, but a set of memoirs written by 'Lord' George Sanger, and memoirs are notoriously unreliable even where they are giving eyewitness accounts of happenings in the past. If I had been Kitson Clark, I should have looked for a contemporary document to verify my claim. It is for this reason, I think, not because it has not been widely quoted elsewhere (except in discussions of Carr's *What is History*),[4] that the status as a historical fact of the gingerbread salesman's murder in 1850 must be regarded as still rather provisional, to say the least. The seconder and sponsors for its membership of the (not very select) club of historical facts awaited by Carr must be not other historians but other, preferably contemporary, documents, and these so far have not been found. Contemporary newspapers reported the fair very fully, but where Kitson Clark stressed the role of drink in leading to acts of violence, the papers noted that 'very few drunken people were seen in the streets at any time during the wakes.' There were descriptions of morris dancers and archery displays and accounts of an ascent in a balloon, but no mention of any violent incidents at all, though one paper did report the arrest of some petty thieves who had come over from Manchester. Kitson Clark cited Sanger's memory of the Wakes as an example of the persistence of rough, brutal and drunken behaviour from the eighteenth century into the early Victorian era. The contemporary sources, which went out of their way to stress the 'large audience' which 'patiently listened' to the speeches of 'a company of tee-totallers' who had come over to the Wakes on the Sunday, would seem to indicate the opposite.[5]

But even if we could find contemporary documents which established the fact of the gingerbread salesman's death, would the historian's account reflect reality in the same way as the contemporary sources did? The answer must be yes and no. When Kitson Clark mentions the incident, his text might theoretically at least be taken as a direct reflection of a real event. But when he uses this fact as evidence for an argument about violence in Victorian England then the matter stands rather differently. Before we can accept his argument, we need a lot more evidence besides. In addition, the likelihood is that Kitson Clark wanted to put forward an argument about Victorian violence, and went looking for the evidence rather than the other way round; and as we have seen, he did not look far enough, or he would have recognized that the evidence he selected was not very sound. In this case, at least, the historian's work does not begin at the archive door, it begins long before. The historian for-mulates a thesis, goes looking for evidence and discovers facts.[6]

Fact and evidence are therefore conceptually distinct and should not be confused with each other, as Carr con-fused them. But the terminological confusion that has bedevilled the whole debate about historical facts does not stop here. A similar misunderstanding to that engendered by Carr can be found in the distinction drawn by White between facts and events. An event, he tells us, is something that happened, but a fact is something constructed by the historian or existing in the remains of the past, in documents.[7]

In historical terms, I think it fair to say, a fact does not have to be an event: for example, it could be a building, now long since disappeared, in a certain place; or a boundary between two states; or a set of stocks and shares owned by a government minister; or a legal prohibition of some activity or other; or a liaison between a politician and a courtesan; or the thickness of armour-plating on a battleship or tank; or any one of a vast range of things, none of which could be described as an 'event', even if it is connected to an event. An event is a fact, but a fact is not necessarily an event. History is not just about events, it is about many other aspects of the past as well, and that applies not just to economic, social, cultural or intellectual history but to much more 'event-oriented' kinds of history, such as political or military history, as well.

Thus White is wrong to imply that historiographical consensus about any event in the past is difficult to achieve and is always open to revision from another perspective, if he means that future historians will start to say that the Stalybridge Wakes did not take place in 1850, or that there were no gingerbread salesmen there (they were in fact recorded in the newspapers already cited), or make some other factual assertion of this kind. Only if new evidence is found to amend or cast doubt on the historian's account of a fact – as in the case of the (now seemingly rather dubious) story of the gingerbread-seller's death at the Stalybridge Wakes – does revision at this level take place. But it is doubtful whether White really does mean this. If he means, as I think he does, that there will always be argument about what the alleged death of the gingerbread salesman meant for the state of public order in Victorian England, and how it is to be interpreted as evidence for larger arguments about the period, then surely he is right.[8]

II

What is at issue, therefore, is how historians use documents not to establish discrete facts, but as evidence for establishing the larger patterns that connect them. Are these patterns, these connections, already there, waiting to be discovered by a neutral process of cognition, or do historians put them there themselves? Some writers on history have argued that historians are deceiving themselves if they imagine their documents to be a kind of transparent window through which larger truths about the past become visible. So great, they suggest, are the problems which the documents present, that the 'traditional confidence' of historians that they can get their facts 'right', or reach through the sources to the 'essential truth' beyond, is completely misplaced.[9] In this view, as the American medievalist Nancy F. Partner has observed, historical 'facts' become 'constructed artifacts no different in cognitive origin than any made thing or "fiction"'.[10] 'The basic claim of historians that their narratives rest on fact,' two of her colleagues have confidently asserted, 'can be, indeed has been, dismantled.'[11] This is not least because documents, as Dominick LaCapra has remarked, 'are texts that supplement or rework "reality" and not mere sources that divulge facts about "reality".'[12] Documents are always written from somebody's point of view, with a specific purpose and audience in mind, and unless we can find all that out, we may be misled. Too often, claims LaCapra, historians unwittingly carry the biases of such documents directly into their own work (or, as he puts it: 'All history, moreover, must more or less blindly encounter the problem of a transferential relation to the past whereby the processes at work in the object of study acquire their displaced analogues in the historian's account.')[13]

'Historians often read texts as simple sources of information on the level of content analysis.'[14] This amounts in his view to a 'reductive use of texts and documents'.[15]

In similar vein, another American historian, Catriona Kelly, has claimed as an achievement of postmodernist theory that 'antagonistic, combative and counter-intuitive strategies of textual reading' have all been 'developed in the wake of deconstructionism'. She urges historians to adopt an 'aggressive attitude' to the sources, 'concentrating not on the most obvious interpretation, but on secondary layers of meaning.' But this injunction has had little measurable effect. 'The impact of non-referential language theory, deconstruction and the exposure of hegemonic interests embedded in what used to pass for neutral description' has not, as Nancy F. Partner has noted, 'left the ancient discipline shattered beyond recuperation.'[16] This is perhaps because 'reading against the grain', as Kelly tells historians they should now begin to do, has been the stock-in-trade of the profession for a very long time.[17] Historians, as Lawrence Stone has protested, were even in his youth ('forty or fifty years ago') taught 'that documents – we did not call them texts in those days – were written by fallible human beings who made mistakes, asserted false claims, and had their own ideological agenda which guided their compilation; they should therefore be scrutinized with care, taking into account authorial intent, the nature of the document, and the context in which it was written.' Since he also says in the same article, written in 1992, that he was taught 'forty or fifty years ago' that 'we should follow the advice of E. H. Carr and before we read the history, examine the background of the historian,' and since Carr did not proffer such advice until the publication of *What is History?* in 1961, or in other words only thirty years before, we may perhaps doubt whether Stone really was taught all these things in his youth. But he clearly believes them now, and indeed he is right to say that these are all assumptions on which historians conventionally operate. He also claims to have been taught 'that perceptions and representations of reality are often very different from, and sometimes just as historically important as, reality itself,' and this too is a fact of which any historian dealing with original source-material is often only too painfully aware, since it makes the task of writing history a good deal more complicated than it would be if sources were indeed the kind of one-to-one reflection of the real world that postmodernists claim historians think they are.[18]

'The whole art of historical research, in many cases,' as Raphael Samuel pointed out in one of his last writings, 'is to *detach* documents from the "discourse" of which they formed a part and juxtapose them with qualitatively different others.' This involves not ignoring or discounting the language in which they are written, but comparing it with the language of the other documents in question. Ever since the Ancient Greek historian Thucydides, historians have grappled with the problem of 'measuring words against deeds', as Samuel says, 'and attempting to judge their representativity.' It might be illuminating in some cases to juxtapose seemingly unrelated events, or to range freely through history, as the French philosopher-historian Michel Foucault does, ignoring questions of historical specificity unless they can be assimilated to free-floating discourses. But the general value of such an exercise is limited. 'Instead of grubbing about in the archives,' Samuel complains, 'they (i.e. postmodernists) can take the higher ground where universes of meaning clash and craggy peaks dispel the clouds of unknowing. Instead of painstakingly documenting the past, they can imaginatively re-invent it.'[19] Samuel's feeling that this kind of freedom can only be achieved by a measure of irresponsibility is palpable.

The real question at issue here is *what enables us* to read a source 'against the grain', and here theory does indeed come in. Theory of whatever kind, whether it is a general set of theses about how human societies are structured and human beings behave, or whether it is a limited proposition about, say, the carnivalesque in history, or the nature of human communication within a pre-industrial village, derives from the historian's present, not from the historian's sources. It is vital for the historian to use it. Without anthropological theory developed in the study of African rural society in the twentieth century, for example, the history of European witchcraft in the seventeenth century would not have made the huge leaps in understanding it has achieved in the last twenty-five years, gains which have only come about because theory enabled Keith Thomas (for instance) to read the sources in a new and original way.[20] Without Marxist theory, urban and labour history would be enormously impoverished, and a major, influential classic such as E. P. Thompson's *The Making of the English Working Class* would never have been written.[21] Without modern economic theory, historians would have no understanding of industrialization, and would not have known how to read or use the quantitative and other evidence it generated.

If ideas and theories in the historian's own time are what allow a reading of documentary material in a way that cuts across or runs counter to the purposes of the people who wrote it, then it follows that the same document can be legitimately used as evidence for a variety of purposes by different historians. It is manifestly not the case that there is always a one-to-one correspondence between the *evidence* provided in a source or a document and the *fact* to which it refers. Thus for example in his famous book *Montaillou*, the French historian Emmanuel Le Roy Ladurie read inquisitorial reports for different evidence and in many cases different facts than those quarried from them by previous writers. While they had been interested in the inquisition itself, and in the Cathar heresy it was attempting to extirpate, Le Roy Ladurie was interested in using the *incidental* details the heretics revealed about their everyday lives to construct an intimate portrait of human relationships and human existence in a medieval village.[22] Characteristically, Sir Geoffrey Elton criticized him for doing this, considering he should have stuck to the inquisition, as his predecessors had done.[23] But it is difficult to see any justification for this argument. Elton is completely wrong in his view that there is only one legitimate way to read a given document. Documents can be read in a variety of ways, all of them, theoretically at least, equally valid. Moreover, it is obvious that our way of reading a source derives principally from our present-day concerns and from the questions that present-day theories and ideas lead us to formulate. Nor is there anything wrong in this.

Critics of 'documentary fetishism' have homed in on this point and treated the Eltonian position as if it were a universally accepted orthodoxy. The intellectual historian H. Stuart Hughes has levelled the charge that historians in the USA 'seem to have forgotten – if they ever properly learned – the simple truth that what one may call progress in their endeavours comes not merely through the discovery of new materials but at least as much through a *new reading* of materials already available.'[24] Hughes of course has a strong vested interest in asserting this 'simple truth', since he has never discovered any new material himself in any of his publications, but has devoted his entire career to going over old ground. His view is shared by William H. McNeill, of the University of Chicago, who used the occasion of his presidential address to the American Historical Association in 1986 to castigate his colleagues for practising a 'historiography that aspires to get closer and closer to the documents – all the documents and nothing but the documents' because this meant 'merely moving closer and closer to incoherence, chaos, and meaninglessness'.[25] Coming from a historian whose lifelong specialism had been in the history of the whole world from the beginnings of humanity to the present, and whose acquaintance with original documents was correspondingly limited, this view was perhaps unsurprising, if somewhat tactlessly expressed.

In a slightly wider sense, perhaps Elton was right to note that criticisms of 'documentary fetishism' and the advocacy of reinterpretation as the primary task of the historian have mainly emanated from intellectual historians. After all, they use sources in a different way from most historians: as interpretative vehicles for ideas, not as clues to an exterior reality. Moreover, they work with a very limited number of classic texts, written by a handful of authors, or in other words, in a field where new documentary discoveries have inevitably become extremely rare. Reinterpretation is therefore almost the only option available to them.[26] When an intellectual historian reads Hobbes's *Leviathan* or Marx's *Das Kapital*, it is not in order to use their writings to reconstruct something outside them, but in order to construct an interpretation of what they mean or meant. There are indeed many interpretations of these thinkers' ideas, not least because the systems of thought Hobbes and Marx established were so wide-ranging that they never became completely closed. But the possibility of reinterpreting them by means of new documentary discoveries has almost ceased. (Though one can never be completely sure that no new documents by or about Hobbes or Marx will turn up, scholars have been combing every conceivable archive for them for decades, and it seems rather unlikely.)

The impatience of intellectual historians with their colleagues' concern for the discovery of original documentation seems understandable, but it is also reasonable to call for a little academic tolerance here: historical knowledge and understanding can surely be generated both by the discovery of new documents and by the imaginative reinterpretation of old ones. The discovery of the Dead Sea Scrolls in 1947, for instance, imposed a new agenda of interpretation irrespective of contemporary political assumptions. At the same time, Charles Beard's reinterpretation of the American Constitution owed little to newly discovered documents, yet transformed our knowledge and generated massive debate that led to a real advance in historical understanding.[27] Historians are always led by their present-day concerns; the truth does not simply emerge from an unprejudiced or neutral reading of the sources, even if such a thing were possible; the Dead Sea Scrolls themselves have been the subject of huge controversy almost since their discovery. Not all sources are equally open to a variety of interpretations or uses, and some indeed can only reasonably be interpreted in a single way. Others, like philosophical texts, can be, and have been, subject to almost constant reinterpretation over the years. Some sources are used to get at a historical reality beyond themselves; others are studied for their own sake. Historians work in a variety of ways, and specialists in one field should not tick off their colleagues in another for failing to conform to the pet methods they employ in their own.

III

The traces left by the past, as Dominick LaCapra has observed, do not provide an even coverage of it. Archives are the product of the chance survival of some documents and the corresponding chance loss or deliberate destruction of others. They are also the products of the professional activities of archivists, which therefore shape the record of the past and with it the interpretations of historians. Archivists have often weeded out records they consider unimportant, while retaining those they consider of lasting value. This might mean for example destroying vast and therefore bulky personnel files on low-ranking state employees such as ordinary soldiers and seamen, manual workers and so on, while keeping room on the crowded shelves for personnel files on high state officials. Yet such a policy would reflect a view that many historians would now find outmoded, a view which considered 'history' only as the history of the élites. Documents which seem worthless to one age, and hence ripe for the shredder, can seem extremely valuable to another.

Let me give an example from my personal experience. During research in the Hamburg state archives in the 1980s, I became aware that the police had been sending plain-clothes agents into the city's pubs and bars during the two decades or so before the First World War to gather and later write down secret reports of what was being said in them by socialist workers. The reports I saw were part of larger files on the various organizations to which these workers belonged. Thinking it might be interesting to look at a wider sample, I went through a typewritten list of the police files with the archivist, and among the headings we came across was one which read: 'Worthless Reports'. Going down into the muniment room, we found under the relevant call-number a mass of over 20,000 reports which had been judged of insufficient interest by the police authorities of the day to be taken up into the thematic files where I had first encountered this material. It was only by a lucky chance that they had not already been destroyed. They turned out to contain graphic and illuminating accounts of what rank-and-file socialist workers thought about almost every conceivable issue of the day, from the Dreyfus affair in France to the state of the traffic on Hamburg's busy streets. Nobody had ever looked at them before. Historians of the labour movement had only been interested in organization and ideology. But by the time I came to inspect them, interest had shifted to the history of everyday life, and workers' views on the family, crime and the law, food, drink and leisure pursuits, had become significant objects of historical research. It seemed worth transcribing and publishing a selection, therefore, which I did after a couple of years' work on them.[28] The resulting collection showed how rank-and-file Social Democrats and labour activists often had views that cut right across the Marxist ideology in which previous historians thought the party had indoctrinated them, because previous historians had lacked the sources to go down beyond the level of official pronouncements in the way the Hamburg police reports made it possible to do. Thus from 'worthless reports' there emerged a useful corrective to earlier historical interpretations. This wonderful material, which had survived by chance, had to wait for discovery and exploitation until the historiographical climate had changed.

The survival or otherwise of historical source-material is undeniably a matter of history itself. The record left us by the past is fragmentary, and the process of selection has not always been arbitrary. But historians have always known this, and have always thought it important to situate the surviving fragments in a broader context created by other remaining fragments, thus gaining some sense of the whole even where significant parts of it are missing. Doing historical research is rather like doing a jigsaw puzzle where the pieces are scattered all over the house in several boxes, some of which have been destroyed, and where once it is put together, a significant number of the pieces are still missing. The nature of the resulting picture will depend partly on how many boxes still survive and have been tracked down, and this depends partly on having some idea of where to look; but the picture's contours can still be filled in, even when not all the pieces have been located. We *imagine* the contours in this situation, and have to speculate on quite a bit of the detail; at the same time, however, the discovery of the existing pieces does set quite severe limits on the operation of our imagination. If they only fit together to produce a picture of a steam-engine, for instance, it is no good trying to put them together to make a suburban garden: it simply will not work. The fragmentary nature of the traces left to us by the past is thus no reason for supposing that historians' imagination is entirely unfettered when it comes to reconstructing it.

But this raises the further question of how we translate these traces into a language that we ourselves can understand. Often they are written not only literally in a different tongue (Latin, Greek, Anglo-Saxon or whatever it might be) but also metaphorically, so that the same word used in the seventeenth century as in the twentieth or twenty-first may have a subtly different meaning. 'Family' is a case in point: in the seventeenth century it was liable to include living-in servants, which is no longer true even in the rare households where they still exist. So serious is this problem

of source interpretation that one group of German historians has produced a multi-volume encyclopedia tracing the
shifting meanings of such words and concepts (alas, only in
German) through the centuries.[29] But such readings are a
matter of interpretation too. If different historians translate
historical sources from the historical language in which they
are written in two different ways, how do we know which
translation is 'correct'? How can we convey to today's
readers the meaning which such words had for historical
contemporaries? Are these meaningful questions anyway?
Some have argued that they are not; that there is in effect
no means of deciding between one translation and another,
no means therefore of accurately reconstructing the past
meanings of language and therefore the past to which it
refers.[30] But it *is* possible to reconstruct the meanings
which past language had for those who used it because the
individual words and concepts we come across in it were
part of a system of meaning, so their meaning can be
pinned down in terms of the other words and concepts
used in the system. We do not just read a single document
from, say, Tudor England, but hundreds, even thousands of
documents, in the course of a single research project, and
by seeing the same words and concepts used in conjunction
with many others, we can eventually isolate their meaning
in terms of the overall linguistic and conceptual system
being employed.

As a historian who works not only on a very different
society from our own but also one which uses an entirely different language – German – I have of course been faced by
a double challenge in this respect. Yet I do not think the
problem has been insurmountable, not least because many of
the sources I have used – civil service minutes from the
Justice Ministry in Berlin, for example, or surveillance

reports from the police files in Hamburg – employ a stereo-typed and repetitive language in which the same words and concepts appear all the time. In many ways, these sources are linguistically impoverished compared to the writings of the poets and philosophers who were the contemporaries of my policemen and bureaucrats. The kind of translation work the historian does is rather different from that carried out by someone who is translating Heinrich Heine or Immanuel Kant. What the historian is usually concerned with is language and thought at a fairly basic level, unless of course the subject is the history of poetry or philosophy. Relatively few historical controversies turn on the meanings of specific words or concepts or even documents. Insofar as they involve disagreements about the interpretation of source-material at all, they tend, rather, to centre on dis-putes as to what sources are relevant rather than what the sources actually mean. Moreover, it is sometimes possible for one source to have only one permissible interpretation in itself, and therefore to conclude that in a controversy over it, one historian's reading is true and the other's is false. The fact that this is not always the case does not mean that the possibilities of 'translation' are necessarily and inevitably open or infinite.

These points cast a somewhat negative light on the argument, originally put forward by R. G. Collingwood and subsequently elaborated by E. H. Carr, that all history is the history of thought, because ultimately, as Carr put it, 'no document can tell us more than what the author of the doc-ument thought.' When we read a source, we re-enact in our minds the thought of the person who wrote it.[31] But this is not necessarily true. Historians are accustomed to elicit meaning from documents by comparing them with other documents, and in this way a document can indeed be made to reveal more than its author thought. The gaps in a document, what it does not mention, are often just as interesting as what it contains. A statistic in a document can look quite different from what its author thought when we put it together with other statistics of which the author was unaware. We bring our own thoughts to bear on documents, and these can have a material effect on how the document is read. Many sources are not written at all. Getting inside the head of someone who buried treasure in a grave in the fourth century, or made a newsreel in the twentieth, is far from easy. Collingwood's notion of historical explanation is far too closely tied to the explanation of political events. If we are looking at the causes of the price-rise in sixteenth-century Spain, for instance, it does not make much sense to say that we are re-enacting the thoughts of the contemporaries who compiled the sources from which we derive the statistics.[32] Moreover, as two American historians have pointed out:

> Documents cannot be viewed as simple manifestations of a creator's intentions; the social institutions and material practices which were involved in their production played a significant part in shaping what was said and how it was said. The historian's meticulous reading of the evidence may therefore have little in common with what the author intended to say or what the contemporary reader understood to be said.[33]

Historians have to know about these institutions and practices, of course, and must bear this context in mind even while they detach the document from it. Otherwise they run the risk of violating the boundaries of its possible meanings in the service of their own particular interpretation.

Still, in the end, as Carr conceded, the conscious motive or thought of the writer of a document might be quite irrelevant to the purposes for which we wish to use the document, though we always have to take it into account.[34] What the historian writes, and what the documents say, are two different things, or at least, most historians have hitherto supposed them to be. But this distinction too, as we shall now see, has come under fire from critics of historical method.

IV

How do we derive historical facts from historical sources? The great Italian historian of the Ancient World, Arnaldo Momigliano, once described the foundations of modern historical scholarship in the following terms:

> The whole modern method of historical research is founded on the distinction between original and derivative authorities. By original authorities we mean statements by eye witnesses, or documents and other material remains that are contemporary with the event they attest. By derivative authorities we mean historians and chroniclers who relate and discuss events which they have not witnessed, but which they have heard of or inferred directly or indirectly from original authorities.[35]

This distinction, for which the terms 'primary' and 'secondary' sources are more commonly used, was introduced above all by German scholars in the nineteenth century. The contrast between their practice of always going to the primary or original sources, and that of, say, the Enlightenment historians, who relied heavily though not exclusively on chronicles and other secondary or derivative sources, has led many if not most historians to date the establishment of the subject on a professional or scientific basis to the nineteenth century and not before. It is this distinction which postmodernist critics of this historical tradition are now radically calling into question.

Perhaps the most far-reaching, comprehensive and explicit challenge to history as a discipline in this sense has been mounted by the French linguistic theorist Roland Barthes and the philosopher Jacques Derrida. As early as 1968, Barthes charged that historians' claim to reconstruct past reality rested on a pretence. History as written by professionals (or for that matter by anyone else) was, he said, 'an inscription on the past pretending to be a likeness of it, a parade of signifiers masquerading as a collection of facts'. Objectivity was 'the product of what might be called the referential illusion'. The illusion lay in the fact that the past was only *imagined* to be out there, waiting to be discovered: in practice it was an empty space waiting to be filled by the historian. Verbatim quotations, footnote references and the like were simply devices designed to produce what Barthes described as the 'reality effect', tricking the reader into believing that the historian's unprovable representations of the past were no more than straightforward reporting. Historians' own understanding of what they did remained, as Jacques Derrida noted, stubbornly 'logocentric', that is, they imagined they were rational beings engaged in a process of discovery. But this too was an illusion, like all forms of 'logocentrism'.

Such ideas derived — at some distance, to be sure — from theories originally advanced by the Swiss linguist Ferdinand de Saussure, who had noted early in the century that the relation of words to their meanings was usually completely arbitrary: the word *dog*, for instance, no more suggested in itself a carnivorous, barking quadruped than *chien* did in French, or *Hund* in German. Saussure argued therefore that words, or what he called signifiers, were defined not by their relation to the things they denoted (the signified) but by their relation to each other (e.g. 'dog' as opposed to 'cat'). But while Saussure regarded language as a system of differentiation constructed from signs, in which the signifiers were consistently related to one another in a logical way, subsequent theorists such as Jacques Derrida went much further and argued that the relation changed each time the word was uttered. Language was thus an 'infinite play of significations'. There was no 'transcendental signified' which determined meaning in itself. Everything was a mere arrangement of words, everything was 'discourse' or 'text'. Nothing existed outside language. Because we apprehended the world through language and nothing else, everything was a text.[36]

Advocates and critics alike are right in thinking that such views have radical implications for both literature and history. They imply that authors can no longer be regarded as having control over the meaning of what they write. In the infinite play of signification that constitutes language, the meaning of a text changes every time it is read. Meaning is put into it by the reader, and all meanings are in principle equally valid. In history, meaning cannot be found in the past; it is merely put there, each time differently, and with equal validity, by different historians. There is no necessary or consistent relation between the text of history and the texts of historians. The texts which survive from the past are as arbitrary in their signification as any other texts, and so too are the texts which use them. 'If there is nothing outside the text,' as the Princeton-based British historian Lawrence Stone has remarked, 'then history as we have known it collapses altogether, and fact and fiction become indistinguishable from one another.'[37] The medievalist Gabrielle Spiegel noted that 'if texts – documents, literary works, whatever – do not transparently reflect reality, but only other texts, then historical study can scarcely be distinguished from literary study, and the "past" dissolves into literature.'[38] This is not merely an alarmist diagnosis on the part of disciplinary conservatives. Postmodernists themselves have taken a similar view. Patrick Joyce, for example, has argued that because 'the events, structures and processes of the past are indistinguishable from the forms of documentary representation, the conceptual and political appropriations, and the historical discourses that construct them,' the idea of the social as something separate from discursivity disappears, and with it social history too.[39] In practice, his argument would seem to undermine the enterprise of history as commonly understood on a still wider scale.

For present reality can be felt and experienced by our senses; but the past no longer exists, it is not 'real' in the same sense as the world around us in the present is real. It too has become a text. Documents are the texts through which we apprehend the past, and there is no reality beyond them except other texts. 'Historians,' complains the philosopher Hans Kellner, '. . . routinely behave as though their researches were into the past, as though their writings were "about" it, and as though "it" were as real as the text which is the object of their labours.' This he declares to be 'naïve realism'.[40] Moreover, in principle historical documents are no different from the writings of historians themselves. The reader, the historian, invests documents and history books alike with meaning; there is no meaning there otherwise. So the distinction between primary and secondary sources is abolished, and with it the principle, enunciated by Momigliano, on which most modern historical scholarship effectively rests goes out of the window too. The primary/secondary distinction, charges Keith Jenkins, 'prioritizes the original source, fetishizes documents, and distorts the whole working process of making history.'[41] It is therefore time to abandon it.

It follows from this, Jenkins argues, that 'when we study history we are not studying the past but what historians have constructed about the past. In that sense,' he continues, 'whether or not people in the past had the same or different natures to us is not only undecidable but also not at issue. In that sense, the past doesn't enter into it. Our real need is to establish the presuppositions that historians take to the past.' It is thus 'more constructive' in his view to 'get into the minds of historians than the minds of the people who lived in the past and who only emerge, strictly speaking, through the minds of historians anyway'.[42] This view echoes that of the Dutch philosopher Frank Ankersmit, who argues that differences of historical opinion cannot satisfactorily be resolved or explained in terms of research; it is, rather, a matter of style. Differences of opinion between historians are in his view grounded in aesthetics. 'Content,' he says, 'is a derivative of style.' What the historian should do, therefore, is to stop investigating the past and start instead to think about ways in which it figures in the present. 'History . . .' he says, should 'no longer [be] the reconstruction of what has happened . . . but a continuous playing with the memory of this.'[43] In a similar way, Jenkins says that it is wrong to insist that history students should properly look at history itself rather than what historians have written about it. 'If history is interpretation, if history is historians' work[s], then historiography is what the "proper" study of history is actually about,' because history itself is simply a discourse, a 'congealed interpretation'.[44] History and historiography are the same thing. The point of history is to study historians, not to study the past.

Thus, as commentators have been quick to note, the historian's conventional concern with the past would be replaced in a postmodernist history with a focus on self-reflexivity and on problems of literary construction: how does the historian as author construct his or her text, how is the illusion of authenticity produced, what creates a sense of truthfulness to the facts and of closeness to past reality (or the 'truth-effect')? The implication is that the historian does not in fact capture the past in faithful fashion but rather, like the novelist, only gives the appearance of doing so. In literary theory we do not study the characters and actions Jane Austen wrote about in her novels as if they were something that existed outside her mind; why should we proceed differently with historians and the characters and actions they write about?

Such an approach follows a prominent vein in postmodernist thinking, in which the secondary rather than the primary becomes paramount: rather than study Shakespeare, it is often argued, we should study what critics have written about him, because one reading of Shakespeare is as good as another, and the text itself has no particular priority above interpretations of it, since all are forms of discourse, and it is wrong to 'privilege' one discourse over another. What all this might mean in practice is exemplified in a recent book by the feminist historian Diane Purkiss on *The Witch in History*. Purkiss explicitly rejects the idea of even attempting to answer 'the empirical questions that preoccupy many of my contemporaries' because of 'the impossibility of defining the witch'. Her purpose, rather, is to 'tell or retell the rich variety of stories told about witches'. The sources are too fragmentary to say with any degree of certainty why people believed in witches. Her interest in the treatment of witches by academic historians who have studied the sources under the illusion that they can say something meaningful or certain about witches is therefore to delineate the role the witch plays in their 'academic self-fashioning'. She makes no attempt to assess the relative merits of these historians in relation to their empirical accounts and interpretations of the historical phenomenon of witchcraft.

Now of course in practice, Purkiss actually has 'assembled evidence', as she admits, about all these things, and in doing so is not only carrying out the same procedures she so derides in others, but is also carrying them out in the service of an 'overall empirical purpose' she elsewhere deplores as a concept. Although she dismisses historical scepticism about empirical arguments as 'masculine' and the very notion of 'truth' in 'empirical history' as 'male', this does not stop her from criticizing the claims of some feminist historians about witchcraft as inherently 'improbable', thus arrogating to herself a right of scepticism which she denies to men – a sexist double standard if ever there was one, and an impossible one too, for if truth were really a male concept, then Purkiss could never even begin to claim that anything she said herself was true. Such contradictions aside, however, the important point about her account of witchcraft here is its refusal to make any distinction between historical, fictional and poetical accounts of witchcraft, and its concentration on the portrayal of witches in verse, drama, historical texts and other forms of secondary literature, rather than on the witches themselves. In Purkiss's book, all these texts, from

Shakespeare to Keith Thomas, are treated on an equal. basis.[45]

So in this approach there is no real difference between history and fiction. For Hayden White, researching and writing a history book is much the same as researching and writing a novel. Both are made up of elements of real human experience. Both have to meet the demands of correspondence to that experience and coherence in the way they present it. Both use language as their means of representing reality. Just like novelists, historians, says White, prefigure their field of enquiry by selecting and evaluating the evidence with the very linguistic and imaginative tools that will be used in the construction of the resulting narrative.[46] There is something to be said for White's observation that the great nineteenth-century historians whose work he analysed in his first major book *Metahistory* – Michelet, Ranke, Tocqueville, Burckhardt – had a great deal in common with their contemporaries among the novelists, like Balzac, though given the dominance of literary realism in the novel of the first half of the nineteenth century, this was hardly surprising. But White goes on to argue that the literary and linguistic forms by which different historians and novelists construct their work are all equally valid ways of representing the past.

There is in consequence no single correct view of any event or process, he argues, but many correct views,

> each requiring its own style of representation . . . When it is a matter of choosing among . . . alternative visions of history, the only grounds for preferring one over another are moral or aesthetic ones . . . One must face the fact that, when it comes to the historical record, there are no grounds to be found in the record itself for preferring one way of

> construing its meaning rather than another . . . We can tell
> equally plausible, alternative, and even contradictory sto-
> ries . . . without violating rules of evidence or critical
> standards . . . One can imagine not only one or two but any
> number of alternative stories of . . . any . . . culturally sig-
> nificant event, all equally plausible and equally authoritative
> by virtue of their conformity to generally accepted rules of
> historical construction.

Thus White not only denies the possibility of objective knowledge about the past, he also claims that it is pointless to argue about it, since each version forms a closed system of thought which is as valid as any other as a form of historical representation (however it may be judged on other grounds). Fictional narratives do not displace one another if both are written about the same subject. We do not say that one is true and the other false. White and those who follow him say that the same holds good for historical narratives.[47] 'No given set or sequence of real events,' White declares, 'is intrinsically tragic, comic, farcical, and so on.' Events can only 'be constructed as such' by the historian,[48] who is bound by the limited possibilities of literary representation to follow one or other of these models in constructing events, and to draw on a strictly finite number of metaphors and forms of emplotment. Literary models, in other words, construct the interpretation, rather than interpretation emerging from the sources and finding a form of literary expression appropriate to the truth of the argument and the material.

In all this theorization, historical fact more or less dis-appears from view. The distinction between primary and secondary sources, on which historical research rests, is abolished. The historian becomes an author like any other fabulist, the object of literary criticism and analysis. The boundaries between history and fiction dissolve. The demarcation line between history and historiography, between historical writing and historical theory, is erased. Whatever useful opportunities this line of thinking offers history as a discipline, there is no doubting the hostile intent towards traditional norms of historical judgment on the part of many of those who have developed it. How far their ideas can stand up to critical scrutiny is the question we now have to address.

4

SOURCES AND DISCOURSES

I

Belief in the historian's almost unlimited power to shape interpretation derives from the perception in postmodernist theory that a historical text, as the intellectual historian David Harlan argues, can no longer be regarded as having a wholly fixed and unalterable meaning given it by its author. But it is doubtful whether anyone, in fact, has *ever* believed that meaning can be fixed in this way. Anyone who has published a book and read the reviews of it will be well aware that various different interpretations of a text are possible. Some of them – whether motivated by malice, carelessness or simple stupidity on the part of the reviewer – are only remotely related to the interpretation intended by the author. An awareness of the multiple meanings of texts, and their relative autonomy from the intentions of the author, has long been part of the stock-in-trade of the historian. That most traditional branch of historical scholarship, diplomatic history, has been largely built on the analysis of the ambiguities of diplomatic documents – not all of them intentional – and has taken much of its analytical power from its awareness of the possibility, even likelihood, that a treaty, or a protocol, could, and often would, be interpreted by different states in different ways. Political historians have always known that a speech by an individual statesman can often have the opposite effect from that intended; and they have always been aware that a politician may frequently fail to make his meaning clear to his audience, and produce in consequence what Harlan describes as the post-structuralist paradigm of an 'unruly text spewing out its manifold significations, connotations and implications'.[1]

The language of historical documents is never transparent, and historians have long been aware that they cannot simply gaze through it to the historical reality behind. Historians know, historians have always known, that we can only see the past 'through a glass, darkly'. It did not take the advent of postmodernism to point this out. What postmodernism has done is to push such familiar arguments about the transparency or opacity of historical texts and sources out to a set of binary opposites and polarized extremes. To an imagined historian believing that the language of texts is a transparent window on to the mind of its author, they oppose the equally unreal picture of a situation in which the author has no relevance to the content of a text at all. The French theorist Paul Ricoeur argues for example that because 'the reader is absent from the act of writing, the writer is absent from the act of reading . . . the text thus produces a double eclipse of reader and writer.'[2] But this is not so. A text is always written for a readership and framed according to the writer's expectations of how the intended readers will take it. Similarly, the reader is always mindful of the purposes and intentions of the writer during the act of reading. All this remains true even when people read a document not addressed to them – people like historians, in fact.

When we read, for example, a diplomatic dispatch from, say, Lord Palmerston to the Prussian Foreign Minister in the early 1860s, we bear both reader and writer in mind; it would be foolish to do otherwise. We remain aware of the fact that the Prussian Foreign Minister may have taken the dispatch to mean something slightly different from what Lord Palmerston intended, so to understand the text, we have to know not only other texts of both writer and reader, but also the political and diplomatic contexts in which they operated, knowledge which requires the reading of yet further texts. Moreover, we know what happened to Anglo-Prussian relations in the course of German unification in the 1860s and 1870s (they deteriorated), and in a wider sense we know what happened to Anglo-German relations from the period of unification up to the middle of the twentieth century (they culminated in two world wars). We cannot help reading the dispatch in the light of this knowledge, whereas it was written not only without the knowledge of these later developments, but also without much idea of what was going to happen in the weeks and months after it was written, although obviously Palmerston had some idea of what he *hoped* would happen as a result of writing the dispatch. In this sense it would not make much difference if we could by some magic summon both gentlemen before us and grill them in person on what the dispatch actually meant: we would still have to read those other documents to make sense of it and to inform ourselves sufficiently to ask intelligent questions. Even if they were made aware of later developments too, we still could not wholly rely on the answers they gave, for who can wholly rely on what diplomats and politicians say in any case?

As historians, we clearly cannot recover a single, unalterably 'true' meaning of a dispatch simply by reading it; on the other hand, we cannot impose any meaning we wish to on such a text either. We are limited by the words it contains, words which are not, contrary to what the postmodernists suggest, capable of an infinity of meaning. And the limits which the language of the text imposes on the possibilities of interpretation are set to a large extent by the original author. Postmodernist theorists are simply being unrealistic here. The fact is, as Dominick LaCapra sensibly remarks, that historical research is a dialogue between two kinds of significances – the historian's and the document's. 'The historian enters into a "conversational" exchange with the past and with other enquirers seeking an understanding of it.' Historians have to 'listen attentively to possibly disconcerting "voices" of the past and not simply project narcissistic or self-interested demands upon them'. Thus in any history book there is in fact a multiplicity of voices, and the historian may also be using several.[3] Something like this can be seen in Roy Porter's description of Gibbon's *Decline and Fall of the Roman Empire*:

> Gibbon coped with bias by revealing it; by exposing the prejudices of his sources, and presenting, rather than suppressing, the personality of 'the historian of the Roman Empire'. Impartiality arose not out of a fetishism of facts but from the operations of the mind, from analysis, imagination, wit and a capacity to hold judgment in suspense. Gibbon's 'great work' reads like a chorus of voices. The contemporaries speak; Gibbon's sources comment on them; Gibbon adds his glosses, often scolding away in the footnotes; and the reader is invited to listen and participate in the intellectual symposium.[4]

Reading any history book necessarily involves listening to this chorus of different voices sounding through the text.

Postmodernist critics have alleged by contrast that historians adopt an omniscient position, using the language of scholarship to suggest to readers that the knowledge they are conveying is neutral, objective and derived from a transcendent source rather than linked to the historian's own purposes. Thus they claim to have succeeded in alerting 'an unwary public, as well as their peers, to how the different perspectives of historians enter into their books'.[5] But have the readers of history books, whether professional or otherwise, always been so 'unwary'? It simply isn't the case that readers gullibly swallow everything the historian writes as if it were the absolute truth. Too many commentators, postmodernist and otherwise, seem to harbour an arrogant underestimation of the sophistication and critical discernment of those who read history books. As Roy Porter has remarked, 'The reader seems to be a missing person in so much history-writing today, presumably because academic historians have largely lost all sense of writing for a public.'[6] This goes *a fortiori* for writers on historiography, who seldom pause to think how their work, or, still more, that of the historians they are writing about, is actually read.

In practice, surely, no reader comes to a history book naïvely willing to believe everything it says. Postmodernists are right to say that readers bring to history their own presuppositions, their own beliefs and purposes. The point, however, is that these no more completely shape their reading of the book than do the intentions of the author. Reading is a matter of interaction between reader and writer, in which neither is necessarily or inevitably dominant. Moreover, historians on the whole do not write as if *everything* they say is *absolutely* true. On the contrary, the conventional language of historians has *always* made a specific point of detailing the varying levels of certainty or probability attaching to what they say. It is not just that the words 'probably' and 'perhaps' occur fairly frequently in historical work; the careful historian in fact deploys a large variety of stylistic devices to indicate the relative strength or weakness of the argument advanced, and to indicate how tentative or otherwise are the conclusions reached. When, exceptionally, a historian like A. J. P. Taylor made what he liked to call 'snap judgments' and issued statements of seemingly dogmatic finality about complex historical issues, it is clear that these were intended to provoke his readers into thinking about the subject, rather than to bully them into believing that he was telling the absolute truth about it.

By making their own preconceptions and purposes explicit, historians have customarily tried to provide readers with the knowledge to read their books against their own intentions if so desired. Moreover, in teaching undergraduates and graduate students alike, university historians' primary aim is to get them to adopt a critical and questioning attitude to the books and articles they read – including their own (otherwise what value would teaching be to a historian, and why do so many historians acknowledge in the prefaces to their own books the crucial contribution of their students in having forced them to rethink or reformulate many of their arguments?). One postmodernist writer, Beverley Southgate, has claimed that the 'traditional' model of history as the pursuit of the truth about the past means 'that students of history will be taught not so much to question as to conform to existing dogma'. Nothing could be further from the reality of the situation; one wonders whether Southgate's colleagues in the History Department at the University of Hertfordshire, where he teaches, would recognize their own teaching techniques in this description. One hopes not.[7]

Historical writing as well as teaching makes a point of conveying the provisional and uncertain nature of interpretation, and the need to test it constantly against the source materials used as evidence in its favour. This is why it is important not to confuse what happened with how we find out about it. Patrick Joyce may assert that 'the events, structures and processes of the past are indistinguishable from the forms of documentary representation, the conceptual and political appropriations, and the historical discourses that construct them.'[8] But this is self-evidently not the case. Discourse does not construct the past itself; the most that it is possible to argue is that it constructs our attempts to represent it. Joyce himself confounded his own theoretical claims in a book published at the same time as his polemic against Lawrence Stone in *Past and Present*. Whilst arguing for a 'semiology of the social order' in this work, Joyce also noted that 'conceptions of the social order were related to attempts to bring order and decency to the experience of poverty, insecurity and labour.'[9] However Joyce interprets the concept of 'experience' here, the implication that poverty was materially real is clear enough. He insists, indeed, on underlining his belief, as expressed in his book, that discourses in the past structured perceptions 'only because they articulated the needs and desires of their audiences'.[10]

As Joyce's own historical work suggests, the historian's voice is important, but so too are the voices of the past which the historian is trying to transmit. It is perfectly true to say, as Keith Jenkins does, that most school and university students learn history almost exclusively through reading secondary work.[11] But this is not really relevant to arguments about the nature of historical knowledge, which relate in the first place to the extent to which it is possible to reconstruct the past from the remains it has left behind – or, in other words, to historical research based on primary sources. It is certainly true that to a large extent we use the same procedures in reading secondary sources as we do in reading primary materials: we ask who has written the document, and why, and to whom the document is addressed, and why, we check it out for internal consistency and for consistency with other documents relating to the same subject, and if it contains information derived from other sources, we ask where this information comes from and do our best to check it out too. But this does not mean the *objects* of these identical procedures (primary and secondary sources) must be identical too.

To call the past a 'text' is of course to use a metaphor, not to attempt a description.[12] The past is much more than a mere text, and to attempt to read it as a text is to capture only a small part of its reality. Social and political events are not the same as literary texts. Gabrielle Spiegel has claimed: 'No historian, even of positivist stripe, would argue that history is present to us in any but textual form,'[13] and elsewhere she has referred to 'the literary nature of all historical documents'.[14] But a historical source is not the same as a literary text. It is not necessarily, indeed it is not usually a description of an event or a state of mind or a story. From Mommsen's use of Roman inscriptions through to the Rankeans' analysis of diplomatic documents, from the cliometricians' number-crunching of parish records of births, marriages and deaths to the medievalists' surveys of field systems, buildings and archaeological remains, historians have long been skilled in dealing with sources that do not directly tell a story themselves, or report events even in the most recent past. Moreover, radio and cinema, videotapes and camcorders, computer printouts, photocopying, microfilm, faxes, electronic databases, the Internet and the World-Wide Web are all generating new forms of source-material for future historians, even if a large proportion of it gets lost. It is foolish to suppose, as John Vincent does, that because the written word is declining as a form of communication, history is dying too.[15]

The textual metaphor can easily be unhelpful to the discussion of history, by suggesting that history depends on the analysis and composition of literary texts just as much as literary criticism and scholarship does. Even where the historian's sources are written down, they very often bear little resemblance to any form of literature. They may be statistical series of corn prices or criminal offences, they may be lengthy lists of individuals belonging to this or that organization, they may be brief inscriptions or graffiti carved into a Roman wall. The conventional tools of literary analysis are of little use in dealing with such materials. On the other hand, historians do not simply take such materials as direct reflections of past reality. Maps can deceive, as Mark Monmonier has pointed out in his entertaining manual *How to Lie with Maps*.[16] So too can figures and graphs. Statistical series and lists, like visual materials, were all compiled by human beings with specific purposes in mind, and the methods used to gather serial data in the past were often somewhat haphazard and uncertain. But that is to say no more than that they have to be treated with the customary scepticism with which the historian treats more conventional written sources, and the same kind of source-criticism has to be applied to them as well.

II

Some writers have claimed that it is impossible for historians to enable the past to 'speak for itself' because if the past were to express itself it would have to re-enact itself.[17] This assertion would seem to depend on the belief that when you or I think we are expressing ourselves in speech or writing, we are not really doing so at all, but producing an arbitrary set of words that has no determinate relationship to ourselves at all. However, even if we develop, perhaps even 're-invent' our identity during our lifetime, and even if we have not one unitary self but an identity that is multifaceted, it is still usually possible to discern some consistency in our utterances over time, and indeed most people, unless they are politicians, go to some trouble to make sure that they do express themselves in a reasonably consistent and non-contradictory way. We do in fact invest our words with meanings which have a real relationship to our own life and our own existence; life would be very difficult for us indeed if we did not.

Language and grammar are in fact not completely arbitrary signifiers, but have evolved through contact with the real world in an attempt to name real things. In a similar way, historical discourse or interpretation has also evolved through contact with the real historical world in an attempt to reconstruct it. The difference is that this contact is indirect, because the real historical world has disappeared irrecoverably into the past. It has to be established through a reading of the documentary and other fragments which the real world of the past has left behind. Yet these are not arbitrarily configured discourses either, but were themselves created in a much more direct interaction with reality. Language is not in the end purely self-reflective. Experience tells us that it mediates between human consciousness and the world it occupies, as Hayden White himself noted in 1975.[18] If it did not describe and inform us about the past, then we would not be able to know that the past had any real existence at all. Hence admitting the existence of the past as extra-textual reality implies recognizing that language can describe things external to itself. Content is not a derivative of style: it is possible to describe the same thing accurately in a number of different styles, just as it is possible to give a full and fair account of, say, Gibbon's argument about the causes of the rise of Christianity without making a misguided attempt to imitate the literary style in which he put it.[19]

Moreover, a postmodernist such as Jenkins or Ankersmit would also presumably wish to maintain that he is expressing his own beliefs in a consistent and rational way in what he writes, even if this is not always the case in reality. Now there is no real difference in principle between Jenkins writing something in 1995 in a book which I am reading in 1997, and, say, King Henry VIII of England writing something in a letter in 1532 which I am reading in 1997. Both have written these texts in the past, even if Henry VIII's past is more remote than Jenkins's. Both wished to express a meaning or meanings which had a bearing on their own life in some way. When King Henry writes to Ann Boleyn of 'the great affection I have for you',[20] he does not have to re-enact this affection in person in order to express himself, however much he might have wished to, any more than when Jenkins says his 'new work is addressed primarily (though obviously not exclusively) to advanced and under-graduate students and their teachers' he has to gather a group of such people together and start haranguing them in order to give them access to the reality of what he is saying. In other words, taking Jenkins's book *On 'What is History?'* as a historical text, it is simply not true to say, as he does, that we cannot have access to his meaning because the past, in its incarnation in the Jenkins of 1995, cannot express itself.

The postmodernists are caught in a paradox of their own making here. They want to argue that all texts are essentially the same, that there is no difference, for example, between a primary source and a secondary source, between Henry VIII's letter or Jenkins's book and what someone else has written about either of these documents later on (for example, J. J. Scarisbrick's standard biography of King Henry, or my own account of Jenkins's book in the pages which you are now reading). Yet there is a very real difference between what somebody writes and the account someone else gives of it. I would like to think that I have quoted Jenkins fully and fairly in these pages, and given an accurate representation of his views. But if he wishes to check whether in fact this is the case, then surely he is going to go back to the book itself rather than to some other person's account of it. The principle at work here is no different from that operating in the case of Henry VIII's letter and the account of it given in a later biography.

The same kind of contradiction catches Jenkins's attempt to deal with Gabrielle Spiegel's argument that the 'dissolution of the materiality of the verbal sign means the dissolution of history'.[21] According to Jenkins, history as a discipline never did rest on a verbal sign whose materiality was not dissolved, since all verbal signs are immaterial anyway. But for Jenkins to attack Spiegel's position by calling it the product of 'ideology and mystification' is disingenuous, because he himself is on record as saying that *everything* is ideology, which means that his own position must be ideological too.[22] Why should we therefore accept his invitation to be 'suspicious of the motives' of those with whom he disagrees, and not be suspicious of his own motives as well? The point here is not merely the failure of postmodernist writers such as Jenkins to engage in the self-reflectivity they so passionately advocate for others; it is also the manner in which they take an unproven assumption from their own arsenal of beliefs (in this case, the immateriality of the sign) and berate their opponents for advancing arguments which are not based on an acceptance of it. If we believe that signs – words, language, concepts, arguments, books – do bear some relation to material reality, then Spiegel's fears begin to seem a lot more reasonable.

Because the past is constantly generating its own material remains, some have argued, 'it can and does constrain those who seek to find out what once took place,' even if those remains can never really speak for themselves. In their qualified defence of the historian's belief in past reality and the possibility of reconstructing it, Professors Appleby, Hunt and Jacob reject the idea that the past can impose its reality on the historian through these remains, and prefer instead to argue that the constraints which they impose on the possible variety of interpretations depends on the existence of 'a scholarly community whose principal task is to reconstruct, interpret, and preserve artifacts from the past', and which operates a 'complex set of rules' in so doing. But surely the past does impose its reality through the sources in a basic way. At the most elementary level, one cannot simply read into documents words that are not there. Moreover, it is highly dangerous to make objectivity in this sense dependent on the existence of a scholarly community. There was, after all, a scholarly community in Germany in the 1920s which remained in existence, largely unaltered in personnel and ideology, under Hitler's Third Reich; scholars nowadays are generally in agreement that the set of rules it operated in approaching the German past was seriously flawed and delivered an interpretation of history that was highly distorted. If we accept that this was because these rules were themselves faulty, however, we also have to accept that good rules transcend scholarly communities and do not therefore depend on their acceptance by them.[23] Those rules might include very basic precepts such as not altering documents, or not leaving out or suppressing material damaging to one's argument or purpose. In this sense, the documents do have an integrity of their own, they do indeed 'speak for themselves'. The constraints that past reality imposes through them on the historian are more than merely negative. That is why, as E. P. Thompson once said, 'the historian has got to be listening all the time . . . If he listens, then the material itself will begin to speak through him.'[24]

III

These issues, and others besides, were made painfully concrete in the American historical profession in the 1980s by the so-called Abraham affair. When the young American history professor David Abraham's book *The Collapse of the Weimar Republic* was published by Princeton University Press in 1981, many reviewers (including myself) hailed it for its originality, while at the same time finding its structural Marxism rather too schematic. Indeed, I thought that its central arguments were at such a high level of abstraction that they could not really be empirically validated at all, and that the book was best regarded as a work of political science rather than history, conforming therefore to a set of rules and conventions that were not strictly historical.[25] Other, more specialist reviewers were critical in a very different way. In particular, the conservative and avowedly anti-Marxist American historian Henry Ashby Turner, who had himself worked on the same source material, went on record accusing Abraham of deliberately inventing and falsifying archival material in order to discredit German capitalism and blame it for the collapse of the Weimar Republic. Appalled at these allegations, Abraham went back to the archives to check his sources, and replied to Turner admitting some minor errors but rejecting the main charges levelled against him.[26]

At this point, another American specialist in the history of big business in the Weimar Republic, Gerald Feldman, entered the fray with a further string of accusations. Feldman had originally recommended the book for publication by Princeton University Press, despite numerous errors which he had said should be corrected. But after learning of Turner's charges, he also learned that a graduate student, Ulrich Nocken, had checked all the quotations in Abraham's book for a review. Nocken reported that there were hundreds of egregious mistakes, including the printing of inaccurate paraphrases as if they were direct quotations from the documents, wrongly attributed letters and documents, mistranslations, misconstruals, inventions and falsifications of the sources. This persuaded Feldman that he had been wrong to assume that because Abraham had been awarded a PhD, his scholarly integrity could be trusted. As if to atone for his earlier gullibility in passing the manuscript for publication, Feldman now unleashed a ferocious campaign of denunciation, in which a large number of specialists in modern German history, including myself, were sent circulars exposing the errors in Abraham's work and declaring him unfit to be a member of the scholarly community. Abraham replied with a vigorous self-defence, lobbying the German history community on both sides of the Atlantic in his turn. But in the face of Feldman's campaign, which included denunciatory letters and phone calls to universities considering Abraham for an assistant professorship, this was, in the end, to no avail. As a result of Feldman's untiring hostility, Abraham was hounded out of the profession and went to law school, where he graduated with distinction and duly re-entered university employment, this time as a lawyer rather than as a historian, and therefore in a subject which is perhaps more comfortable with the manipulation and tendentious interpretation of evidence than history is.[27]

The affair raised three crucial issues apart from that of the professional ethics of the participants in the row. First, the relationship between Marxist and non-Marxist views of history. Was Hayden White right to argue that 'the Marxist view of history is neither confirmable nor disconfirmable by appeal to "historical evidence", for what is at issue between a Marxist and a non-Marxist view of history is the question of precisely what counts as evidence, and what does not?'[28] Was this, as Abraham's defenders maintained, an attempt by anti-Marxists to discredit him for political reasons, by rubbishing his scholarship without justification? Was a Marxist construal of a document inevitably a misconstrual in the eyes of an anti-Marxist? There was no doubt about Turner's anti-Marxism, and it is relevant to note that he himself was about to publish a large book on *Big Business and the Rise of Hitler* which constituted a massive demolition of the Marxist view that capitalists brought Hitler to power. On the other hand, Turner was on record as respecting those Marxist historians, notably Tim Mason, whose scholarship he held to be sound. Mason himself went into print distancing himself from Abraham and endorsing the importance of historical accuracy in research.[29] And Feldman had been generous in his praise of 'good Marxist and neo-Marxist history' and could in no sense be seen as anti-Marxist.[30] The controversy could not therefore be reduced to the status of a political disagreement. It was a disagreement over evidence and its uses.

The second issue that it raised was the relationship between fact and interpretation. Abraham's defenders claimed that his mistakes of detail made no difference to his overall interpretation. And indeed, when Abraham himself, having been back to the archives and checked over all his sources again, issued a 'corrected' second edition of the book, it was only the quotations, attributions, footnotes, references and other matters of detail that were corrected; he did not alter or amend one single aspect of his interpretation.[31] The critics of the second edition were able to point out that the citations and much of the evidence no longer supported the argument at a number of points. But in a sense they never had. Abraham's schema of rival agrarian and industrial power-blocks in the Weimar Republic was taken straight from the Greco-French Marxist political theorist Nicos Poulantzas. Abraham, it seems, had merely scoured the archives for 'evidence' that would back it up. When combined with Abraham's self-confessedly poor research skills and excessive haste in research, this had led to misreadings that, in more cases than not, supported his argument, and in many instances actually went beyond it in the direction of the old agency theory (that capitalists were directly, instead of merely indirectly, supporters of Nazism) – a theory which, ironically, he was claiming to transcend.

This leads on to the third point, namely the importance or otherwise of evidence, and the falsifiability of historical interpretations by means of an appeal to it. At one point in his book, Abraham cited a major German industrialist as writing in a private letter in the early 1930s that it was desirable 'to crystallize the bourgeois right and the Nazi Party into one', a declaration which admirably supported his overall interpretation. But the original document, cited accurately by Feldman, contained the crucial word 'not', so that it actually said the reverse of what Abraham said it did, and therefore went against his general argument.[32] On innumerable occasions, Abraham, Feldman showed, invented evidence by supplying additions or glosses from his research notes as part of actual quotations. Abraham indeed admitted that while in the archives he had failed to fence off quotes from original documents with inverted commas in his notes, so that he was frequently unable to distinguish them from his own (often, as it turned out, rather tendentious) summaries of other parts of the same documents. Thus he frequently quoted the latter as if they were the former. The book was so riddled with errors that some of them, as Abraham himself was quick to point out, actually went against the argument he was advancing.[33] But it is hard to quarrel with Feldman's conclusion that the general tendency of the mistakes was 'to exaggerate the evil role played by industry, to overdramatize its power and self-assurance, and to make arguments far beyond what the evidence would allow'.[34]

Abraham wrote in self-defence that as he carried out his research, there seemed to be 'an exemplary fit' between his initial hypotheses and the evidence he found.[35] But every working historian knows how unlikely that is. The first prerequisite of the serious historical researcher must be the ability to jettison dearly-held interpretations in the face of the recalcitrance of the evidence. If a letter from an industrialist says he does not want any crystallization of the bourgeois right and the Nazis, then no amount of theorizing will alter that fact, and there is no way round it. There is nothing mysterious about this; historians are perfectly used to trying out ideas on the evidence and throwing them away when they don't fit. Evidence running counter to the argument cannot be omitted or distorted, but must be explained, even at the cost of amending the argument or abandoning it altogether. Many historians and reviewers have commented on this point. Thus when the British Marxist historian Christopher Hill remarked in the preface to one of his books: 'I was advancing a thesis . . . I picked out evidence which seemed to support my case,' his critic J. H. Hexter rightly commented: 'Far from just looking for evidence that may support his thesis, he (i.e. the historian) needs to look for vulnerabilities in that thesis and to contrive means of testing them. Then, depending on what he finds, he can support the thesis, strengthen its weak points, or modify it to eliminate its weaknesses.'[36] It is clear that Abraham had failed to follow this basic procedure.

My own view is that while Abraham did not deliberately falsify evidence, he was extremely careless with it, far more so than is permissible in a work of serious historical scholarship, or indeed in any work of history; and that he *subconsciously* moulded the evidence gathered in his research notes in order to fit the interpretation he had worked out beforehand. It was not a question of middle-aged 'fact fetishists' against youthful champions of 'historical imagination', as some of Abraham's partisans claimed. Both in his book, and in his replies to Feldman, Abraham proved distressingly unable to tell fact from fiction. This was not, therefore, as Abraham himself and his supporters such as Peter Novick implied, a methodological dispute between theoretical and empirical historians in which the 'objectivists' demonstrated their continuing and, by implication, malign and stultifying grip on the American historical profession.[37] Abraham and his defenders maintained that any history book would reveal as many errors as his if it were subjected to the same level of intense, detailed scrutiny. Lawrence Stone, for instance, said:

> When you work in the archives you're far from home, you're bored, you're in a hurry, you're scribbling like crazy. You're bound to make mistakes. I don't believe any scholar in the Western world has impeccable footnotes. Archival research is a special case of the general messiness of life.[38]

But this too was a debatable point. For Stone was far from being an unimpeachable witness on this issue. When he was Abraham's age, in 1951, his own work had been subjected to a series of devastating and merciless attacks by his Oxford colleagues Hugh Trevor-Roper and J. P. Cooper in the *Economic History Review*, which had shown a similar catalogue of gross error to that discovered in Abraham's work. Stone had published an article arguing that English aristocratic landowners in the early seventeenth century were extravagant, financially inept, and declining in economic power. The conclusion was that this hastened the 'rise of the gentry' which was regarded by left-wing historians like R. H. Tawney as one of the main causes of the English Civil War. Trevor-Roper, however, pointed out that Stone had confused different generations of aristocrats with the same title, got many if not most of his sums wrong, and altogether misunderstood the nature of landownership at the time. In arguing that aristocratic ownership of manors had declined, for instance, Stone took county samples without realizing that aristocrats owned land in many different counties, and would readily sell their holdings in one to build up their estates in another; moreover, manors differed substantially in size, a factor Stone ignored completely, so that his figures showing a decline in the number of manors held by aristocratic landowners in some cases concealed an actual growth in the acreage and quality of land they possessed overall.

Trevor-Roper's critique was described variously as 'terrifying', 'brutal', and 'one of the most vitriolic attacks ever made by one historian on another'. Stone himself was forced to admit that there were 'very serious mistakes' in his article, and confessed to his 'unscholarly treatment' of much of the evidence.[39] When I was an undergraduate in Oxford, indeed, the dons, sniffy as ever about American universities, even Princeton, where Stone had gone to teach, were wont to sneer that he had been forced to seek employment in the USA because his position in Oxford had become untenable as a result of the controversy. Although he in fact went on to a highly successful career, publishing a series of major (though never less than controversial) works in the process, his mauling at the hands of Trevor-Roper clearly rankled even more than thirty years afterwards, as his defence of Abraham, with whom he evidently had a certain fellow-feeling, seems to suggest. More to the point, however, was the fact that Stone had recovered from this early débâcle and during his later career had exercised a major and undeniably significant influence on the study of early modern English history, and, through his perceptive and readable review articles, the study of history in general. To deny Abraham the same chance of making amends, as Feldman ultimately did, was surely wrong.

IV

The Abraham affair was taken up into the debate on post-modernism not least because it touched on the issue which was proving the crucial test of the claim that history was incapable of establishing any real facts about the past. Nazi Germany seemed to postmodernism's critics to be the point at which an end to hyper-relativism was called for. Postmodernists realized this. In replying to critics, Hayden White pointed out (in a footnote to one of the essays in *The Content of the Form*) that the Jewish historian Lucy Dawidowicz had attacked all previous writers on Nazism for misrepresenting, neglecting or trivializing the Holocaust, thereby implying that they too were writing more in literary than in factual terms, and that the Third Reich was no different from any other historical subject in this respect. But Davidowicz's views on this subject have rightly been generally viewed as distorted, exaggerated, over-polemical and uninformed about modern German and international historical scholarship. There is in fact a massive, carefully empirical literature on the Nazi extermination of the Jews. Clearly, to regard it as fictional, unreal, or no nearer to historical reality than, say, the work of the 'revisionists' who deny that Auschwitz ever happened at all, is simply wrong. Here is an issue where evidence really counts, and can be used to establish the essential facts. Auschwitz was not a discourse. It trivializes mass murder to see it as a text. The gas chambers were not a piece of rhetoric. Auschwitz was indeed inherently a tragedy and cannot be seen either as a comedy or a farce. And if this is true of Auschwitz, then it must be true at least to some degree of other past happenings, events, institutions, people, as well. What then are the implications of this for postmodernism?

In a set of conference papers devoted to this subject, *Probing the Limits of Representation*, edited by Saul Friedländer, a number of postmodernists and their critics sought to address this problem. Hayden White in particular retreated from his earlier position in order to defend himself against the accusation that his hyper-relativism gave countenance to the 'revisionist' enterprise of 'Holocaust denial'. He conceded that the facts of the Holocaust closed off the possibility of using certain types of emplotment to describe it. But in making this concession, he explicitly acknowledged the primacy of past reality in shaping the way historians write about it, thus abandoning his central theoretical tenet. The past turned out not to be completely at the mercy of historical narrativity and emplotment after all.[40]

White himself summed up his change of position by saying that in his early writings he was more concerned to point out the ways in which historians used literary methods in their work, and in so doing inevitably imported a 'fictive' element into it, because their written style did not simply report what they had found, but actually constructed the subject of their writing. In his later work he came to draw a sharper distinction between fiction on the one hand and history on the other. Rather than imagining the object first, then writing about it in a manner that was therefore mainly subjective, history existed only in the action of writing, involving a kind of simultaneous production or identification of the author of the discourse and the referent or thing about which he or she was writing. White made this shift of position essentially in response to the debate on the Holocaust, and it certainly seems to me to sum up more realistically than his earlier arguments the way in which historians actually go about their business. Historical imagination, he says, calls for the imagining of 'both the real world from which one has launched one's enquiry into the past and the world that comprises one's object of interest'.[41] This is a view from which it is hard for any historian to dissent.

What does the whole debate add up to in practical terms, then? According to Russell Jacoby, when postmodernists such as White and LaCapra deign to descend from the lofty heights of abstraction to offer concrete criticisms of actual works of history, 'what begins as a call for a radical departure in historical thought comes out sounding very familiar: the importance, complexity, and ambiguities of the text are continuously reiterated.'[42] This is perhaps taking too negative a view. Even Lawrence Stone admits that the 'linguistic turn' has 'taught us to examine texts with far more care and caution than we did before, using new tools to disclose covert beneath overt messages, to decipher the meaning of subtle shifts of grammar and so on.'[43] All this is to the good. And if Hayden White has had few direct imitators, his influence has been none the less real for being all the more diffuse. It can to some extent be traced in the use by other historians of terms such as 'emplotment' and the like, terms originally used by White himself, but more generally it can be seen in a growing awareness on the part of historians of the literary and narrative elements in their own work – research as well as writing – and that, surely, is no bad thing. Yet most of White's earlier arguments do not stand up. The distinction between primary and secondary sources on the whole has survived the withering theoretical hail rained down upon it by the postmodernists. The past does speak through the sources, and is recoverable through them. There is a qualitative difference between documents written in the past, by living people, for their own purposes, and interpretations advanced about the past by historians living at a later date.

Keith Jenkins has argued that historical method does not lead to historical truth. But in saying this, he confuses theory and method. Historical method is not what he says it is – feminist, neo-Marxist, structuralist, *Annaliste*, Weberian or whatever.[44] These things are *theories*. Historical *method* is based on the rules of verification laid down by Ranke and elaborated in numerous ways since his time. It is common to all historians working in all these various theoretical modes, as a glance at their heavily footnoted works will easily show. Even major methodological differences, for example between cliometricians churning quantitative data through their computers, intellectual historians engaged in a close reading of a small number of texts, or medieval historians deciphering archaeological finds, still fade into the background in comparison with the shared duty of 'getting it right' – of copying out and punching in the figures accurately, of verifying the wording and authorship of the text, of reporting the correct location of each find in the dig. It is not true to say that historians are 'not too concerned about discrete facts'.[45] On the contrary, whatever the criteria for the facts' selection, the vast majority of the historian's efforts are devoted to ascertaining them and establishing them as firmly as possible in the light of the historical evidence. Even Jenkins uses footnotes. Footnotes and bibliographical references really are designed to enable the reader to check the sources on which a historian's statement is made and to see whether or not they support it. They are not mere rhetorical devices designed to produce a spurious 'reality effect'. Postmodernists have claimed that

> Although historians often frame their criticisms of colleagues' work in terms of evidence – sources overlooked, misplaced emphasis, inappropriate categorization – such

criticisms cannot demonstrate the superiority of one interpretation or story-type over another. These debates over
evidence are largely diversionary; they are carried on as if
the choice and use of evidence will determine a historian's
perspective rather than that the historian's perspective
counts as evidence.[46]

This claim is misconceived. As the Abraham controversy –
and others too, such as the famous 'storm over the gentry' in
the 1950s – showed, interpretations really can be tested and
confirmed or falsified by an appeal to the evidence; and some
of the time at least, it really is possible to prove that one side
is right and the other is wrong. What counts as evidence is
not determined solely by one historian's perspective, but is
subject to a wide measure of agreement which transcends
the individual. Still, it has undeniably been a frequent cause
of dispute, above all, perhaps, when historians have come to
deal with the problem of causation, as we shall now see.

5

CAUSATION IN HISTORY

I

In his book *What is History?*, E. H. Carr famously declared
that 'the study of history is a study of causes.'[1] Historians
had to look for a variety of causes of any given event, work
out their relationship to one another if there was one, and
arrange them in some kind of hierarchy of importance.
Causes had to be ordered as well as enumerated. Carr
poured scorn on the views of Sir Isaiah Berlin and others
who argued, in the style of Cold War attacks on Soviet historical 'determinism', that history was governed by
chance, accident and indeterminacy, and that individuals
were autonomous and endowed with unfettered free will,
and were thus morally responsible for their own actions,
which therefore could only be explained as the outcome of
their will and not of some larger impersonal 'cause'. In
everyday life, Carr noted, not unfairly, people did not proceed on such extreme assumptions. To adduce causes was
not to deny moral responsibility; nothing was less true than
the dictum that 'to understand everything is to excuse

everything'. Morality and causation were two distinct categories which should not be confused.

Admittedly, Carr conceded, accident and contingency in history were real enough. It would be futile, for example, to argue that Lenin's premature death at the age of fifty-four had had no effect on the subsequent course of Russian history. But, Carr insisted, broader trends were more important. Insofar as the essence of being a historian was to generalize, and accidents of this kind were not generalizable, then they were in practice of little interest; they belonged to the 'facts' which it was the historian's duty to get right, not to the interpretations which it was the historian's real purpose to advance. It might be the case, for example, that Mark Antony would not have fought and lost the battle of Actium if Cleopatra had had a big nose and so had failed to attract him (an example quoted by J. B. Bury from Pascal's *Pensées*). Thus if Cleopatra had not been beautiful, Octavius would not have founded the Roman Empire. Carr said: 'It is true that Cleopatra's nose had results. But it makes no sense as a general proposition to say that generals lose battles because they are infatuated with beautiful queens . . . Accidental causes cannot be generalized . . . they teach no lessons and lead to no conclusions.'[2]

Carr thought that historians operated a kind of common-sense approach to explanation, which might not satisfy the philosopher but would operate perfectly well in everyday life. If Mr Jones ran over Mr Robinson on a blind corner, driving a car with defective brakes, Carr said, we might explain the incident in terms of the corner, or the brakes, or by reference to Mr Jones's excessive consumption of alcohol at the party from which he was returning; but we would not get much credence if we argued that the cause lay in the smoking habit which had led Mr Robinson to cross the road to buy a packet of cigarettes at the corner shop. For Carr, this last-named cause lay in the realm of chance and contingency, and therefore effectively had to be ruled out of court. You could say that blind corners, defective brakes or drunk-driving made road accidents more likely, but you could not say that cigarette smoking by pedestrians did.[3]

Carr's example of Mr Jones and Mr Robinson has been re-examined recently by Professors Appleby, Hunt and Jacob. 'Doesn't any analysis of this case,' they ask, 'depend on whether Mr Robinson and Mr Jones were white or black, homosexual or heterosexual (perhaps one of them was on his way to a gay bar and was preoccupied), or even accident-prone or rock-steady?'[4] This is a very American gloss on Carr's analysis, one that objects to it because it is not a politically correct way of approaching history in the 1990s. But Appleby, Hunt and Jacob's argument is itself open to objections which point to the limitations of rewriting history from a particular political perspective. In the first place, while it might indeed have been important that one of the two men in question was thinking about the bar he was going to visit instead of the oncoming traffic, if indeed he was, and if indeed this could be proven, it is not immediately apparent why it should matter whether the bar in question was straight or gay. In any case, however, we know that Mr Jones was on his way home and that Mr Robinson had simply popped out to buy cigarettes, so Appleby, Hunt and Jacob simply haven't read the evidence correctly, and we can rule out their speculative point as factually wrong. As far as the ethnicity of the two gentlemen is concerned, this too is irrelevant to an explanation of the accident unless we can show that Mr Jones was a racist and deliberately ran down Mr Robinson because he belonged to a different ethnic group. But there is no evidence for this in Carr's account, since

Jones clearly stepped on the brake pedal when he saw Robinson crossing the road (otherwise it would not have mattered that the car's brakes were defective, since he would not have tried to use them). So we can rule this out too as factually incorrect as well as irrelevant.

The British historian A. J. P. Taylor used to delight in provoking more sober historians by positing tiny causes for vast events. The First World War, for instance, in his view was caused by railway timetables, because this locked the belligerent powers into a sequence of troop mobilizations and war declarations from which they could not escape.[5] Even in his autobiographical writings he liked to emphasize the element of chance in his life.[6] Doubtless he would have been sorely tempted by the idea that Mr Robinson was killed because he smoked cigarettes. But it is less than certain that he intended to be taken entirely seriously in this kind of thing, and more likely that he intended to irritate his more pedestrian colleagues, an activity at which he was generally very successful.

A more fruitful way of indicating the importance and limitations of chance (or contingency, as the more theoretically inclined like to call it) in history is to imagine what might have happened had things been slightly different. Suppose, for example, that Hitler had died in 1928 and the Nazis not come to power; would there have been a Second World War? Most historians would agree that war would have broken out anyway. The chances of the Weimar Republic surviving were very small after the Depression began in 1929, and a far-right dictatorship of someone like Franz von Papen, who in the event became Hitler's chief conservative collaborator in 1933, or a restoration of the Hohenzollern monarchy, which was what Heinrich Brüning, Chancellor from 1930 to 1932, seems to have wanted, would almost certainly have led to a similar sequence of events to that which took place anyway: rearmament, revision of the Treaty of Versailles, *Anschluss* in Austria, and the resumption, with more energy and determination than ever before, of the drive for conquest which had been so evident in Germany's war aims between 1914 and 1918. However, these things would probably not have happened in the same way; and in particular, though all the conservatives were antisemitic,[7] and might well have imposed restrictions on the human rights of Jews similar to those which were put in place by the Nazis during peacetime, and indeed by conservative regimes in Poland and Vichy France too, it is far from certain that they would have launched the systematic programme of extermination which constituted the 'Final Solution' of the 'Jewish problem' envisaged by Hitler, to whose world view antisemitism was far more central. Even here, if one accepts the view that the genocide emerged 'from below', in the experience of military men, police units and SS confronted by a large Jewish population in the occupied territories of Eastern Europe in 1941, it is however at least arguable that there would have been large-scale massacres at the very least, though not the systematic, Europe-wide programme of destruction launched by the Nazis under the name of the 'Final Solution'.

Of course, we can never know for sure what would have happened. The relevant point here is that despite very significant differences, it is unlikely that the overall pattern of events would have diverged totally from what actually happened had Hitler died in 1928. Accident, chance and contingency certainly have a real effect, but that effect is almost always rather limited in practice. As far as this goes, therefore, Carr's argument, though put in a rather extreme way, certainly has a good deal to recommend it. But there are problems with it too. To begin with, Carr went on to argue that causality is a matter of interpretation, and therefore inevitably bound up with value judgment. History must serve the present, and so too must our view of the causes of historical events. In the case of Mr Jones and Mr Robinson, for example, we can cite the blind corner, the defective brakes, or the alcohol intake of the driver, because we can do something about these things – alter the corner, for instance, or introduce tougher laws about the standards of maintenance and repair of motor vehicles and the level of alcohol at which people are permitted to drive them. But although we could ban cigarette smoking and thus prevent Mr Robinson from killing himself in another way, this would have no effect at all on traffic accidents of the kind which took place when Mr Jones ran him over. The enumeration of accidental causes, therefore, concluded Carr, is 'from the point of view of the historian dead and barren', because it cannot contribute anything to our ability to shape the future.[8] Our search for the causes of Mr Robinson's death is guided by our objective of reducing deaths on the road.[9]

But while the citation of accidental causes may be dead and barren from the point of view of the politician or the social reformer, it is difficult to see why it should be dead and barren from the point of view of the historian, whose primary purpose is to understand the past. If your main aim is to shape the future, then it is not a good idea to devote your life to studying history; it would be far better to avoid academic or intellectual life altogether and go into politics or business or the civil service or some other kind of practical career. If the sources suggest that an accidental cause was at work, it would not be right to rule it out just because it could not be made to serve our purposes in the present. Indeed, an even greater danger lurks here: supposing a cause, accidental or otherwise, suggesting itself powerfully from the documents, goes against our ideas about the present and the future? Was Carr really saying that we should suppress it in the interests of present-day ideology?

It is hard to escape the conclusion that Carr did not really think his argument through. Nor, in the end, was the example of Mr Jones and Mr Robinson particularly well chosen. For historical explanation is not just about finding causes for discrete events like car crashes or world wars. Historians are just as interested in what events or processes decide, and what they mean, as in what causes them. Consequences are often more important than causes.[10] 'Why?' is far from being the only question historians ask. Categorizing past societies or political systems or structures of belief is no less legitimate than enquiring into the causes of past events. Historians can explain something by putting it into a context (i.e. arguing it was part of this movement rather than that, belonged to one period or trend rather than another, and so on). Nor is explanation itself all that history is about. Allan Megill's view is typical: 'It is a rather widely-held opinion among professional historians that the truly serious task of historiography, making it a contribution to knowledge and not a triviality, is the task of explanation.'[11] But are description and the recovery of empirical fact really no more than trivialities? Few historians would wish to concede this point in practice, given the enormous amount of time they spend on these activities. Moreover, some historians at least have become somewhat dismissive of the search for causes in recent years. Geoffrey Barraclough, a specialist on medieval Germany whose experiences in the Second World War converted him to the idea that history had to be relevant and oriented towards the present, argued in 1967 that historians should stop teaching their pupils about causes, which could only be speculated upon and had no relevance to the present, and concentrate on results instead.[12] More recently, John Vincent has declared that the search for causes is futile; it is better in his view to look for explanations, though he never makes the distinction between the two very clear. 'Cause,' he says, 'is a constriction on historical thought; let it be unbound.'[13] Writing in 1976, Theodore Zeldin rejected narrative history and the search for causes in favour of what he called a *pointilliste* method, which would compose a picture out of unconnected dots, between which the reader could make 'what links he thinks fit for himself'.[14] 'Causation,' he observed, 'has been almost as merciless a tyrant to historians as chronology.'[15] He too thought it was time for historians to escape its clutches.

In his own great work, *A History of French Passions* – originally published as *France 1848–1945* in the *Oxford History of Modern Europe* – Zeldin looks at French society over the century in question under a variety of novel perspectives – ambition, love, politics, intellect, taste, anxiety – and includes surveys of almost every aspect of French life, illustrated with telling and often entertaining examples of individual French men and women whose lives seem to come into the perspective in question. The book is indeed remarkable for its refusal to engage in large-scale theories or explanations, and its rigorous avoidance of narrative and chronology. But at the same time all is not quite so innovative as it seems. Often, for example, the novel-sounding titles conceal quite old-fashioned subjects; 'Ambition', for example, introduces the reader to a masterly synthesis of recent research on French social structure, with chapters on the peasantry, the bourgeoisie and the working class. A chapter on 'Hypocrisy' turns out to be mainly about the

Communist Party. And so on. The book's section on politics
not only has a chronology concealed beneath the thematic
approach, moving from Legitimism and Orleanism via
Bonapartism to Republicanism and so on, but also in practice
delivers numerous quite cogent and persuasive explanations
of French political history, for example of the reasons why
the Third Republic managed to last so long. Since Zeldin's
previous experience had been as a straight political historian
specializing in the Second Empire, it is perhaps hardly surprising that the political coverage was the most coherent in
the book. But the rest, too, consists not only of attacks on
historical orthodoxies but of numerous explanations of the
subjects with which it dealt.[16] There is indeed a refusal to
put forward any overarching thesis to bind the various parts
of the book together. But perhaps this is inevitable in a
survey of a century of French history that aimed to be totally
comprehensive in its coverage.

At the opposite end of the spectrum, other historians
have continued to emphasize the importance of causation
and the prominent role of accident and personality in history. Geoffrey Roberts, an expert on Soviet Russia, has
argued for a

> human action approach to the study of history [which]
> emphasizes the freedom of individuals to act, the impor-
> tance of reconstructing what happened from the actor's
> point of view, and the role of accident, miscalculation and
> unintended consequences in shaping historical out-
> comes . . . The idea that people do things for a reason, that
> their individual and collective actions are the stuff of history
> and that it is possible to construct an evidence-based
> account of why past actors acted as they did is, for most of
> us, plain common sense.

But this is not true at all. Historians by and large do not concentrate on the accidental, do not assume that individuals
have unfettered freedom of choice, and do not confine themselves to reconstructing the past actor's point of view.
Moreover, while 'common sense' may not exactly be coterminous with 'prejudice' and imbued with 'a potential for
repressive bigotry', as Christopher Lloyd has charged, it certainly varies wildly from epoch to epoch and culture to
culture.[17] 'Common sense' in the medieval and early
modern periods, for example, included the notion that
human action was guided by divine (or diabolical) inspiration, and that disease was frequently caused by black magic
or witchcraft. The recounting of miracles was part of the
'common sense' of medieval historiography. The give-away
here is, of course, Roberts's phrase 'for most of us', which
implicitly ejects from the community of historians those who
do not write political or diplomatic history and are therefore
not one of 'us'. This does not really do justice to the breadth
and diversity of historical scholarship today.

II

While Roberts would have us concentrate on explaining historical events in terms of their relation to the aims and
intentions of the people who took part in them, Carr's concept of causation has often been labelled 'determinist', that
is, it rests on the assumption that events are generally caused
by factors independent of the will of the people involved in
them. In an early piece, written in 1966, for example,
Hayden White declared that history's claim to discover true
patterns in the past trapped human beings, as it were, in an
inescapable net of causation and robbed them of freedom of

action in the present; if this was abandoned, then people could use history to assert their control over the future, and this indeed should be history's primary purpose.[18] White's argument rested on the idea that it did not matter whether the history we used to further our present concerns was true or not. Any history beyond the merely antiquarian was by definition a 'metahistory' the truth or otherwise of which could never be determined, since it was essentially the creation of the historian.[19] 'Explanation' in history really consisted only of theories made up by historians without reference to the source material and imported into it from outside. It rested on a series of poetic insights into how things happened, formalized into a philosophy of history which was to be found, if only implicitly, in every historical work, in one variant or another.[20]

This argument collapsed a number of clearly related phenomena into each other, abolishing the distinctions between them, and reducing them all in the end to the phenomenon of the poetic insight. Empirical research into the causes of specific events is arguably more than the expression of a philosophy of history, though admittedly the historian has to have some basic theory of how and why things happen, some fundamental idea of human motivation and behaviour, to begin with. Moreover, White did not say why historians' explanations of the causes of things were 'poetic' rather than rational. Given the dull and pedestrian manner in which many historians write, 'poetic' seems something of a misnomer. His argument was also remarkable for its trivialization of questions of evidence and its elevation of interpretation to a position of almost exclusive pre-eminence in the nature of historical scholarship. Historians, according to White, are less concerned to establish *that* certain events occurred than to determine what certain events might *mean*. But establishing that events occurred is a central part of the historian's business and cannot be dismissed as a secondary problem or a side-issue.

In the hands of some postmodernists, White's argument can be turned into a general criticism of the historian's enterprise as a whole. Thus Keith Jenkins, for example, declares gleefully:

> Historians are not too concerned about discrete facts . . . No, historians have ambitions, wishing to discover not only what happened but how and why and what these things meant and mean. This is the task historians have set for themselves (I mean they did not have to raise the stakes so high). So it is never really a matter of the facts *per se* but the weight, position, combination and significance they carry *vis-à-vis* each other in the construction of explanations that is at issue.

And he proceeds to reprimand historians for this folly. Working historians, he repeats, clearly ought to recognize that interpretations do not just arise from the facts, but are put there by historians themselves and will only have a limited temporal and local validity before they are superseded by other interpretations. The concept of historical causation is itself merely an element in the arbitrarily-constructed discursive formation of professional historiography.[21]

Even more radical criticisms have been levelled at the concept of historical causation by some postmodernists. The idea of a cause depends rather obviously on the concept of sequential time. Something that causes something else generally comes before it in time, not after; thus the causes of the French Revolution of 1789 are to be sought in the years 1788 and before, not 1790 and after. If sequential time is recognized as no more than an intellectual construct, then the consequences of this recognition for historical research are very serious, as a number of writers have argued. Frank Ankersmit expresses a widespread view when he says: 'Historical time is a recent and highly artificial invention of Western civilization.' Writing historical narrative based on the concept of time, he has declared, is 'building on quicksand'.[22] Drawing on Einsteinian physics, many postmodernists are sceptical of the notion of time as even and regulated; in political terms, they see such a view of time as oppressive and controlling, legitimating hegemonic discourse and privileging Western ways of viewing the world over non-Western.[23] A democratic history written according to the precept of abandoning sequential time would be, as one postmodernist writer has argued approvingly, an 'interminable pattern without meaning', rather like some forms of contemporary music or some contemporary experimental novels. This would lead to a new form of history which would abandon 'the time of clocks and capital' altogether.[24]

Yet those who argue in this manner are caught in a paradox. The very use of the concept of '*post*modern' is contrary to the notion that there are no time-periods in history. As a perceptive critic has remarked, when a postmodern writer puts forwards the claim that 'historical time is a thing of the past,' she does not seem to see all the ironies present in the statement; for declaring something to be a thing of the past itself uses the historical concept of time which the statement is intended to dismiss.[25] Besides this, a basically linear concept of time continues to be used the world over by people both in the conduct of their everyday lives and in their preference for, say, novels which narrate a story over novels which do not; for John Grisham over Alain Robbe-Grillet, for example. Historical time is thus in no way merely adhered to as a concept by people who, as some argue, are 'privileged by the prevailing hegemonic arrangements'.[26] It is in essence far too powerful a principle to be dispensed with, even by those who reject it. Indeed any attempt to deny historical time necessarily presupposes the very thing it denies. *How* we count the years – whether we use the Western calendar, or the Jewish, or the Chinese, or whatever – is completely irrelevant to this point, and it is hard to escape the conclusion that postmodernists here are confusing the Western hegemony implicit in the worldwide use of the Christian calendar with the culturally neutral, because universal, sequence of time which calendars are designed to count.

III

Time passes, therefore; yet no historian can hope to capture every passing moment. As I write this, I can hear the click of my fingers on the word-processor, the faint whine of the computer in the background, the dull but constantly varying roar of the traffic in the main road across the garden, the twittering of the birds outside, the light ticking of the clock on my desk, the soft padding of my cat as he comes up the stairs, the sound of my own breathing, and so on: all this in a handful of seconds, and already it is gone beyond any hope of complete or accurate reconstruction, least of all in the exact sequence in which these noises have come to my ears. So we all pull out from the seamless web of past events a tiny selection which we then present in our historical account. Nobody has ever disputed this. The dispute arises when some theorists believe that the selection is largely determined by the narratives and structures which occur in the past itself, and those who think it is imposed by the historian.

Is it the case, as Hayden White has maintained, that most professional historians believe that they are constructing their narratives as simulacra of the structures and processes of real events in the past, not as the product of their own aesthetic sensibilities and purposes?[27] It seems unlikely. Every historian is aware of the complexity of the facts, their irreducibility to a single linear narrative; and everyone writing a work of history, or, come to that, a doctoral thesis, is confronted by the problem of how to separate out the still inchoate material collected – or to be collected – during research into a series of more or less coherent narrative and structural strands, and then of how to weave these strands together into a more or less coherent whole. Often the decisions taken have a material effect on the interpretation itself. What might appear to be a conventional historical narrative is often nothing of the kind, but the outcome of a series of aesthetic and interpretative choices. For example, LaCapra has described *The Defeat of the Spanish Armada* by Garrett Mattingly rather patronizingly as 'a lovely old-style tale', and Le Roy Ladurie's *Montaillou* as a 'highly conventional narrative' presenting a 'traditional story'.[28] But in both cases he misses the point. First, as we have seen, a conventional narrative account of the inquisition register on which Le Roy Ladurie based his book would use it to describe the inquisitorial process in Montaillou. The whole point about Ladurie's book is that it reads it *against the grain*, for a structural analysis of everyday life and relationships in the village, in which a whole battery of modern anthropological theories is brought to bear on everyday life.[29] Similarly, Mattingly's book is a highly complex and sophisticated narrative, moving from one geographical centre to the next (London, Madrid, Antwerp and so on) in a rather Cubist fashion, trying to give us a multiplicity of viewpoints and interweave a number of different narratives. It seems to me to be very much aware of modern novelistic techniques, despite LaCapra's dismissal of it for belonging to a genre of 'traditional narrative' unaffected by the modern novel. Mattingly shaped his classic book in this multi-stranded narrative form because, as an American, he wanted to get away from British historians' common habit of narrating the whole thing from the British point of view. Historical narrative, then, seldom simply consists of a single linear temporal strand.

Perhaps I may illustrate some of the difficulty of interweaving narrative and causal argument by referring to my own work. When I began, in the early 1980s, researching the Hamburg cholera epidemic of 1892, it was because I was attracted by the immense amount of source material this major disaster generated, which revealed the structures and dynamics of everyday life, social inequality, politics and administration, mentalities and behaviour, in a major European city. These are precisely the fine details which remain concealed from the historian's view in more normal times. As I went through the material, it became clear that explaining why a major epidemic happened in Hamburg that year and nowhere else in Western Europe would be even more revealing of the social and political assumptions and practices of nineteenth-century liberalism than the epidemic itself was. A whole range of factors was involved, from the amateurism of the city administration through the overcrowding of the city slums to the peculiar theories of disease transmission held by the city's medical profession. The major cause seemed to be the failure to modernize Hamburg's water supply, and this too required lengthy explanation.

The question then arose of how to present all of these causes over a period stretching from the 1830s to the eve of

the epidemic in 1892. Eventually, after a good deal of experimentation and after shifting great chunks of text around as
I wrote, I came up with a mixture of narrative and analysis
which would, I hoped, generate a growing sense of suspense
and excitement in the reader as we came closer and closer to
the narrative of the epidemic itself in the second half of the
book. So I divided the causes into twelve groups, each of
which was to play a major role in the epidemic itself; narrative tension was generated by withholding information
about precisely what this role was until we arrived at the
epidemic itself. The book narrated each causal group from
around 1830 or so up to the spring or summer of 1892 (the
epidemic began in August), so that in effect it presented
twelve separate narratives, each piling another layer of causation upon the previous ones and modifying them in the
process. Starting with the most general – the amateurish
nature of the city administration – it moved through the
analysis of political inequality, poverty and the various
factors which governed the expenditure priorities of the
city administration, to the growth of environmental pollu-
tion and lack of public hygiene, the failure to build a
properly purified water supply and the inadequacies of popular nutrition. All of these factors, it was implied without
explicitly stating so, would intensify in one way or another
the effects of cholera in 1892 until over 10, 000 people
died of the disease in the city within the space of less than
six weeks. The next six narratives, each once more beginning early in the century and moving up to the eve of the
epidemic, dealt with the unfavourable patterns of death and
disease in the city even in normal times, the *laissez-faire*
dogma which prevented local doctors from intervening in
epidemic situations, the inadequacies of their responses to
earlier, lesser epidemics, and finally the arrival of cholera in

Germany in 1830, its recurrence at intervals thereafter, the medical theories evolved to account for it, and its re-emergence in the course of 1892, setting the scene for the narrative of the epidemic itself.

There was never any doubt in my mind from the very outset that what I was doing was constructing an ensemble of narratives that added up to a set of causal explanations as to why the epidemic broke out in Hamburg and (as comparisons with other cities like Bremen showed) nowhere else in 1892. This set of causal explanations was then recapitulated and weighted at the end of the book in a much briefer, more schematic fashion, where I argued that: the epidemic occurred because the causative agent, the cholera bacillus, brought in by Russian emigrants on their way to America, passed through a series of safety-nets all or some of which were present in other cities, but none of them in Hamburg; the medical scepticism in Hamburg about the infectious nature of the disease prevented proper isolation of the emigrants and delayed notification of the outbreak; the failure to filtrate the water supply sent the bacillus through every household tap; overcrowding, poor sanitation and unhygienic housing aided person-to-person transmission; and administrative inefficiency made it difficult to contain the epidemic once it had broken out. It would have been perfectly possible to have put this argument in a completely different way. My reason for devising twelve parallel causal narratives was mainly aesthetic: it simply seemed the neatest, most economical and above all the most exciting and most interesting way of organizing and presenting the evidence; above all, it seemed the best way of using the wonderfully rich source material generated by the epidemic to explore all the various aspects of daily life, social structure and political action in a city where – and this was the book's overarching thesis – *laissez-faire* liberalism proved incapable of dealing with the problems generated by massive urban-industrial growth and was forced by the ensuing disaster to give way to 'Prussian'-style state interventionism.[30] There could never be any question of presenting a 'simple' chronological narrative in this case – not even of the epidemic itself – because there were far too many events and processes going on at the same time. Arranging it all purely in terms of chronology would have delivered a chronicle with no explanatory power whatsoever. The book's structure seemed to me the most effective way of putting across a mass of empirical evidence to support a series of causal arguments and hypotheses.

Most historical narratives consist of a mixture of revealed, reworked, constructed and deconstructed narratives from the historical past and from the historian's own mind. We start with a rough-hewn block of stone, and chisel away at it until we have a statue. The statue was not waiting there to be discovered, we made it ourselves, and it would have been perfectly possible for us to have made a different statue from the one we finally created. On the other hand, we are constrained not only by the size and shape of the original stone, but also by the kind of stone it is; an incompetent sculptor not only runs the risk of producing an unconvincing statue that does not much resemble anything, but also of hammering or chiselling too hard, or the wrong way, and shattering the stone altogether.

We have to work *with* the limitations of the material. And these limitations are strict and severe. In some cases, the narrative is there in the sources, lived and thought by the people we are writing about: German or Italian unification in the nineteenth century, for example, or the making of the USA in the eighteenth. In other cases it is not. Yet even where historians are aware of the fact that people in the past were consciously living a story they believed in and sought to shape, they can never rest content with simply reproducing it; it must be juxtaposed with others, hidden meanings must be discovered, flaws and contradictions in the story must be exposed. Historians not only deconstruct the narratives of other historians, they also deconstruct the narratives of the past as well.

Hayden White has suggested somewhat condescendingly that history has become 'a refuge' for people who want 'to find the simple in the complex and the familiar in the strange'.[31] If this ever applied to historians in the past, it certainly does not apply today. It may be part of the postmodern turn in historical studies that so much work is now being done on the irrational, the bizarre and the exceptional in the past. But in truth, ever since the early nineteenth century, one of the main purposes of historians has been to find the strange in the familiar, to increase the distance between ourselves and the past. Empirical historians are constantly telling us that the past is far more complex than the great, suprahistorical metanarratives would seem to allow. Back in the 1950s, the liberal American historian Richard Hofstadter was even worried that historians' commitment to the 'rediscovery of the complexity of social interests . . . may give us not only a keener sense of the structural complexity of our society in the past, but also a sense of the moral complexity of social action that will lead to political immobility.'[32] It was precisely this kind of political consequence that conservatives like Sir Geoffrey Elton most welcomed. Professional historians have more often than not been hostile to 'oversimplification' rather than indulging in it.

The postmodernist critic Sande Cohen has gone further

than Hofstadter and argued that historical narrative in itself is inherently anti-intellectual. Historians, he says, 'use narration in order to deflect thinking,' and he condemns their 'outrageous recreation of tutelary narration' where 'the reader is not even allowed to *think*'. Thus history, he thinks, is part of 'the discourse of bourgeois society'. By focusing attention on the past, historians are engaging in 'aggression against the present', which is part of 'capitalism's promotion of thought forms that make the present as something that matters all but inaccessible'. Building on these arguments, Cohen then goes on to condemn the Marxist historian Edward Thompson's polemic against French structuralist Marxism as 'an aggressive rejection of the nonnarrated', demonstrating a 'sad' conformity to 'bourgeois historiography' and a most un-Marxist rejection of 'critical thinking', while even Hayden White's analyses of historians' writings are dismissed as 'defensive protections of the historical discipline', something which would surprise the many historians such as Elton and Marwick who have seen them in a rather different light.[33] Like many postmodernists, Cohen vastly underestimates the critical capacity of people who read history, and hugely overestimates the historian's ability to discipline the reader's thought, even by the use of 'tutelary narration'. By contrast, other versions of postmodernist thought, at the opposite extreme, claim that the reader's ability to impose meaning on narratives is unlimited. Neither the totally passive nor the hyper-active reader of the rival theorists' imagination comes near the reality.

Many historical narratives have set out to provide historical justification or inspiration for political and social movements in the present. Reading and writing about the feminist struggle for equal rights and human dignity for women in the nineteenth century in no way closes off the possibility of contemplating women's situation in the pre-sent, rather the contrary, in fact, which is why present-day feminists have devoted so much attention to them. It is quite wrong to see narratives as constricting and essentially reac-tionary myths that have little to do with historical truth. The official historiography of Soviet Russia and the Eastern bloc was, in the view of the French originator of this particular critique, Jean-François Lyotard, a 'master-narrative', imposed and sanctified by the state. What he termed 'local narratives' were by contrast forms of resistance, individual stories told by prisoners, students, peasants and deviants of various kinds, impossible to incorporate into the state's ver-sion of events, and thus directly subversive of it. Unlike the master-narrative, local narratives did not claim omniscience or universal validity, and they were subjective rather than laying claim to objective historical truth.[34] Hence history in general consisted – and should consist – of a mass of local his-tories. 'Postmodernism' indeed was defined by Lyotard simply as 'incredulity toward master-narratives'.[35] But it is not true to say, as Lyotard tended to, that master-narratives are the hegemonic stories told by those in power. The Marxist master-narrative itself, in many different variants, was developed over decades by an oppressed minority. The same may be said of the master-narratives of feminist his-tory, or gay history, or black history. Master-narratives do not have to be oppressive.

Historians in general have not only always been active in constructing local narratives or counter-narratives, they have also taken special pleasure in attacking master-narratives of every kind. Sir Geoffrey Elton was particularly insistent on the historian's duty in this respect. Many historians have seen their task not so much in creating narratives as in destroying them. 'Ever since historical study became professional,'

Elton declared towards the end of his life, '– that is to say, systematic, thorough and grounded in the sources – it has time and again destroyed just those interpretations that served particular interests, more especially national self-esteem and self-confidence.'[36] The continued prevalence of national historical myths in the Third World was for him a matter for regret. 'The world is now in the hands of adolescents,' he complained.[37] 'Historians,' Theodore Zeldin, echoing Elton in his own, less apocalyptic manner, proclaimed, 'are the counterpart of the social scientists; they say what cannot be done, rather than what should be done. Their function is less glamorous than that of the soothsayer. They are only court jesters.'[38] It was a function of the court jester in medieval times not only to entertain and amuse, but also to tell his audience unpalatable truths. History has always been seen by historians as a destroyer of myths more than a creator of them.

In destroying myths, historians have often sought to substitute for them narratives which are more closely grounded in the sources. But narrative is by no means the dominant mode of historical representation among contemporary historians that postmodernists, fixated on the great narrative histories of the nineteenth century, like to claim it is. Indeed, the sequential presentation of historical material has often been entirely abandoned by modern historical scholarship, under the influence of the social sciences. Probably the majority of histories, other than introductory textbooks in the last three or four decades, have done their best to avoid having their structure shaped by the passage of time, and this is even more true of articles and theses. Moreover, some of the most famous history books of the earlier part of the century have avoided narrative too: Namier's *Structure of Politics* sought to uncover the deep and relatively unchanging structures which underlay the surface froth of events. Eugene Genovese's *Roll, Jordan, Roll*, even Wehler's *Kaiserreich* were all structural histories in which the passage of time was either frozen and change consigned to periods before and after the moment being studied, or abolished altogether in a deliberate assertion of grand continuities. The first injunction history tutors give their students is 'avoid narrative'; thematic analysis gets the grades, a priority which reflects wider beliefs about the presentation and communication of research and scholarship at every level in the twentieth-century historical profession.[39]

IV

Historical narratives do not necessarily have to be bound to a forward direction of time's arrow. Some of the most celebrated historical works of the modern age move backwards in time. The English legal historian, F. W. Maitland, in his book *Domesday and Beyond*, peeled off the layers of time which had accumulated in the returns made about custom and law to William the Conqueror's massive landholding survey of 1086, the Domesday Book, to reveal earlier and earlier patterns of tenure and settlement as he went back through the centuries. 'Beyond' in this sense meant moving towards more and more remote periods of the past, seen from the perspective of the late eleventh century. For the nationalist German historian Hellmut Diwald, writing a history of the Germans in reverse chronological order, starting with the present (in his case, the 1970s), meant moving backwards from what he saw as his country's humiliation, division and impotence in the third quarter of the twentieth century to a more and more glorious past – a past which he clearly hoped the book would motivate his readers to retrieve.[40] Whatever its purpose, writing history backwards has long been part of the stock-in-trade (if a little-used one) of historians, one of a large variety of ways in which they have managed to smash what the French historian François Simiand called at the beginning of the twentieth century 'the chronological idol'.[41]

Postmodernist critics of linear notions of time ignore the fact that historians have long been accustomed to employ a variety of concepts of temporality in their work; indeed, one could say that it is precisely this that distinguishes them most clearly from mere chroniclers, whose notion of time is by definition confined to the tale of years.[42] Even in the most traditional kinds of political history, historians skate quickly over years or even decades when nothing much changed, and concentrate on periods, like the revolutionary years of 1789–94 in France, when as much of political importance happened in a month as happened in a year under the *ancien régime*. There are periods when political history seems to speed up, as in Russia in 1917, others when it seems to move in slow motion, as in Spain during the years of General Franco's dictatorship. Historians are also used to the idea that historical processes of a similar kind occur in different countries at different times. Industrialization, for example, got under way in Britain in the 1780s, but in Germany not until the 1840s or Russia until the 1890s. The 'demographic transition' from a society of high birth and death rates to one of low birth and death rates began in France in the eighteenth century but in Italy only a hundred years or so later.

Nor can working historians be shocked by the notion that there are different kinds of periodization for different kinds of history. Most obviously, economic change moves at a different pace from political change. The history of changes in, say, military technology, also has its own particular tempo, as does that of culture and the arts; recently it has been argued that women's history should also be periodized differently from men's. Change in any one of these areas obviously had an effect on the others, but to cram them all into conventional units of time framed by major political turning-points, although it has been done often enough in textbook surveys of national histories, is artificial and unhelpful, and insofar as the postmodernist questioning of linear notions of time has contributed to a heightened real-ization of this, it is to be welcomed.[43] But conventional, politically-defined periods have always provided their own testimony to the unevenness of historical time and its mal-leability in the hands of the historian: in modern European political history, for example, the nineteenth century is con-ventionally dated from 1815 to 1914, or in some versions from 1789 to 1914; the 'short twentieth century' from 1914 to 1989.

Some historians have also built the notion of different kinds of historical time into their own work; most famously Fernand Braudel, who said that his major problem in writing *The Mediterranean and the Mediterranean World in the Age of Philip II* 'was to show that time moves at different speeds.'[44] At the top level were political events, which Braudel recounted in the third part of his book. Here things happened quickly if unevenly. Battles, treaties, court intrigues and political rival-ries were 'surface disturbances, crests of foam that the tides of history carry on their strong backs'.[45] These tides of his-tory were covered in the second part of Braudel's massive work: slow-moving social and economic trends, often imperceptible to contemporaries, changing military tech-nologies, social structures and state systems. Finally, at the very bottom of the ocean of time, were the still, deep waters 'in which all change is slow, a history of constant repetition, ever-recurring cycles'. Treated at length in the opening section of *The Mediterranean*, this was the level of 'immobile history', the '*longue durée*', in which pre-industrial society's potentialities of change were confined by the unchanging powers of the natural environment.[46]

In turn, this slow-moving, deep stratum of history generated persistent systems of belief or 'mentalities' which other historians, such as Jean Delumeau in his *History of Fear in the West*, charted over a period of several hundred years in which they seemingly underwent little or no change at all.[47] In retrospect, the French historians often seem to have exaggerated the extent to which these things did not alter: Braudel was heavily criticized for taking the natural environment of the Mediterranean littoral as a given, instead of investigating the ways in which it was transformed by human activity, for instance in the massive deforestation carried out to supply wood for shipbuilding, construction and fuel. Nor did he always show very clearly how his three different levels of time related to one another. The *Annales* model was never very good at accounting for historical change at any level: its interest in causation was often rather limited. Nevertheless, for all these undoubted problems, the point here is that it made explicit, in a way that had seldom been done before, the manner in which historical time differs from linear time. It is in many ways the opposite: not a given, unchangeable, taken-for-granted series of dates, but a construct for which the historian has to argue.

Postmodernism's new view of time can be seen in its most concrete form in architecture. Postmodern buildings jumble together the architectural styles of several centuries to achieve a new synthesis; while postmodern novels mix up genres popular at different periods or even interweave actions set in different eras.[48] But this is not really rejecting historical concepts of time, it is simply using them in a new way, rather as the authentic performance movement in music now prefers to perform eighteenth-century music on eighteenth-century instruments, or at least on replicas of them (something which itself raises key questions of authenticity in a more subtle form). This aspect of postmodernism can perhaps be seen as extending an invitation to historians. Why should not we too raid the many and various genres of historical writing which have been developed over the past couple of centuries, to enrich our own historical practice today? Why do we have to stick rigidly, for example, to one particular model; why can't we take what we want from Macaulay, Braudel, structural history and the history of events, diplomatic and economic history, cultural and social history, and so on, and weave them into a new synthesis? Periodization is in large measure a function of teaching syllabuses in universities, with their divisions into neat chronological sections, each of which is then served by a textbook from a multi-volume series, further solidifying the boundaries; and if postmodernism helps us to escape from the strait-jacket which this imposes on our segmentation of past time, that can only be to the good.[49] More generally, if postmodernism makes us more aware of the possible models available to us within the history of historical writing and research, this too can only enrich our own practice as historians in the present.

V

In the end, therefore, time does pass, a fact we experience only too painfully in the process of human ageing to which we are all subject ourselves, and we cannot abolish it by simply declaring, as Ankersmit does, that there is no difference between the fourteenth century and the twentieth, or that time is merely a collection of unrelated presents, or that the textuality of the world abolishes the principle of cause and effect. To argue that we can only know causes from their effects, and that therefore the effect is the origin of the cause, as some postmodernists have done, is to mistake the process of enquiry for its object. History rests on the belief that the present differs from the past and derives from it; it also points to the future, which will be different again. In the end, everybody knows that the present is affected by the past, that what happens today can affect or cause what happens tomorrow or the day after, and that the texts and other material objects which we produce today provide the basis on which the future can attempt to know us. 'It is an illusion,' as Perez Zagorin has concluded, '. . . to assume that historiography can dispense with the concept of causality.'[50]

If time is inescapable in its inexorable sequentiality, that still does not solve the fundamental problem of historical causation, it only makes it possible to contemplate it. It is obvious enough what a cause is; we can have *necessary* causes (if A had not happened, then B could not have happened) and *sufficient* causes (A happening was enough to make B happen). Within the first category at least, we can have a *hierarchy* of causes, *absolute* causes (if A had not happened, then B *definitely* could not have happened) and *relative* causes (if A had not happened, then B *probably* could not have happened). Accustomed as they are to stating their arguments in a careful gradation of assessment of probability and plausibility, historians do not in practice approach the discussion of causation in concrete historical instances in such a schematic way. Most historians will go to some lengths to avoid a 'monocausal explanation'. Almost all historians are used to the idea that historical events are frequently *overdetermined*, that is they may have several sufficient as well as necessary causes, any one of which might have been enough to trigger the event on its own. Generally, however, they see it as their duty to establish a *hierarchy* of causes and to explain if relevant the relationship of one cause to another. 'Opposition to a strict hierarchy of causation,' one defender of this procedure has argued, '*can* lead to a refusal to admit any sense of causative priority, to a mere description of "free-floating", relatively valid and equally significant forces.'[51] This is something most historians usually try to avoid.

Historical explanation commonly proceeds by relating an event or a process or a structure to a broader historical context, for example locating a text in the society in which it was produced, relating the behaviour of a political party to the social identities of the people who belonged to it, or linking rising death-rates to an increase in poverty, malnutrition, environmental deterioration and disease. Some postmodernist theory denies any possibility of separating text from context and so involves a rejection of this procedure. However, if, as we have seen earlier in this book, it is in fact possible to distinguish a historical source from the past reality to which it (in part) refers, and if it is meaningful to set this source and this reality against other sources and other realities, then the procedure remains defensible. It is true that in any case contexts themselves are in a sense infinite. Because time and effort are no more abundant for historians than for anyone else, they cut out a small segment or segments from this infinity, and this is where their own preconceptions and intentions are crucial. Relating a source to its context depends above all on what questions one is asking of it; once the decision has been made to ask one set of questions rather than another, it follows that one particular set of contexts has to be examined rather than another, and in this sense, once more, there are certain inescapable routes the historian has to follow. Historians do therefore, in a sense, reconstitute the historical contexts in which they read sources, but the possibilities of reconstitution are far from infinite once the initial direction of research has been decided; and the process of research usually throws up new contexts of which the historian was originally unaware, but which are of obvious relevance to the project. These new factors can undermine or drastically alter the historian's original conception of the shape of the past.

This does not, however, completely invalidate the process of seeking explanation through context. The contexts which historians choose to bring into play are far from arbitrary, however roughly the seamless web of history is torn asunder. Historians usually stop looking for explanatory contexts once they reach areas that are so remote from what they are trying to explain that the connection becomes minimal. Much more serious for the nature of historical explanation is the question of exactly what kind of context we are looking for. The recent turn to cultural history and *mentalités* has seriously undermined the notion of historical causation as understood by someone like E. H. Carr. The new focus on culture and language undermines the prioritization of causes common to Marxism, the *Annales* school, and neo-Weberian social history, in which economic causes work through the social and are in turn expressed by the political and the cultural. It has replaced it with cultural determination, in which culture is itself a relative concept and so lacks any universal explanatory power. Just as Foucault and Derrida have rejected the search for origins and causes as futile, so postmodern theories of interpretation in general challenge any attempt to interpret cultural artefacts in terms of anything other than themselves, as we have seen, because there is in this view nothing outside the text anyway.[52] While cultural history, intellectual history and even the history of high politics have received a fillip from the new theories and approaches of the late 1980s and 1990s, the principal victims have been social and economic history; precisely the areas, as we shall now see, which experienced the greatest growth and expansion in the 1960s and 1970s.

6

SOCIETY AND THE INDIVIDUAL

I

For a long time political history dominated the concerns of those who called themselves historians. 'History is past politics,' as Sir John Seeley, Regius Professor of Modern History at Cambridge in the late nineteenth century put it, 'and politics is present history.'[1] For political historians, 'history' is often coterminous with the exploration of high politics. Thus when the conservative American historian Gertrud Himmelfarb argues that 'more history has to be put into social history,' she means, of course, 'more politics'.[2] 'History' as a university subject, when it emerged during the professionalization process of the nineteenth century, was emphatically the political history of the nation-state and its relations with other nation-states. The history of high politics and international diplomacy was king. History was made by great men. They were taken to be morally and politically autonomous individuals, whose decisions reflected in the first place the peculiarities of their own personality rather than wider forces of any kind. So dominant was this approach within the profession that social and economic historians actually had to set up their own separate university departments to get a foothold in the academy, and to claim that their own specialism constituted a separate discipline entirely distinct from history proper. Two world wars reinforced rather than undermined the hegemony of the 'kings and battles' approach. Even in the 1990s, the view that history is essentially political history remains widespread within the profession, and the associated belief that it is made by morally autonomous individuals, as we have already seen, is far from dead.

Declarations by eminent historians dismissing the history of the great majority of human beings in the past as trivial, meaningless or impossible to study are legion. The great Sir Lewis Namier, for instance, examining a PhD thesis in London on a popular movement in the French Revolution of 1789–94, asked the candidate pointedly: 'Why do you bother with these *bandits*?'[3] The history of every age, he thought, was shaped by a handful of men who possessed the necessary freedom of will and action for this task; and history was therefore no more than the business of finding out what made them tick. 'Whatever theories of "free will" theologians and philosophers may develop with regard to the individual,' he wrote, 'there is no free will in the thinking and actions of the masses, any more than in the revolutions of planets, in the migrations of birds, and in the plunging of hordes of lemmings into the sea.' The point of history was to study 'people who *mattered*', in the words of Namier's assistant and disciple John Brooke, and 'the workers, the peasants, collectively, had hardly ever mattered,' so 'a historian rarely had to take notice of them.'[4] In this rather snobbish and élitist attitude, Namier was curiously not so very far away from the views of G. M. Trevelyan, a historian who in other ways represented the opposite pole in historical thinking from his own. Trevelyan was a patrician who looked back nostalgically to the ordered world of the eighteenth century in which his own class, the landed gentry, had held sway, and he loathed the industrial revolution and the age of the masses. His paternalistic and condescending stance towards the lower orders in history is the main reason why he is no longer read today, and why he will continue to be neglected in the future, despite the advocacy of supporters such as his biographer David Cannadine.[5]

Historians like Elton and Himmelfarb have strongly advocated a return to traditional political history based on the study of the nation-state.[6] But this is whistling in the wind. Himmelfarb may earn the plaudits of right-wing journalists in the intellectual magazines, but among professional historians her views cut little ice. History has become too diverse for such arguments to stand any chance of damming the new currents in history that have flowed so strongly in the decades since Carr and Elton wrote their books – social history, quantitative history, microhistory, cultural history, women's history, gay history, black history, psychohistory, and so on. Political history is now only written by a minority. In Britain, indeed, ignoring or belittling these trends now seems so eccentric an enterprise that when Professor John Vincent, one of the few historians who still does this, submitted the manuscript of his *Very Brief Introduction to History* to Oxford University Press, who had commissioned it, the publishers rejected it for this very reason.[7]

Yet Himmelfarb, Vincent and the other defenders of the élite view of political history have had some surprising allies in their battle to confine history to the study of the élites and dismiss the thoughts and deeds of the vast majority of people in the past as irrelevant and unimportant. E. H. Carr, for example, thought that it was only over the last two centuries or so that 'the mass of people . . . enter fully into history', because it was only in this period that 'social, political and historical consciousness has begun to spread to anything like a majority of the population.'[8] By 'history' in this context, Carr meant what he called 'the expansion of reason' and the march of progress. Thus he clearly thought the history of ordinary people was not worth studying until they became organized in political movements and so contributed to the making of the modern world. More recently, John Vincent has claimed that because history depends on written sources, and most people in the past could neither read nor write, 'history can only speak directly of minorities.' The history of preliterate or illiterate societies, he has declared, is 'unsound'.[9] These arguments have generally failed to convince the modern historical profession. Historians have displayed great ingenuity in exploiting unwritten sources to construct the history of preliterate social groups, assisted by many kinds of written records compiled about these groups by the state and by their social superiors. There are many reasons why the history of the powerless masses before the modern era is worth studying. The history of their experience of death and disease, marriage and sexuality, belief and emotion, has much of relevance to tell us about the human condition. Historians have stubbornly ignored the advice of Namier and Carr and spent increasing amounts of time and energy over the past few decades on taking notice of that enormous majority of people in history dismissed by élitist sages as unworthy of notice.

Historians have broadened their perspectives in a methodological sense too. At the end of the twentieth century, historians are writing about almost every conceivable kind of human activity in the past, as well as about animals, plants, the natural environment and the built and constructed world of machines and human habitations. Under the influence of the *Annales* school, there have been studies of the history of fear, of smell, of madness, of childhood; under the impact of radical neo-Marxists in Britain, 'history from below' has tried to adopt the perspective of ordinary men and women in the past, to write about their experiences and to look on the state, politics and society with their eyes; under the influence of neighbouring and rather remoter disciplines, there have been studies of the body, of medicine and science, of health and disease, of popular culture, of seemingly irrational and inexplicable folk-beliefs in the past; under the tutelage of the social sciences in Germany and America there have been quantitative structural studies of urban and rural communities in the past, of religious practice, of crime and criminality. Virtually everything of meaning or importance to contemporary humanity now has a written history; and that means everything of importance to all kinds of people, not just to a small élite of the educated and the powerful. However humble or powerless, however illiterate or uneducated, almost every group of people in the past has now been rescued from what E. P. Thompson called, in a phrase which struck a resounding blow against the arrogance of the political historians, 'the enormous condescension of posterity'.[10]

II

The major influence in this broadening-out of the historian's perspective on the past in the last few decades has been the rise of social history. This has taken place in every country.

To begin with, it originated in Britain in the nineteenth century under the influence of the celebrated third chapter of Macaulay's *History of England*, which was devoted to a survey of the state of English society in the later part of the seventeenth century. This spawned many imitations, above all in the work of Macaulay's disciples, right down to the similar accounts of the social history of early eighteenth-century England in the first two volumes of Sir John Plumb's unfinished biography of Sir Robert Walpole. It achieved its apotheosis in the enormously popular *English Social History* of Macaulay's great-nephew G. M. Trevelyan, the bestselling English history book of its time. Trevelyan unashamedly took his cue from the history of English literature, with which he assumed all his readers would be familiar, and entitled his various chapters 'Chaucer's England', 'Shakespeare's England', 'Defoe's England', 'Dr Johnson's England' and so on.[11] The problems of this kind of approach were manifold. It relied too heavily on imaginative literature for source-material, and so was often led astray. Its basis in literary works meant that it concentrated too much on the history of literate minorities. It was entirely innocent of social theory or indeed explanation.

Above all, however, it defined itself negatively, in G. M. Trevelyan's notorious phrase, as 'history with the politics left out'. The history of this approach ultimately went back to Macaulay again, whose third chapter was deliberately written as a contrast or background to the political history which dominated the rest of the narrative. It received its first book-length incarnation in J. R. Green's *Short History of the English People*, published in 1874, in which the author announced that he had 'preferred to pass lightly and briefly over the details' of political history, and to dwell instead 'at length on the incidents of that constitutional, intellectual and social advance in which we read the history of the nation itself.'[12] Yet this approach was soon superseded. Social history in the universities emerged as an adjunct of economic history, and as departments of the latter were set up in the early decades of the twentieth century, they usually included a small minority of historians whose field was the history of living standards, trade unions and the 'labour' side of industry in the nineteenth and twentieth centuries, linked to the history of industrialization (Macaulay, Trevelyan and their followers such as Sir John Plumb had preferred, by contrast, to concentrate their gaze somewhat nostalgically on the rural world).

This pointed to a second root of social history, more common on the European continent, where the term 'social question', coined in the mid-nineteenth century to refer to the emergence of a class of impoverished industrial workers, led naturally on to the concept of the 'social movement' which these workers formed to liberate themselves, the 'social revolution' by which they would supposedly achieve this, and thus the 'social history' which described these conditions and these aspirations. 'Social history' therefore meant in effect for many years the organizational and ideological history of the labour movement, and above all the Marxist labour movement, a version of the term still incorporated for example in the French periodical *Le mouvement social*, the German *Archiv für Sozialgeschichte* and above all the Dutch-based *International Review of Social History*, produced by the International Institute for Social History in Amsterdam, which houses the papers of Marx, Engels and many of the leading German Social Democrats of the late nineteenth and early twentieth centuries. The identification of 'social history' with nineteenth-century labour history is evident even in a more recent periodical such as the British journal *Social*

History, which concentrates heavily on this particular area of investigation and gives prominence to debates and controversies between labour historians working largely within the overall framework of a Marxist, neo-Marxist or post-Marxist approach to the past.

But this concept of social history has long since been outflanked by a far broader approach developed in France and subsequently in Germany and elsewhere. The 1970s and 1980s saw a massive shift from *social history* in this old sense, to the *history of society*, in Eric Hobsbawm's phrase.[13] Not just the proletariat, but other social classes, from the landowning aristocracy and the propertied and professional bourgeoisie to the mass of the peasantry and the criminal underclass, came into its purview. Social institutions such as the family, clubs and societies, leisure organizations and the like, entered the picture. There were studies of social structure in individual towns and villages, of demography and population movements, of generations of men and women, of childhood and old age, of social rituals, mores and beliefs. Before long, social historians were staking a claim to have created a major new discipline, separate from 'traditional' history altogether. A mark of its success was provided by the fact that between 1958 and 1978, the proportion of history doctorates in the USA devoted to social history quadrupled and overtook those focused on political history.[14] Peter Stearns's tenth-anniversary editorial in the *Journal of Social History* in 1976 was a typical example of the aggrandizing political style of social history at this time. Kitted out with sub-headings such as 'Us and Them', and assessments of how many social historians had managed to get appointed in university history departments in Britain and the USA, the article laid out ambitious claims for the dominance of social history ('social history *is* history') over the rest of historical scholarship.[15] This view was widely shared. 'Social history,' the British historian John Breuilly remarked in the mid-1980s, 'is not a particular kind of history; it is a dimension which should be present in every kind of history.' This, he said, was because every kind of action and institution had a social dimension.[16] 'Social history,' as his colleague Geoff Eley observed, was not just another branch or sub-specialism, it had a 'totalizing' commitment 'to understand *all* facets of human existence in terms of their social determination'.[17]

This kind of claim has led the more aggressive postmodernists to lambaste what one of them has recently called 'the ludicrous nature of the pretentions of the social historians'.[18] And indeed there have been indications for some time that the social history boom has passed its peak. As early as 1976, ironically enough in a companion piece to Stearns's editorial in the *Journal of Social History*, Theodore Zeldin was already proclaiming that social history had failed in its ambition to become the 'central pivot of research' into the past. It had 'lost its direction amid the variety of its achievements.'[19] This was not least because of its growing fragmentation, which reflected the disintegration of history as a whole. Some two decades later, two British labour historians, Jon Lawrence and Miles Taylor, noted similarly that the 'totalizing ambition' of social history had collapsed during the 1980s into a mass of largely unconnected sub-disciplines such as demography, urban history, and so on.[20] 'What is history?' E. H. Carr asked in 1961, and he went on to give an answer that was both clear and coherent and applied to all kinds of history everywhere, no matter what the subject covered or who the historian covering it. A quarter of a century later, when the editor of the magazine *History Today* came to ask the same question of a number of its contributors, all of them professional historians and many of them distinguished practitioners of the discipline in their own right, she found it impossible to elicit a single answer and instead split the question up into a series of no fewer than twelve sub-questions, covering issues such as, 'What is social history?', 'What is women's history?', 'What is intellectual history?', and so on. Introducing the collected answers, she voiced the fear that the subdivision of the discipline in this way 'fragments and atomizes the past so that we are left with nothing but the loose change of history . . . the chances of a coherent narrative history, the possibility of putting the story of the past back together again, are lost forever.'

But this, she went on, was no cause for despair. Rather, it was time to celebrate 'a new pluralism' which had been animated by 'the retreat from faith in impartial "truth", the loss of the belief in the past as a jigsaw which will one day be complete'.[21] Other commentators on this phenomenon have not been so sanguine. Even in 1961, E. H. Carr deplored the fragmentation of knowledge and ascribed the 'vast and growing mass of dry-as-dust factual histories, of minutely specialized monographs of would-be historians knowing more and more about less and less, sunk without trace in an ocean of facts' to the continuing influence of the nineteenth-century idea 'that history consists of the compilation of a maximum number of irrefutable and objective facts'.[22] But this was unfair. Even the most dauntingly specialized of monographs usually has an argument of some kind or other. And the sources of the growth of specialization are far more complex than Carr would have us believe. He ascribed it to a failure to distinguish between what was important and what was not in the past; yet his own ideas of what was important were in fact quite narrow, as we have seen, and excluded the history of the vast majority of the human race throughout recorded time. It may not have been surprising, therefore, that he dismissed as unimportant the new wave of social-historical studies which was just beginning as he was writing. Yet whatever their subject-matter, it is doubtful whether they were as narrowly factual as he claimed. To conclude, as Frank Ankersmit has done, that historical interpretation is impossible, and historians should therefore confine themselves to the minute study of tiny 'historical scraps' is to advocate a new antiquarianism that few would be interested in pursuing and fewer still in reading.[23]

The historical profession, and with it the generation and further specialization of historical knowledge, has undergone a vast expansion since the early 1960s. Membership of the American Historical Association, the national organization of professional university and college historians in the USA, which numbered a few hundred in the 1950s, had climbed into the thousands by the 1980s. It has been calculated that there were already more historians alive in 1960 than in all previous ages put together; and the expansion of the profession has continued at an even faster pace since then. In Britain, the new universities founded in the wake of the Robbins Report in the late 1960s almost all established history departments, some of which – as at York, for example, or Warwick – quickly won a reputation for important and innovative research. Similar developments took place in West Germany and France. It was never so easy to get a job as a paid, professional historian as it was in the second half of the 1960s. This meant, however, that historical knowledge was increasing so fast that it became more and more difficult to hold it together in a single discipline. New, increasingly specialized journals were founded, from the *Journal of Transport History* to the *Journal of Holocaust Studies*, and new specialized groupings of historians were established, such as the German History Society, or the Society for the Social History of Medicine, in which the majority of historians spent their entire professional careers.

In 1979 an American commentator lamented what he called the 'truly awesome' degree of subdivision within the historical profession:

> Historians are subdivided quadruply, by nation or region of the globe, by time period, by thematic category . . . and by cognitive predilection . . . All that unites historians is a concern for the evolution over time of whatever it is they study . . . This is something . . . to be sure . . . But it is far less compelling as an attribute in most contexts than the diversity of outlooks and interests that splinter historians into minute subgroups, each with its own hierarchy of respected authorities.[24]

What this meant was that historians were finding it increasingly difficult to agree about what was important about the past. Take E. H. Carr's claim, for instance, that while millions of people have crossed the river Rubicon, the historian is only interested in Caesar's crossing of the river, because it affected the course of history. By the 1980s, Carr's statement was manifestly untrue; social historians would have been interested precisely in those millions of ordinary people, and the patterns of communication their crossings and re-crossings of the river Rubicon revealed; economic historians would have been interested in the trade patterns and cycles of these millions of crossings; medical historians would have been interested in the ways in which the masses' crossings of the river communicated disease; and so on.[25] The confidence of the Rankeans and their successors that the political history of the nation-state was the central object of study had gone.

So too has the assumption of E. H. Carr that what was significant in history could be defined by its contribution to social progress. Each sub-specialism of the discipline nowadays has its own definition of what is important, and several historians may study the same object, or the same documents, with completely different questions in mind, and without having the least interest in the questions that other kinds of historians have asked. History, many now believe, is no longer an integrated body of knowledge; it has fragmented almost beyond recall. Historical scholarship has become vastly more diverse, and the sheer volume of historical knowledge generated by the thousands of historians at work in the last thirty years makes it impossible for any one person even to master the literature in a relatively specialized field such as, say, nineteenth-century American history or even the history of the French or Russian Revolutions. In view of this proliferation of historical knowledge, it is scarcely surprising that there seems to be a greater demand for historical syntheses than ever before. A glance at the catalogues of any academic publisher will reveal a plethora of multi-volume general textbook series, from the *Oxford History of Modern Europe* and its companions the *Oxford History of Early Modern Europe* and the *Shorter Oxford History of the Modern World* to the *Cambridge Medieval History* and its companions such as the *Cambridge History of India*, from the new *Penguin History of Britain* to the *Longman's History of Italy*, the *Fischer Europäische Geschichte*, and many, many more. In Germany, the appetite for multi-volume histories seems undiminished, and the ghost of Ranke stalks the corridors of academe, driving senior historians to emulate his monumental stature by putting

similarly serried lines of books on the library shelves alongside his. To the late Thomas Nipperdey's three huge
volumes on Germany from 1800 to 1918 one can now add
Hans-Ulrich Wehler's three even larger tomes. Both authors
attempt to cover social and cultural history as well as the
political and economic spheres. In France, the preference
seems to be for multi-volume surveys dealing with large
subjects over extremely long time-spans and co-authored by
teams of historians rather than by individuals. Here too the
aim is to be broadly comprehensive.[26]

Yet these syntheses are all to a greater or lesser extent
self-consciously selective in the treatment they accord to
their subjects. The contrast, for example, between the
Cambridge Modern History, published at the beginning of the
century, and its successor the *New Cambridge Modern History*,
which began to appear fifty or so years later, is instructive.
In 1900 the authors commissioned by the series-editor Lord
Acton still shared the basic post-Rankean assumptions about
the subject-matter of history, and delivered detailed empirical narratives of the political history of European
nation-states and the relations between them that made a
coherent and satisfying whole. If you want to find out which
party was in government in Denmark in 1895, or what
were the diplomatic objectives of the Austrians in the Seven
Years' War, you can safely turn to the relevant volume and
find what you want. By the time the *New Cambridge Modern
History* came to be written, however, all consensus on the
subject-matter of such a history had disappeared, and what
resulted was a disparate collection of essays covering a
rather haphazard variety of subjects, so that you can never
be quite sure what you will find there. The fact that it gives
far more room to interpretation than its predecessor also
ensures that it has dated far more quickly. If I want to get

basic information about European political history, it is to the old Cambridge volumes that I turn, not the new ones.

The whole idea of a multi-volume and 'authoritative' synoptic history is out of date. It is not surprising that the latest series of this kind, the sixty-volume *Fischer Europäische Geschichte*, makes no pretence at being comprehensive, but instead aims to provide a series of comparative studies covering broad aspects of European history, in which authors are given their head and allowed to express their individuality: indeed this is reflected in the very title, which claims not to be a 'history of Europe' but simply 'European history'. In other series currently in production, the coverage varies widely according to the predilections of the author of each individual volume. In the new *Penguin History of Britain*, for instance, the volume on the seventeenth century, by the American historian Mark Kishlansky, sticks largely to an old-fashioned narrative of high politics, while the coverage of the twentieth century, by the Cambridge historian Peter Clarke, is much broader (though still giving the 'view from Westminster' and neglecting the crucial determining factor of Britain's imperial crisis and decline). What is safe to say is that the publisher's claim that 'these volumes will furnish the definitive history of Britain for our day and generation' will not be fulfilled. There can be no definitive history any more. Sensible readers and teachers will select the best volume on any given period from the range of multi-volume series available; and their judgment as to which is the best will vary according to how they think history should be studied and taught.[27]

The notion of a complete synthesis of historical knowledge in a particular field has all but disappeared. Those written in the present day, like Norman Davies's panoramic *Europe: A History*, tend to present an avowedly personal view of the field, and to provoke as much as to inform.[28] We take from them what we want — in Davies's case, the argument that Europe should be seen as a whole, stretching across as far as the Urals, and not just identified with 'the West' or the current membership of the European Union — and their idiosyncrasies encourage us even more than before to read with a critical and sceptical eye. The virtual disappearance of the idea of a complete and comprehensive synthesis is one reason why Peter Novick concluded in 1988 that 'as a broad community of discourse, as a community of scholars united by common aims, common standards and common purposes, the discipline of history had ceased to exist.'[29]

III

Despite the increasing specialization and fragmentation which many have observed in the historical profession in recent decades, there is still in some respects reason to doubt Novick's pessimistic view of its future as a community of scholars united in a single discipline. With the globalization of communication, more historians in more countries are saying more to audiences in other countries than ever before. Certainly, for instance, the translation of books by French and German historians into English has been undertaken on a far greater scale in the last two or three decades than previously, while English and American historians now find a much wider readership in other languages than they did even a generation ago.

Historians in every country have been steadily more influenced by their colleagues elsewhere. Nothing could be further from the truth than John Vincent's assertion that historical writing 'remains conspicuously national in character.

French, Germans, Americans, English, go their separate ways.'[30] In fact, the *Annales* school has had an enormous influence on scholarship in England and America, while the work of the British Marxist historians has had a similar international impact, despite Vincent's curious belief that E. P. Thompson has had no influence on other historians or in any way 'affected historical practice'.[31] Postmodernist theories have been imported into the United States from France and spread back from there to the historical profession in Europe. Cheap international travel and transcontinental communication through e-mail have effectively abolished the boundaries between scholars of different nations; conferences and seminars on an international basis are held almost daily increasingly by electronic means; the Internet is now enabling scholarly research and debate to be disseminated worldwide almost instantaneously; international scholarly centres have sprung up everywhere, from the Institute of Advanced Study at Princeton to the *Wissenschaftskolleg* in Berlin, from the *Maison des Sciences de l'Homme* in Paris to the Humanities Research Centre in Canberra; and no historian's curriculum vitae can be held to be complete without the now virtually obligatory listing of lectures and seminars given in London, New York, Jerusalem or San Francisco. In the international marketplace of ideas, no one can afford the luxury of intellectual autarky.

The fact that Novick's own excellent book on the 'objectivity question' in the American historical profession has been so widely debated in so many different branches of the profession in the United States is itself a persuasive falsification of his views. Just because we all have a different idea of what history is, or should be about, does not mean that we no longer read each other's work. But there is no denying that this has become more difficult: for over the last thirty years in history there has been an almost exponential increase in the total volume of historical knowledge, occasioned not least by the unprecedented growth in the sheer number of historians over the same period. The expansion of history's subject-matter has also been reflected in a widening of the historian's geographical horizons from the days when the profession in the West wrote mainly on the political history of the European and North American nation-state. Recognition of this fact has still not dawned on a number of stubbornly parochial specialists in European history, above all perhaps in Britain. Hugh Trevor-Roper, writing as Regius Professor of Modern History at the University of Oxford in 1965, declared that Africa had no history, merely 'the unrewarding gyrations of barbarous tribes in picturesque but irrelevant corners of the globe'.[32] As late as the early 1990s, John Vincent was still writing off Asian history as an impossibility ('We do not understand Asia and will not need to'),[33] surely a rather unwise statement in an age when the rampant growth of the new Asian economies was already beginning a major shift of the global power balance away from the West. All of this underlined the commitment of some grandees of the historical profession in Great Britain to the view that history was properly the study of literate minorities in the West, preferably minorities with political power.

Nearly thirty years after Trevor-Roper, another British historian, the seventeenth-century specialist John Kenyon, observed with satisfaction that in 'history departments, hastily cobbled-up courses on Indochina or West Africa faded away as soon as these areas ceased to be of immediate current concern; students also found,' he added, 'that such arcane courses, for which external examiners at degree level could rarely be provided, left them at the mercy of their tutor's whims and prejudices.' But this observation, reflecting a now-fashionable tendency among British conservatives to deride the 1960s, and delivered from the safe distance of a 'Distinguished Chair' at the University of Kansas, merely reflected the mental insularity and prejudice of its author, even more than his equally misguided claim that the contribution of British historians to European history did not 'constitute an important or influential corpus of work'.[34] Far from European and overseas history being on the decline in Britain, it has grown and flourished in the 1990s as never before, and the number of distinguished publications, ground-breaking theses, learned journals, university courses and even competent external examiners is greater than ever. Even in 1961, E. H. Carr had poured withering scorn on 'the parochialism of English history, which already weighs like a dead hand on our curriculum', and argued for an expansion of continental European and indeed non-European history on a considerable scale.[35] Thirty-six years on, there is a good deal of evidence that his plea has been heard.

Here too Carr ran into criticism from Sir Geoffrey Elton, who devoted his Inaugural Lecture as Regius Professor of Modern History at the University of Cambridge to a plea that English history be placed at the centre of the university curriculum.[36] Others have echoed this view, particularly during the debate on the contents of the national history curriculum introduced by Britain's Conservative government into schools.[37] There has been a parallel debate in the United States, too, though it has scarcely found any echoes on the European continent, where history has on the whole remained obstinately insular. To demand that more time be spent on domestic history in France or Germany for instance would be entirely superfluous. In France, the assumption of cultural superiority has guaranteed that the vast majority of historians do not really consider the history of other countries worth studying, although there is a partial exception in the case of Britain, where French historians such as Halévy and Bédarida have made a notable contribution.[38] Synoptic French surveys of aspects of the history of 'the West' have too often been devoted mainly to the history of those particular topics in France, which has been taken axiomatically – and of course quite wrongly – as typical of the history of Western humanity as a whole; and treatment of other countries has been extremely cursory. Books by French historians claiming to deal with general trends in the history of 'the West' have in practice been based almost entirely on French evidence and have completely ignored the experience of any country east of the Rhine.[39] In Germany, the understandable obsession with national self-examination after the genocidal débâcle of Hitler's Third Reich has ensured that virtually no one can make a successful career in the historical profession by studying the history of another country; and despite the opening of German historical institutes in London, Paris, Washington and Rome, to assist German scholars studying the history of these countries, the fact remains that the contribution of German historians to the history of other countries in recent decades has been negligible. By contrast, no German historian can afford to ignore the vast corpus of first-rate work produced on modern German history by historians in Britain and America. The cosmopolitanism of the historical profession in Britain and America contrasts starkly with the national narrowness of the profession on the European continent.

In the twentieth century, the study of European history has always been strong in Britain and America, driven by the involvement of the countries in two world wars fought to a large extent on European soil and centring in considerable measure on European great-power rivalries. In Britain, decolonization has led to a shift of perspective from imperial history – also a long-established tradition – to the history of Africa and Asia from an African or Asian rather than a European perspective, while in the USA and Australasia, the attention of historians has been shifting for some time away from Europe and towards the Pacific Rim. Even in Germany there are at last signs that, as the obsession with explaining the causes and consequences of the Third Reich becomes a little less central, historians are beginning to make a reputation for themselves with serious research on other European countries. Interest in the history of extra-European civilizations is growing, and books like those of the Anglo-American historian Jonathan D. Spence on the history of modern China are reaching a wide audience.[40] Historical scholarship is thus not only more eclectic than ever before, it is also becoming gradually less Eurocentric in its coverage and approach. And if this has meant greater fragmentation of history as a field of knowledge, anything we have lost has also been balanced out by the greater opportunities which modern communications and the modern organization of historical scholarship provides for specialists in different fields to talk to one another, and to exchange ideas with colleagues in other countries.

IV

The battles that have raged over the nature of history have often been fought between different kinds of historian – economic, political, intellectual and social. In practice each of these branches of historical enquiry has a somewhat different methodology, and the assumptions which these generate have been translated into different attitudes to theory and epistemology. Political historians like Elton and Himmelfarb have advocated a return to traditional political history based on the study of the nation-state and denigrated other approaches as trivial, irrelevant or misguided.[41] Economic historians like Robert Fogel, Morgan Kousser or Christopher Lloyd have urged history to focus on structural or quantitative questions and regard their own discipline of economic history as the only truly scientific, and hence reliable, way of studying the past. Social historians, like Peter Stearns or Arthur Marwick condemn the dullness of traditional political history, excoriate the impudence and ignorance of the postmodernists, and claim that social history is the only approach that combines intellectual excitement with scholarly solidity. Intellectual historians like Hayden White or Frank Ankersmit assert that all the world's a text and want to make us all into intellectual historians since the text is all that can meaningfully be studied. In this sense, history has become a multicultural domain, where different groupings struggle for intellectual supremacy on the battleground of ideas, courses and university history syllabuses. It is surely not out of place in this situation to plead for a little intellectual tolerance, and to warn any one particular orientation against the arrogant assumption that its own methods and procedures are necessarily better than those of its rivals.

Such a warning is particularly apposite at the moment in the case of intellectual and cultural history. Here, as the American labour historians David Mayfield and Susan Thorne have pointed out, the 'linguistic turn' has sought in effect to dethrone society and the economy as the moving forces in history and to reinstate politics and the state. Ideas and institutions become central instead of social and economic structures and processes. Society-centred explanations are sweepingly dismissed as 'reductionist', because they allegedly either ignore politics altogether or reduce it to a direct and unmediated product of the social. The result is a 'paradigmatic shift' which is bringing about 'nothing less than the dissolution of the dominant modes of interpretation, both liberal and Marxist, which have informed social analysis for most of this century and much of the last'. Mayfield and Thorne suggest that this may simply herald a 'full circle' return to old-fashioned political history, in which political historians no longer feel they have to pay any attention to the 'social factors' which some of them at least have been forced to take account of in recent decades. It might therefore be a step backwards instead of a step forwards; alternatively, the focus on the social which has been so influential in history over the years might be seen as a pointless detour rather than a significant advance in understanding.[42] Yet, as Mayfield and Thorne remark, it is 'quite wrong to suggest, as is commonly done in revisionist polemics, that the old social history simply neglected the constitutive effects of politics, language and culture'.[43] This is true even though much of the debate has taken place within the tradition of Marxist-oriented labour and social history. Indeed, Marx himself was very conscious that the behaviour of many political groups could not be reduced to a one-way product of the economic or social, as even a cursory glance at his classic studies of mid-nineteenth-century French politics, the *Eighteenth Brumaire* and the *Class Struggles in France*, will confirm.

Despite all the various pronouncements of its demise by postmodernists, social history is not dead. What has happened, undeniably, is that it has lost, or is in the course of abandoning, its universalizing claim to be the key to the whole of historical understanding. To this extent, the post-modernist critique has been not only successful but also liberating. By directing historians' attention to language, cul-ture and ideas, it has helped free them to develop more complex models of causation and to take seriously subjects they may have neglected before. There is much to be said for paying closer attention than ever to the surface patterns and meanings of language. At its best, the work that is now appearing under the influence of postmodernist theory pro-vides a new dimension of understanding that moves well beyond the limitations of social history. Studies of popular mentalities, of memory, commemoration and celebration, of the cultural dimensions of power and authority, of gender and the micropolitics of everyday life, and of many other subjects, have added significantly to historical knowledge. The achievement of cultural history in the postmodern mode is not merely additive; it has helped reorient our understanding of many areas of political and social history, from the French Revolution to the First World War and beyond.

But this does not mean that we should abandon social history altogether. There is no reason, for example, why historians should not continue to use concepts like class as a means of understanding the behaviour of human groups in the recent past.[44] Or why they should not carry on believing that the experience of poverty, misery and oppression under which it is reasonable to suppose that some groups in the past had to suffer, had some relevance to their culture and beliefs, and to their political allegiance as well. We should not forget the fact that the poor in the past paid for their poverty in the real, physical coinage of disease, suffering and death. There is a real danger that the 'linguistic turn' in history may make us forget this brute fact. One postmodernist author, Elizabeth Deeds Ermarth, for example, has realized that by reducing everything to text and discourse, she has eliminated the notion of society as something real and with it 'what used to be called social justice'. The term 'social', she says, has its origins in the nineteenth century and is thus one of the many classical notions which postmodernism has rendered obsolete. Aware of the embarrassing political implications of this, she claims that 'other gains' have been achieved to make good the 'loss of the terms "reality", "truth", and "man"'. As one of her critics acidly remarks, however, quoting from the relevant passages of her work,

> It is very unclear what those gains are. Perhaps the following: 'To restore health to psychic and social life and to heal the damage done by long-term and ever-increasing discursive emphasis on the symbolic, syntactical, thetic disposition of language at the expense of the semiotic, paratactic, rhythmic disposition' (147). Since Ermarth is one of those who believes that 'everything is writing' (177), perhaps this is how we are now supposed to refer to 'what used to be called' poverty, hunger, torture, oppression.[45]

Thus the postmodernist concentration on words diverts attention away from real suffering and oppression and towards the kinds of secondary intellectual issues that matter in the physically comfortable world of academia. It has become commonplace to argue, for instance, that words do matter just as much as deeds; that, for example, reading about an execution is the same as attending one or even carrying it out; or that pornography is indistinguishable from rape.[46] But while the pornography of sex and violence should not be trivialized or treated lightly, to equate it with real physical assault, bodily violation and death is to restrict one's vision to the imaginative world of reader and writer and to give this a grossly inflated significance. For most of the time, the majority of people are neither readers nor writers. Such a restriction avoids any examination of the real world of people in history and society.

That is not to say that 'mere words' have no effect, just that they should not be enthroned as the supreme beings of modern life and experience. In practice, most people recognize that there is some connection between people's standard of living, occupation, gender, sexual orientation, ethnicity, and social status – all of which have real physical referents of one kind or another – on the one hand, and their social, moral and political attitudes and general view on life, and the language in which they express these things, on the other. What postmodernism has helped us do is to underline the fact that this connection is not one-way. All these lessons can be useful when applied to the past. But their usefulness diminishes when the ideas in which they originate are pushed too far, so that we get an intellectual reductionism instead of a socio-economic one, or we abandon anything other than politics and ideas as irrelevant to an understanding of human motivation and action in history.[47]

V

In one respect at least, the clash between social history and postmodernism does not seem so stark as some of the combatants would have us believe. In particular, both, in contrast to traditional political and diplomatic history, have an apparent tendency to downplay the importance of the individual.

As a champion of a particular social interpretation of history, E. H. Carr for example thought that the cult of the individual was a pervasive Western myth which it was time to debunk. Mass democracy had brought it to an end.[48] Neither historians nor the people about whom they wrote were isolated individuals; they were all social beings. Carr argued that to distinguish between individuals and impersonal historical forces was false, for the former were the product and indeed the embodiment of the latter. He exemplified this principle well in his own *History of Soviet Russia*, following Trotsky in depicting Stalin as the product of the new Soviet bureaucracy of the 1920s rather than as an individual with any marked personality traits of his own. But had he lived to carry his *History* on into the mid-1930s, Carr would have been confronted with the phenomenon of Stalin as the ruthless, paranoid dictator of the great purges and the reign of terror which killed untold millions of Soviet citizens for the most trivial of reasons or for no reason at all. Perhaps he would have subscribed to the view, advocated by some American historians in the 1980s, that these events were the products of the structure of Soviet rule, driven on 'from below', rather than the consequence of Stalin's own individual pathology.[49] We cannot really know.

Carr himself actually included a chapter on 'Personalities' in the fifth volume of his *History of Soviet Russia*, where he dealt with the major players in the intraparty power struggles of the 1920s – Trotsky, Zinoviev, Kamenev, Bukharin and Stalin. The chapter opens with a general statement about the role of the individual in history:

> The events of history are set in motion by the wills of individuals. But what individuals will is governed in part by the historical conditions in which they find themselves; and

these conditions impose still narrower limits on what they can effectively will. Hence the explanations of events given by the historian cannot be confined to simple statements of the will of the individuals concerned, and tend for this reason to create the illusion of 'impersonal' forces at work in history, though the historian is well aware that the acts through which these forces find expression are the acts of individuals and are set in motion by the individual will.

In a similar way, Carr thought that a 'great man' was great because he embodied on a larger than normal scale the wills and aspirations of his contemporaries or anticipated those of their successors. Thus Trotsky represented Westernizing tendencies among the Bolsheviks, Stalin their anti-Western phobias. Carr believed that the key to the ambiguities of Stalin's character – 'an emancipator and a tyrant, a man devoted to a cause yet a personal dictator' – could not be found in the man himself. They had to be found in his environment. 'Few great men have been so conspicuously as Stalin the product of the time and place in which they lived.'[50]

Carr thought that 'great men' gave expression to their times, and were always representative of wider historical forces. Hitler, for example, would have remained a disregarded figure on the lunatic fringe of German politics but for the Depression of 1929–33 and the attendant crisis of the Weimar Republic. However, once such an individual attains a significant degree of power, then personality traits come into play which may have little or nothing to do with 'vast impersonal forces', and Carr was perhaps a little too quick to dismiss them. In the years after he wrote *What is History?*, Carr came in fact to concede a somewhat greater role to the individual in history than he had previously done. He thought for example that Lenin, had he remained in power, would have managed the industrialization of Russia more humanely than Stalin did.[51] Nevertheless, the social-historical approach which he championed undeniably left relatively little room for the individual actor in history.

On the face of it, postmodernism, with its dethroning of the author and its elevation of impersonal discourses to the centre of historical analysis, would seem to echo this view. Yet ironically, in view of its suspicion of the notion of individuality, postmodernism has also done a great deal to re-establish the place of the individual in history, though this has been in a very different mode from the political historians' traditional cult of 'great men'. Postmodernism's suspicion of the mainstream, its privileging of the marginal, the bizarre and the obscure, has produced a large amount of historical work recreating the world of little-known individuals such as Mennochio the Italian miller in Carlo Ginzburg's *The Cheese and the Worms*.[52] One of the very great drawbacks of generalizing social-science history, with its reliance on averages and statistics, was its virtual elimination of the individual human being in favour of anonymous groups and trends. To reduce every human being to a statistic, a social type, or the mouthpiece of a collective discourse is to do violence to the complexity of human nature, social circumstance and cultural life. On the other hand, to claim that an individual such as Stalin was simply a monster and a freak does little to help us understand why he behaved the way he did, and hugely overestimates the freedom of manoeuvre that people, even dictators, have to impose their individual will on others.[53] In the end, no one has managed to better Marx's dictum that people make their own history, but they do not do it under circumstances of their own choosing. It is precisely the interaction between the individual and his or her circumstances that makes the study of people in the past so fascinating. Postmodernist history's return to the individual, to the human element in history at every level, redresses the balance and is a major gain in this respect.

7

KNOWLEDGE AND POWER

I

It is time, one postmodernist writer has recently declared, to abandon the kind of history that

> lets us think we know the past. History in the postmodern moment . . . asks: Whose history gets told? In whose name? For what purpose? Postmodernism is about histories not told, retold, untold . . . Histories forgotten, hidden, invisible, considered unimportant, changed, eradicated. It's about the refusal to see history as linear, as leading straight up to today in some recognisable pattern – all set for us to make sense of. It's about chance. It's about power.[1]

Some of these were sentiments with which E. H. Carr might have felt a certain sympathy. He thought that 'the function of the historian is neither to love the past nor to emancipate himself from the past, but to master and understand it as the key to the understanding of the present.'[2] Needless to say, such arguments did not cut much ice with Sir Geoffrey

Elton. He admitted that one could learn at least a few lessons from the past, about the possibilities open to human thought and action, and the 'magnificent unpredictability of what human beings may think and do.'[3] But essentially, however difficult it may be, historians had to make the effort to understand in a cognitive sense the actions, ideas and motivations of people in the past without direct reference to their own beliefs in the present.

Yet for most historians, in practice this can never be enough in itself. Consciously or unconsciously, we also want to use our knowledge of the past for our own purposes in our own time. Marxist historians for example have always given present politics primacy in their approach to history. Nor should it be thought that such arguments apply only to Marxism. The historians of the *Annales* school in France insisted on scientific rigour in their research, and were busily engaged in trying to construct an alternative set of ideas to Marxist historicism. None of this was politically neutral. Fernand Braudel wrote his *magnum opus*, *The Mediterranean and the Mediterranean World in the Age of Philip II*, in a German prisoner-of-war camp, according to his own confession, in order to recapture some of the deep structures of history and identity which he hoped and believed had survived the defeat of France by the Germans in 1940. Towards the end of his life, he returned to this ambition in his study of *The Identity of France*, in some ways a profoundly conservative, nationalist text. It argued that France and its borders had not changed in essence since the thirteenth century, and declared that French blood had not been diluted since prehistory. This claim went together with Braudel's racist belief that between the French and other nations, including by implication all kinds of immigrants, 'there may be some intermingling but there is no fusion.'[4] Pierre Chaunu, another *Annales* historian, can also be located on the right. Chaunu has described legalized abortion as 'absolute murder' which will have 'disastrous demographic consequences' for France.[5] The links between the pioneering role of French demographic history and the conservative-nationalist obsession with the traditionally low birth rate in France becomes explicit in Chaunu's work. Thus behind the seemingly scientific neutrality of these historians there lurk some disturbing political purposes.

Even Elton, for all his protestations of objectivity, brought a political agenda and political preconceptions to his historical work. In the preface to his first book, *The Tudor Revolution in Government*, he argued that 'government must be strong to be worth having,' and he devoted much of his subsequent career to building up a positive assessment of the 'strong rule preventing anarchy and preserving order' which he saw as having been created under Henry VIII and his minister Thomas Cromwell. He attacked the fact that 'our history is still much written by whigs, the champions of political freedom,' and declared his intention of stressing instead 'the need for controlling that freedom'.[6] His was far from being a history which sprang naked from the sources; on the contrary, it was clothed from the outset in strongly held conservative political beliefs. Elton's arguments about the historian approaching the documents free from all present-day assumptions were refuted by his own explicit recognition of the role such preconceptions played in his own historical work.

In his book *Policy and Police*, Elton tried to exonerate his hero Thomas Cromwell from the charge that he practised a 'reign of terror' in his implementation of Henry VIII's Reformation decrees, the dissolution of the monasteries, the seizure of church land, and so on. The book relied heavily on denunciations of Catholics and opponents of these policies sent in by ordinary citizens. ('Without such activities,' he commented, 'society collapses.') In a devastating critique, Lawrence Stone observed:

> Dr Elton seems to be totally unaware of the damage done to the fabric of a society when governments positively encourage denunciations of neighbours by neighbours, thus opening up a Pandora's box of local malice and slander. No one who has read a little about life in occupied Europe under the Nazis, or has seen the movie *Le Chagrin et La Pitié* could share the satisfaction of Dr Elton as he triumphantly concludes that his hero encouraged private delation rather than relying on a system of paid informers. (Incidentally, it is on this issue that a serious case of *suppressio veri* occurs. In his discussion of whether or not Cromwell was planning or operating a police state, Dr Elton omits altogether to mention that sinister little sentence in one of his memoranda to himself in 1534: 'to have substantial persons in every good town to discover who speaks or preaches thus' (i.e. 'in favour of the Pope's authority').)

Elton, charges Stone, considers that if a law was passed, the actions it sanctioned were therefore justified and cannot have amounted to terror or tyranny. This included a statute of 1536 which allowed persons spreading rumours contrary to the royal policy to be executed by torture on the denunciation of a single witness. Elton's preconceived partiality for strong government led him to engage in a distorted reading of the documents.[7] What is noticeable about this dispute is the way in which not only Elton's views but also Stone's derive from political positions occupied in the present. Yet this does not of itself invalidate Stone's critique or reduce the clash of views between the two historians to a mere difference of opinion about politics which cannot be resolved by recourse to the original historical documents. Ultimately, Elton had to answer Stone's charge of *suppressio veri* by reference to Cromwell's memo of 1534, not by talking about the practice of delation in Nazi Germany.

II

All history thus has a present-day purpose and inspiration, which may be moral or political or ideological. The question is, to what extent is this purpose paramount? Is it what history is really about in the end? It is one thing to admit that historians are swayed by their moral or political views in the present, or to accept that theories derived from neighbouring disciplines like sociology, anthropology, economics or linguistics can be useful or even crucial in the study of the past. But it is going a major step further to argue that whatever historians might say or believe, the *main* purpose of all historical writing and research is to gain power for historians or for those they represent in the present. This widely held postmodernist argument derives principally from the writings of the French philosopher-historian Michel Foucault, who saw truth and knowledge as the products not of cognition but of power. In every age, he argued, there was a dominant 'discourse' among the sciences, which – in the language and terminology it employed – framed and restricted the possibilities of thought and its expression in such a way as virtually to exclude the possibility of disagreement. Texts – novels, histories, and so on – were not, in Foucault's view, the outcomes of individual thought, but 'ideological products' of the dominant discourse. History was a fiction of narrative order imposed on the irreducible chaos of events in the interests of the exercise of power. And if one version of the past was more widely accepted than others, this was not because it was nearer the truth, or conformed more closely to 'the evidence', but because its exponents had more power within the historical profession, or within society in general, than its critics.

The Foucauldian linkage of power and knowledge went together in the 1970s and above all the 1980s with the rise of explicitly politically committed forms of historical writing and research. The model for these was labour history, which had developed out of the socialist movement in the nineteenth century and was written explicitly from the point of view of the industrial working class. Labour historians sought to recover the history of workers and their organizations as a means of strengthening their class-consciousness and political commitment in the present and their hope of eventual triumph in the future. They told a story of resistance to oppression and of the forward march of the organized working class towards the twin goals of political power and personal emancipation, to be gained by the socialist transformation of capitalist society and the state. Labour history was thus a matter of recovering precursors of present-day socialist and labour organizations and charting the rise of the movement up to the present, from which its further rise was implicitly extrapolated into an imagined, triumphal future.

The model of labour history was taken up by other interest-groups from the late 1970s, but it was increasingly stripped of any over-arching theory of historical progress or indeed to any claim to historical objectivity at all. Black history, women's history and feminist history, gay and lesbian history, all of which became increasingly assertive in the

USA in the 1980s, began with an initial recovery of 'lost' or even deliberately suppressed historical facts about their own particular group which had been 'hidden from history' and were now 'becoming visible'.[8] But by the late 1980s they had broken free from this largely empirical model and were expending much of their energies in offering a self-consciously partisan reinterpretation of wider and more familiar historical territory from the point of view of their particular group interest. At the same time, they condemned all previously existing historical writing as partisan, representing a white, male, heterosexual, Eurocentric point of view, purveying the discourse of the culturally dominant élites. The point of historical discourse, they argued, was to empower people – specifically, to empower the particular group or groups of people they represented. What made the difference between different ways of viewing the past was the framework of politics and morality, not the accuracy of the historical vision itself, which was in the end impossible to determine.

This development reflected in part the decline of the old working class in advanced industrial and post-industrial societies. The ebbing tide of Marxism and revolution in the West left labour history increasingly stranded as the 1980s progressed. Other sources of inequality in society – gender, ethnicity, sexual orientation – grew in relative importance, rendering social cleavages more complex. The changing nature of historical scholarship on the left began to reflect these wider changes in society at large. Moreover, the situation of the university academics who wrote history was changing too. E. H. Carr's confident belief in historical objectivity as an accurate judgment of the direction in which history was moving had arguably become popular among historians in the 1960s and 1970s not least because this had been a time of vast and rapid expansion in the university systems of all the major Western nations, and thus in the historical profession as well. Much of the excitement, optimism and intellectual confidence of the generation of historians – above all, social historians – who entered the profession at that time stemmed from this fact. More confidence came from a belief in the possibilities of radical political reform created by the Democratic presidencies of Kennedy and Johnson in the USA, the Labour governments of Harold Wilson in the UK, the Social Democratic coalition led by Willy Brandt in West Germany, and the events leading to the fall of General de Gaulle in France. History seemed to deliver the key to the future; the universities seemed to be the powerhouses of political and social change; and the recovery of whole, forgotten areas of human struggle and human existence in the past through the huge expansion of social history in these years gave liberal and left-wing historians the feeling that they were engaged in a crusade to restore human dignity to the neglected masses of the past, as a means of making society more democratic in the present and the future.

At the end of the twentieth century, however, it no longer seems possible to most radicals to hold up the vision of a total transformation of society; instead, all that is attainable is the assertion and recognition of particular interests. The dominance of assertive right-wing governments in the Reagan-Bush-Thatcher years gave the academic left in Britain and America a feeling of impotence which was underlined by the crisis of academia which began in the 1970s and reached its height in the 1980s. The conservative governments of the 1980s held the universities in scant respect and preferred to look to privately-run 'think-tanks' for advice, often rejecting a good deal of received academic wisdom in the process. The expansion of the academic profession came to an end. The wave of new university foundations was over. Competition for academic jobs, which had been so easy to find in the 1960s, was now extremely severe, as all the new institutions began to produce PhDs who were unable to find posts. The numbers of PhDs in all Western countries fell sharply by the middle of the 1980s as a result. The relative economic position of academics declined, as their salaries now fell behind those of other groups, such as lawyers or civil servants, with whom they had traditionally been compared. Increasingly, the autonomy of the academic profession was eroded by the growing power of professional university administrators, the declining influence of democratic institutions such as university senates, the replacement of a collegial by a managerial ethos within universities, and the ending of a professional hierarchy based on professorial power, status and prestige to which all, in theory at least, could aspire. Government checks and controls on universities, especially in the UK, added further to the declining autonomy of the academic profession.[9] History is no longer seen as having any overall direction or making any larger sense. The working class, with which so many historians on the left identified, has turned out to be a broken reed, both declining in numbers with the coming of post-industrial society and transferring its allegiance at least in part to ideologues of the right such as Mr Reagan and Mrs Thatcher.[10]

Many aspects of postmodernism can be understood, sociologically speaking, as a way of compensating for this loss of power within the world at large, and within the university as an institution. For it places enormous, indeed total intellectual power in the hands of the academic interpreter, the critic and the historian.[11] If the intentions of the author of a text are irrelevant to the text's meaning – if meaning is placed in the text by the reader, the interpreter – and if the past is a text like any other, then the historian is effectively reinventing the past every time he or she reads or writes about it. The past no longer has the power to confine the researcher within the bounds of facts. Historians and critics are now omnipotent. To underline this, the postmodernists have developed a new level of specialized language and jargon, borrowed largely from literary theory, which has rendered their work opaque to anyone except other postmodernists. The enterprise thus seems not only self-regarding but, ironically in view of its criticism of hierarchy and prioritization, élitist as well. Its narcissism and élitism can both be seen as compensatory mechanisms for the loss of real power, income and status suffered by its academic practitioners over the past ten to fifteen years. It all reminds one of Oscar Wilde's saying that any fool can make history, but it takes a genius to write it.

The narcissism of much postmodernist writing can be even more directly personal than this. Postmodernism's legitimation of subjectivity in the historian's work encourages historians to intrude into the text to such a degree that in some cases their presence all but obliterates the historical subject. The word 'I', 'me' or 'my' appears no fewer than eighty-eight times in the first four pages of the postmodernist historian Diane Purkiss's book *The Witch in History*, for instance. Where is the witch herself in all this? Purkiss attacks male academic historians of witchcraft for instrumentalizing the witch in pursuit of their own academic careers, but does not pause to think how she is doing precisely the same thing herself.[12] Another recent article by an avowedly postmodernist historian, Rudy Koshar, is only a little less excessive in including thirty-two references to himself in the first five pages.[13] The prioritizing of historical debate and prescriptive writings about the study of history over the study of the past itself also encourages a self-regarding obsession with where the historian stands on these issues, at the expense of the issues themselves. If historians begin to regard themselves as more important than the people they are writing about, if they start to refer to each other – and to themselves – more than they refer to the past, as theorists like Ankersmit and Jenkins would like them to, then inflated self-importance, solipsism and pretentiousness can be the only results. A return to scholarly humility is surely called for here. It was, after all, Sir Isaac Newton who reminded his fellow-scientists that if he could see further, it was because he was standing on the shoulders of giants; what he was doing was only possible because of the work carried out by his predecessors.[14]

A modicum of humility would be in order not least because it is not just the postmodernists, but also in their time the quantifiers, the psychohistorians, the Marxists, feminists and many others, who have arrived on the intellectual scene arrogantly proclaiming all previous ways of doing history to be redundant, biased, useless, or false because they had unsophisticated theories or methods, because they neglected central organizing concepts, or because they were simply unscientific. The originators of this rhetoric in modern times were of course the Rankeans of the nineteenth century. Seen in terms of the sociology of professionalization, such claims might be regarded as a way of legitimating the professionalism of those who advance them, and of convincing the rest of the scholarly world that they are important. Ironically, they are part of the culture of modernism, in which to gain a hearing, intellectuals have to claim that they are saying something radically new.[15]

But the pattern of such interventions in the past has been that after an initial period of controversy, in which its universalizing pretensions are disputed, the new approach settles down to become yet another sub-specialism. When 'cliometrics' appeared, for example, its adherents claimed that it rendered all previous approaches obsolete, and that *all* historians would in future have to be trained in its methods. Twenty years or so later, in the 1990s, the debate has calmed down, the claims of the cliometricians to solve fundamental historical problems by the application of statistics have largely been discarded, and quantitative history has become a sub-specialism with its own societies, its own journals, and its own specialized language, coexisting reasonably happily with all the other sub-specialisms. The same has happened at various times with other new waves of historical theory and practice.

As a classic example of this process, one can take the case of social history, which as we saw made extensive claims to permeate the whole of historical study when it first arrived in the 1960s. The opening article in the *Journal of Social History* by its editor Peter Stearns, written in 1967, used the language of the pioneer ('few significant topics have been explored in any depth'), talked of the subject's 'advancement', and proclaimed its ability to 'recast . . . traditional questions of historiography'.[16] In 1976, however, Stearns was already complaining after a decade of the journal's existence that 'social historians are viewed with misgiving or are simply mislabeled, so that a history department can merrily do what it has traditionally done while adding the word "social" to a few course descriptions and research projects.' 'The rigidity of traditional historians' was to blame in his view for this sorry state of affairs, alongside 'conventional historical thinking' which perpetuated 'the common assumption that social history is another topic rather than a total approach'. Thus 'the resolute desire of traditional historians to put social history into another neat cubby hole' was being effectively realized. In something of a despairing mood, Stearns called for the foundation of separate social history departments to escape the 'boring' nature of 'conventional history', and achieve proper equality as a 'recognized discipline'.[17] Fortunately, perhaps, no one heeded his call.

Here therefore was a crucial retreat from social history's hegemonic claims to dominate the whole of historical study towards the more modest demand for its recognition as a legitimate sub-specialism. This process, replicated with many other sub-specialisms in history, is very similar to the phenomenon which the jazz singer George Melly encountered in his study of popular music in the 1950s and 1960s: groups like the Rolling Stones or the Beatles began with a revolt, which within a short space of time was reduced to a style.[18] The same process is currently happening with postmodernist history. In the guise of a specific kind of cultural and intellectual history, it is already equipped with its own apparatus of specialized journals and associations. Rather as history departments, especially in the USA, thought it necessary to hire one or two quantitative historians in the 1970s and one or two women's historians in the 1980s, so they now think it necessary to hire one or two postmodernist cultural or intellectual historians in the 1990s. These are likely to add in the long run to the already bewildering postmodern diversity and fragmentation of the historical profession, rather than revolutionize its theory and practice as a whole.

III

Is history as practised by professionals in countries like Britain, France, Germany and the United States no more than a dominant, bourgeois form of ideology? Are professional historians just engaged in producing justifications for things as they are, including the maintenance of their own privileged position as middle-class academics? Many postmodernists argue that this is the case, for 'in the end,' as one of them says, 'history is theory and theory is ideological and ideology just is material interests.'[19] A postmodernist perspective, in the words of Keith Jenkins, sees

> professional historians . . . as being not so much outside the ideological fray but as occupying very dominant positions within it . . . professional histories as expressions of how dominant ideologies currently articulate history. It seems rather obvious that, seen in a wider cultural and 'historical' perspective, multi-million pound institutional investments such as our national universities are integral to the reproduction of the on-going social formation and are thus at the forefront of cultural guardianship (academic standards) and ideological control; it would be somewhat careless if they were not.[20]

Confronted with what they see as an entrenched academic Establishment, many postmodernists rail against the imagined intolerance of the historical profession, in which, according to one of them, 'non-conformists, doubters, and non-believers have been treated as heretics fit only for the stake'.[21] They seek therefore to destroy the notion that 'the profession can duly be applauded as having some importance' which rests on its claim to be engaged in uncovering an 'objective' historical truth, for the professionals' truth is no more true than that of any other group in society. Postmodernist history would dispense with professional university historians altogether in this vision, and encourage instead the 'empowerment' of oppressed social groups by showing how 'our own history' can 'serve as a validating foundation' for political programmes in the present and the future.[22] The rules of historical research and the belief in the attainability of historical truth would be jettisoned because the 'distinction between propaganda and good history serves mainly to delegitimize histories which challenge dominant ideology.' Historical writing and teaching would thus be based on the belief 'that history is propaganda, that it is about the present'.[23]

Yet this is the voice not of postmodernism *per se*, of which, as we have already seen, there are many different varieties, but of vulgar postmodernism, transforming into the jargon of the 1990s the crude reductionist Marxism of the Stalinist era. That Keith Jenkins sees university historians in this jaundiced way may, if one wishes for a moment to borrow his own mode of argument, have something to do with the fact that he is only a lecturer in an institute of higher education, and so feels excluded from the multi-million pound university institutions he is criticizing so aggressively. Doubtless this would be an unfair charge, but no more unfair than the charges he is levelling at the university historical profession as a whole. It is in any case simply naïve to see cultural institutions such as universities functioning as mere transmitters of dominant values; they are, rather, one of many sites of contradiction within society, bases for the launching and debating of new and often disturbing, subversive knowledge and ideas. The very notion of a dominant discourse or ideology – liberalism, in

Jenkins's formulation – is itself a sweeping oversimplification in our multifaceted and fragmented postmodern society. Many of the advocates of postmodernism itself, after all, are located at major teaching and research institutions like Cambridge and Manchester, Princeton and Cornell, Berkeley and Yale, the Collège de France or the Sorbonne. There are numerous examples of historians and philosophers, not to mention politicians, who have enunciated and stuck to principles that run counter to their material interests. One could do worse than start with the middle-class intellectual Karl Marx and the factory-owner Friedrich Engels. A primary thrust of postmodernism is to stress the independent force of ideas and to uncouple them from material factors altogether, and it is difficult to avoid the conclusion that Jenkins and those popularizers who think like him do not really understand what postmodernism is about if they regard ideology as just a way of expressing material interests. In any case, there are and always have been many reasons why historians choose one theory, method or interpretation rather than another; often the impulses driving them are hidden deep inside the subconscious mind and cannot be explained in terms of any kind of rationality, let alone economic interest.

If history is a 'bourgeois' ideology, then how does it function as such, and what is its importance in society? According to another postmodernist writer, history is a 'disciplined means for the production of a "historical past" which exercises a regulatory function in relation to the "public past". Its role in this regard is enormously important,' he goes on, because the historical debates conducted by professional historians 'decisively influence the public face of the past over the long term.'[24] Wulf Kansteiner, a German observer of the postmodern cultural scene, has identified 'the growing insignificance of traditional historiography' in public discourse as a major source of history's current malaise.[25] But both these arguments miss the major point, which is that public knowledge of the past – public memory, in other words – has always been structured by influences other than professional historians, from folksong, myth and tradition to pulp fiction, broadsheets and the popular press. The thrust of professional history has more often been towards puncturing the clichés of popular historical myth than towards sustaining them. Moreover, from the outset, professional historians have usually addressed themselves only to an educated minority. To regard university-trained professional historians as simple one-way producers of historical knowledge which structures public perceptions of the past is to overestimate their public influence several times over.

Nevertheless, this is what a number of postmodernist writers persist in doing. Jenkins argues that 'the bourgeoisie' believes history to be a neutral academic discipline above and beyond politics. The bourgeoisie does not need a historical trajectory (such as progress) which has not arrived at its ultimate future destination since it has long since arrived at its own: namely the bourgeois dominance of society and the exploitation of everyone else in it. History thus serves the interests of the bourgeoisie. The notion that history serves the interests of the past cannot be true because 'the past does not have a self'.[26] Like many postmodernist critics of history, Jenkins lumps all historians together into a single category ('bourgeois liberals') and refuses to recognize the enormous variety of political and methodological positions that characterize the profession as it is today. Moreover, the 'bourgeoisie' does not have 'a self' either, any more than does the 'proletariat', or come to that, 'women' or 'gays' or

'African-Americans'; in all these cases the 'self' is just as much constructed ideologically as the past is, and just as hotly contested by different varieties of liberalism and conservatism, rival doctrinal interpretations of socialism, mutually hostile concepts of feminism, and so on.

It is quite wrong to suppose that professional historians all agree on certain aspects of history because these conform to a 'dominant ideology' which helps them keep their posts and their salaries. Visions or versions of history are not simply accepted because their authors have power within the historical profession or the universities. Consider for example E. P. Thompson's book *The Making of the English Working Class*, published in 1963. Its author could scarcely be called an adherent of liberalism or an academic careerist. At the time of writing the book, he was not a university historian at all, but taught mainly in extra-mural studies and at the Workers' Educational Association, and the only spell he ever spent as a fully-paid-up academic historian, at Warwick University, ended in chaos when he led a group of radical students in an occupation of the university's administration and published an excoriating attack on the academic world's subservience to capitalism in his book *Warwick University Limited*.[27] Yet *The Making of the English Working Class* has surely been one of the most influential works of English history published in the last forty years.

Consider in contrast the thesis of Sir Geoffrey Elton that Thomas Cromwell inaugurated a 'Tudor Revolution in Government'. For all the cogency and learning and persistence with which this thesis was advanced by its author, it was never generally accepted by scholars in the field, and indeed was sharply attacked not long after its enunciation, in a major debate in *Past and Present*.[28] Writing in 1980, Lawrence Stone noted that Elton had 'failed to persuade more than a minority of his colleagues in the profession that the changes that took place at that time can reasonably be described as a "revolution in government",' and although Stone added that 'every serious student of the period' had to 'grapple' with Elton's argument, the fact is that this does not add up to Elton's thesis having become an accepted part of historical orthodoxy.[29] Yet its author was for decades a pillar of the academic establishment; he was President of the Royal Historical Society, Regius Professor of Modern History at Cambridge, and was given a knighthood on the recommendation of Mrs Thatcher's Government. Power and knowledge seem only indirectly related in both these cases.

It is perfectly possible to take a rather different view of the relationship between historians and power than that advocated by many postmodernists. As John Vincent has remarked, historians nowadays are mostly state employees in universities, who have experienced a perceptible decline in income and status over the last few decades of the twentieth century:

> Historians today are not holders of power – power over men, over money, over opinion. They live among the foothills of society, where they engage anxiously in downward social mobility. They see very little of power in their own lives; they do not catch its reflections in the lives of others. From the life of action in its modern form – business – they are quite especially remote. Their disconnection from things, their want of rootedness, their poverty of commitment, are those of the minor official class the world over.[30]

To regard them, in other words, as some kind of hegemonic élite is sadly inaccurate.

This may be true; but what of the conclusion which Vincent draws from all this? He argues that because they depend on the state for their employment and pension, historians today are congenitally biased in favour of the big state, social reform and (of course) pensions, and deride 'market forces' in history, for 'left to the market, there would be few historians and little history'. Thus it is extremely difficult for the historian to regain the intellectual position of a 'freebooter or lone adventurer'.[31] It may be, of course, that Vincent's own experience of earning big money as a columnist for the *Sun* newspaper encouraged him in his favourable view of freebooting tendencies. But in practice, anyone who knows his early historical work can testify to the fact that it was refreshingly unconventional in its approach.[32] If we really believed his somewhat reductionist view, we would only expect robust right-wing opinions from historians who lived off a private income, and while it is certainly true that there are some individuals, such as Andrew Roberts, author of the neo-Thatcherite text *Eminent Churchillians*, who fit into this pattern, there are many more who do not. And there is a big market for history and historians in the universities where students have not deserted this subject as they have some others, such as physics. Within the universities, there is as wide a variety of political views among historians as there is among other sectors of the population, not least because the universities which employ them have been deliberately created by society as intellectual spaces where a wide variety of thoughts can flourish. Such a role is not merely cherished by radicals. In Britain, when the Conservatives' Educational Reform Bill of 1989 proposed to abolish tenure for university lecturers, it was a *Conservative* revolt in the House of Lords which succeeded in writing in a clause stating that academics were not to be dismissed because of their beliefs.

IV

The argument that each group in society creates its own history as a means of building its own identity has some problematical implications. As the American historian Laura Lee Downs has noted,

> The politics of identity, feminist and otherwise, rests on a disturbing epistemological ground, in which the group's fragile unity, rooted in an emergent sense of identity as an oppressed other, is shielded from white male colonization by asserting the inaccessibility of one's experience. Only those who share the group identity and have lived its experience, whether seen as biologically given or socially constructed, can know what it means to be black, a woman, blue-collar, or ethnic, in an America constructed as white, Anglo-Saxon and Protestant.[33]

One might argue that it follows that none of these oppressed groups can possibly write the history of white, Anglo-Saxon Protestant males, since they in turn have not shared the experience which makes the writing of such a history possible. The ultimate implication indeed is that no one can know anything beyond their own bodily identity. Experience is the sole arbiter of truth. There is no universal truth, only truths particular to specific groups of people.

Thus white male historians can only write about dead white males, which indeed is why in the opinion of many

postmodernists the dominant perspective on the past pur-
veyed by the historical profession has blocked so many
other groups out of the picture. Indeed, some professional
historians have explicitly defended this practice and argued
that history is, and always *should* be, basically about the
dominant (and in Western society, therefore, white, male)
group or groups in society, because their 'truth' is historically more important than that of subordinate groups. E.
H. Carr was absolutely clear that those who had (in his
view) contributed little or nothing to the creation of historical change as he saw it, such as women, or the
pre-literate and politically unorganized masses, were not
really deserving of the historian's attention. John Vincent
agrees with Carr on this point: 'History is about winners,
not losers . . . History is deeply male . . . History is about
the rich and famous, not the poor.'[34] But this is really a
confession of the writer's deep ignorance of other kinds of
history than the history of British high politics in the nineteenth century which he himself writes. In the broader
world of historical scholarship in Western Europe and the
USA over the past three decades and more, this kind of history has been increasingly in the minority, and it has been
precisely the poor and the unknown, the losers and,
indeed, the female, who have attracted the largest number
of historians and been the subject of the greatest number of
books.[35] This is only partly connected with the rise of
'identity politics'. The historians who have written about
vagrants have almost certainly not been vagrants themselves, and the same (one hopes) goes, *mutatis mutandis*,
for the history of crime. The recovery of the history of
oppressed groups has had far more to do with the desire to
expose fundamental structures of inequality in society than
with any attempt to bolster political, social, ethnic or

gender identities in the present. When a postmodernist historian argues in the mid-1990s for a 'rediscovery of history's losers', one wonders what planet he has been living on for the last thirty years.[36]

The idea that each group in society writes its own history breaks down in practice. By and large it is *not* the case that professional historians, who are still overwhelmingly white, male and middle class, spend their time writing the history of other middle-class white males, even if some of them, like John Vincent, argue that they should. Moreover, the argument that white, middle-class men who write women's history or black history, heterosexuals who write gay history, and so on, were 'appropriating' the history of other groups in an illegitimate manner, because they lack the experience necessary to do so, is itself unsustainable on a number of grounds. For the ultimate implication of such a view would be that the history of religion would have to be left to clergymen, of war to the generals, of fascism to fascists. In the end, no history would be possible, only autobiography. That such a view can have right-wing implications was illustrated by Carl Bridenbaugh's Presidential Address to the American Historical Association in 1962, for instance, when he charged that 'many of the younger practitioners of our craft, and those who are still apprentices, are products of . . . foreign origins . . . They find themselves in a very real sense outsiders on our past . . . They have no experience to assist them.'[37] Nationalist historians have frequently argued in this manner that they own the past of their own country, and that foreigners have no business in trying to appropriate it. Even Fernand Braudel, much of whose work had been devoted to the history of Spain, Italy and other parts of the Mediterranean, argued paradoxically in his last work, on *The Identity of France*, that 'the historian can really be on an equal footing only with the history of his own country; he understands almost instinctively its twists and turns, its complexities, its originalities and its weaknesses.'[38]

But French history is too important a matter to be left to the French, German history has affected other histories too greatly for it to be left to the Germans. Nor should anybody suppose that insisting on the principle that only Bosnians were capable of writing Bosnian history, or Serbs the history of Serbia, would be a way of guaranteeing the production of good, accurate and untendentious historical research. History is as much about the obviously other as it is about the seemingly familiar. It is about bridging a series of gaps, in time, culture and experience, through the use of a disciplined historical imagination. Certainly, the historian can gain by bringing personal experience to bear on the study of the past. Edward Gibbon, for example, was wont to remark that the time he had spent serving in the local militia had not been wasted when it came to writing the military history of the decline and fall of the Roman Empire. Similarly, David Knowles's experience as a monk was clearly helpful to him in writing the history of the religious orders in England, though it skewed his interpretation in a particular way, as we have seen. But there can be losses too, from a narrowing of perspective, or a facile sense of identification which obscures some of the crucial differences between past and present. Much if not most military history written by generals, for example, is hopelessly narrow and ignorant of the wider social, political and diplomatic aspects of the subject; the many books by one of the most reputable writers in this genre, Major-General J. F. C. Fuller, are a case in point.[39] The cultural gap which separates women in the 1990s from women in the 1790s or 1590s or 1390s is very much greater in some respects than the cultural gap which separates men and women in the present.

Moreover, no one would surely claim that women were not entitled to write the history of men or masculinity, or gays the history of heterosexuality, simply because they lacked the personal experience of being male or heterosexual which made this possible. Why should the oppressed not write the history of their oppressors? Yet this is the implication of such arguments. 'If the powerful can't criticize the oppressed,' the philosopher Paul Boghossian has observed, 'because the central epistemological categories are inexorably tied to particular perspectives, it also follows that the oppressed can't criticize the powerful.'[40] In practice, this has not happened. There has been a great deal of important work on masculinity written by female historians in recent years.[41] Imagination makes good the experience which is lacking. Distance may even lend a useful degree of detachment. The historian's identification with the object of study is by no means unproblematical; it caused widespread unease in Germany, for instance, when one senior historian and Second World War veteran remarked that he empathized with the soldiers of Hitler's army on the Eastern front during the Second World War in 1944–45. His sense of identification led him to equate their sufferings with those of the Jews, and the mass expulsion of millions of Germans from Eastern Europe after the war with the mass murder of the Jews in the Holocaust, in a way that most people found both distasteful and unacceptable.[42]

A growing awareness of the problems caused by the claim that experience and identification are necessary for the writing of history has led some historians at least to shift their attention from the empathetic reconstruction of the history of the oppressed groups they identify with to the linguistic analysis of the concepts which they perceive as having structured that oppression: from women, for instance, to gender. But this too can have its pitfalls. In championing the postmodernist use of gender as a concept, the American historian Joan Scott, in Laura Lee Downs's view, has begun to pursue a project in which gender identity is not grounded in the experience of oppression, but is acquired 'solely through a process of differentiation analogous to that which Saussure identified as the structural ground of linguistic systems of meaning'. In this process, the powerful – white middle-class males – created their own identity by setting themselves off against negatively defined others, such as women, non-whites, and the poor. Thus women's gender identity was created by men, not by their own experience, which was merely forced on them by white middle-class males. Paradoxically, therefore, the implication of Scott's championing of gender as a useful concept for historians is that feminists should stop pursuing the illusion of a history of women's experience and devote themselves instead to examining the history and operation of 'the inner workings of the ideological system which placed one in the unhappy position of the "other" to begin with': gender, as a system of differentiation, rather than women, as a group; racism as an ideology, rather than non-whites as a category, and so on.[43]

Since Scott sees language as constituting social being, and providing the only source of agency in history, she is unable to explain historical change at all, since there is nothing in her system of analysis which tells us how language may change itself, or why. Thus she offers no hope that the structures of inequality inherent in concepts of gender can be broken down. What we need, Downs argues, is to take account of the social and, one may add, political and economic context, in analysing language in history, so that we can begin to explain why things changed in terms of the mutual influences of language and its context in the real world.[44] Scott's reply to these charges was vehement but unconvincing and failed to address any of the central points at issue.[45] Downs's plea for the restoration of a real historical context to language and thought was a powerful one.

History written by men about women is no more necessarily written from a male or masculine point of view than history written by women about men is female or feminine in perspective. One can point to many women historians who have written major works on political or diplomatic history in which there is nothing at all that might betray the fact that they are female except the name on the cover: Ragnhild Hatton's biography of King George I of Hanover and England comes to mind, for instance, or Olive Anderson's study of suicide in the Victorian era, or Annie Kriegel's book on French Communism, or indeed the writings of Gertrude Himmelfarb discussed at various points in the present book.[46] Postmodernists may argue that every historical work inevitably embodies both an interpretation and a philosophy of history, and that this makes them essentially incommensurable and therefore incapable of generating any kind of controversy that can be meaningfully resolved. However, this does not commit them to tolerating other perspectives than their own. When the feminist historian Diane Purkiss attacks the account of seventeenth-century witchcraft given in the standard work by Keith Thomas, she argues not that it is empirically flawed, but that Thomas's portrayal of witches as powerless old beggar-women is designed principally to purvey an 'enabling myth' in which (men's) 'historical identity is grounded in the powerlessness and speechlessness of women'. At the same time, Purkiss castigates what she sees as Thomas's studious avoidance of the question of why so many witches were women as an example of male arrogance and indifference towards women's history.[47] Thus Thomas's work is delegitimized on political grounds; the question of whether witches really were mostly beggar-women is regarded by Purkiss as irrelevant because, as history, it can never be finally determined.

In practice, Purkiss's arguments are both contradictory and empirically flawed. Thomas's argument, backed by a mass of telling contemporary evidence, was that poor, single old women were often accused of witchcraft because, far from being speechless, they cursed those who refused them alms. Guilt then drove the latter to link any subsequent accident or misfortune with the curse, and to bring an accusation of witchcraft against the woman in question. This was an attempt to *explain* why so many witches were women, not an attempt to *avoid* the question. And to say that such women were powerless in the face of witchcraft accusations, or that they had little status or influence in the local community, is to make an empirical observation of a strictly limited historical scope. There is no evidence at all to warrant Purkiss's charge that what Thomas was really doing was using these arguments to 'ground' male identity in the present; only the sexist assumption that he must have been doing so because he was a man. Other postmodernists are wont to claim that postmodernism has replaced the historian's supposed certainties of objective knowledge with 'tentative' and 'circumspect' hypotheses which are 'subject to continual revision',[48] but histories such as that of Purkiss, written with the explicit purpose of political empowerment in the present, are anything but tentative and circumspect, least of all in the handling of the empirical evidence on which they base their claims. Feminist history, like any other kind of history, has to be based on the facts if it is to carry conviction.

Postmodernists may claim that 'there is no real object "history", only a philosophy of history; the historian's work reduces to its ideological positions,'[49] but neither of these statements is true. Ultimately, if political or moral aims become paramount in the writing of history, then scholarship suffers. Facts are mined to prove a case; evidence is twisted to suit a political purpose; inconvenient documents are ignored; sources deliberately misconstrued or misinterpreted. If historians are not engaged in the pursuit of truth, if the idea of objectivity is merely a concept designed to repress alternative points of view, then scholarly criteria become irrelevant in assessing the merits of a particular historical argument. This indeed is the ultimate goal of postmodernists such as Ellen Somekawa and Elizabeth Smith, who argue that because 'within whatever rules historians can articulate, all interpretations are equally valid', it is necessary for historians to 'shift the grounds for the assessment of integrity from the absolute or objective truth to the moral or political. That is,' they continue, 'rather than believe in the absolute truth of what we are writing, we must believe in the moral or political position we are taking with it.' They add that they 'reject the assumption that if we abandon our claim to objective truth we must be writing in bad faith (writing propaganda in the most pejorative sense of the word)'[50] but they offer no reason to suppose why this should not in fact be the case. In fact, in classic postmodernist fashion they are caricaturing the position they are attacking by pushing it out to an extreme. No historians really believe in the *absolute* truth of what they are writing, simply in its *probable* truth, which they have done their utmost to establish by following the usual rules of evidence. In the end, it simply is not the case that two historical arguments which contradict one another are equally valid, that there is no means of deciding between them as history because they are necessarily based on different political and historical philosophies. It is one thing to say that different historians use the same sources to ask different questions,[51] quite another to say that they use them for the same question and come up with diametrically opposed answers. If one historian argues that big business put the Nazis into power in Germany in 1933 and another argues that it did not, these arguments cannot both be correct. Claiming that each is true according to the perspective (in this case, Marxist or non-Marxist) from which it is written is a meaningless statement.

As Paul Boghossian has observed: 'To say some claim is true according to some perspective sounds simply like a fancy way of saying that someone, or some group, believes it.' Supposing, he goes on, we apply this view to itself:

> If a claim and its opposite can be equally true provided that there is some perspective relative to which each is true, then, since there is a perspective – realism – relative to which it's true that a claim and its opposite cannot both be true, postmodernism would have to admit that it itself is just as true as its opposite, realism. But postmodernism cannot afford to admit that; presumably, its whole point is that realism is false. Thus, we see that the very statement of postmodernism, construed as a view about truth, undermines itself; facts about truth independent of particular perspectives are presupposed by the view itself.

Similarly, if it is argued that these claims are using different, and essentially incommensurable rules of evidence from one another, so that there is no agreement about what might constitute the kind of evidence that would prove or disprove one or the other, then any claim could be justified simply by making up rules of evidence designed to provide such a justification. It would follow from this, as Boghossian observes,

> that we could justify the claim that not every rule of evidence is as good as any other, thereby forcing the postmodernist to concede that his views about truth and justification are just as justified as his opponent's. Presumably, however, the postmodernist needs to hold that his views are better than his opponent's; otherwise what's to recommend them? On the other hand, if some rules of evidence can be said to be better than others, then there must be perspective-independent facts about what makes them better and a thoroughgoing relativism about justification is false.[52]

Once postmodernism's principles are applied to itself, many of its arguments begin to collapse under the weight of their own contradictions.

In a number of cases, political commitment, freed by postmodernist relativism from the shackles that normally bind historians to the facts, has produced deeply flawed work which clearly distorts or misinterprets the source material in the service of present-day ideology. One example is *Black Athena*, ironically written by a radical white male European scholar, Martin Bernal, whose argument is that white male European scholars have suppressed the uncomfortable truth that Ancient Greek civilization was derived from Egypt. In place of what he regards as the old Eurocentric view, Bernal offers an Afrocentric version according to which Ancient Egypt was a black African culture. Since European and

American civilization is generally portrayed in the 'Western Civilization' course books used in universities throughout the USA as having derived from the Ancient Greeks, this means that it was ultimately black in origin. But this view was quickly revealed as incompatible with the evidence. The ancient Egyptians and Carthaginians were much as the modern Egyptians are in appearance, that is, most definitely not negroid or Afro-Caribbean. The linguistic and archaeological evidence adduced by Bernal for Egyptian influence on Greece does not sustain the view that Egyptian culture was carried across the Eastern Mediterranean by a series of invasions. Moreover, the argument that white thought was black in origin does not sit easily with the parallel contention that white thought is the source of the African-Americans' oppression. In all this, the point is not that political motivation in historical writing is wrong in itself. Rather, the point is that black history deserves to be treated with scholarly rigour and care as much as white history does, and that this is conspicuously lacking in Bernal's account.[53] Similar things may be said of the gay historian John Boswell's misguided attempt to prove that people explicitly identified themselves as homosexual throughout European history, and that this was generally accepted in the Christian society of medieval Europe. This collapses in the face of a far more convincing historical literature which has located the emergence of homosexual identities at the end of the nineteenth century.[54]

Political commitment has been the source of a lot of good history and will continue to be a powerful influence on historians in the future. But history can only provide reliable support for social and political empowerment in the present if it can convincingly claim to be true, and this in turn demands a rigorous and self-critical approach to the evidence on the part of the historian, who must be willing to jettison political ideas if they prove unworkable without distorting or manipulating the reality of the past. While historians are certainly swayed, consciously or unconsciously, by present moral or political purposes in carrying out their work, it is not the validity or desirability of these, but the extent to which their historical arguments conform to the rules of evidence and the facts on which they rest, by which they must stand or fall in the end. In other words, they have to be objective, and it is to the meaning and validity of this problematical concept that we now turn.

8

OBJECTIVITY AND ITS LIMITS

I

Despite his penchant for relativism, E. H. Carr did not think that all views of the past were equally valid. 'It does not follow,' he said, 'that because a mountain appears to take on a different shape from different angles of vision, it has objectively either no shape at all or an infinity of shapes.' Carr was close enough to the British empirical tradition to protest against the view that 'the facts of history are nothing, interpretation is everything,' and he saw real dangers in 'extravagant interpretations' – such as those produced by extreme Soviet and anti-Soviet accounts of the Bolshevik Revolution – that 'ran roughshod over the facts.' Carr's account of the process of historical research and interpretation gave equal weight to both:

> The historian starts with a provisional selection of facts, and a provisional interpretation in the light of which that selection has been made – by others as well as by himself. As he works, both the interpretation and the selection and

ordering of facts undergo subtle and perhaps partly unconscious changes through the reciprocal action of one on the
other.

'History,' he concluded, was thus 'an unending dialogue
between the present and the past.'[1]

This brought Carr to another crucial point. An objective historian was thus not one who simply got the facts
right. That was mere antiquarianism. A chronicler could do
that. To be an objective historian you had to take a larger
view.

> When we call a historian objective, we mean two things.
> First of all, we mean that he has a capacity to rise above the
> limited vision of his own situation in society and in his-
> tory . . . Secondly, we mean that he has the capacity to
> project his vision into the future in such a way as to give him
> a more profound and more lasting insight into the past than
> can be attained by those historians whose outlook is entirely
> bounded by their own immediate situation.

Like Ranke, Carr believed that history differed from chronicle because it tried to grasp how discrete historical facts
were interconnected. Unlike Ranke, however, he thought
that all history was therefore teleological, or in other words,
to put it in more contemporary terms, history was only history if tied to a meta-narrative. The historian had to find
objectivity not by virtue of some moral or religious criterion
outside history, nor by eschewing any wider generalizations
and sticking to a mere recital of the facts, but by looking for
a larger meaning within history itself, an ongoing history
moving from past through present to future.[2]

In his book, Carr enjoined his readers to 'study the

historian before you study the facts.' Let us follow this advice and study the man himself before we go on to a critique of his views on history. Edward Hallett Carr was born in 1892. Shortly before his death some ninety years later, he wrote: 'I must be one of the very few intellectuals still writing who grew up, not in the high noon, but in the afterglow of the great Victorian age of faith and optimism, and it is difficult for me even today to think in terms of a world in permanent and irretrievable decline.'[3] This was an understatement of a very considerable order. Carr believed in Progress with a capital P; and after a career spent partly in the Foreign Office, where he was a supporter of appeasement in the 1930s, and partly in academia, where he taught international relations at Aberystwyth, he became a leader-writer for *The Times* during the Second World War. Here his enthusiasm for Britain's ally Stalinist Russia and his conversion to the belief that the planned economy was the way to the future caused him to be known as 'the Red Professor of Printing House Square'.

After the war ended, he moved to Cambridge and began work on a *History of Soviet Russia*, published over the following decades in fourteen volumes, taking the story from 1917 up to its culmination in *Foundations of the Planned Economy* in the early 1930s. As he indicated in an interview given to the *New Left Review* towards the end of his life, Carr never lost his faith in the Soviet Union as the embodiment of human progress. His multi-volume history reflected this belief. As Carr said, his intention was 'to write the history not of the events of the revolution . . . but of the political, social and economic order which emerged from it'. The book offered, he wrote, 'not an exhaustive record of the events of the period to which it relates, but an analysis of those events which moulded the main lines of development'.

Thus for example he provided extensive coverage of 'events and controversies before 1917 which, even if their immediate consequences appear small, played a vital part in the later history of the revolution'.[4] By contrast, his three volumes on *The Bolshevik Revolution* ignored the drama of the revolution itself, the defeat of the opposition to Lenin and the Bolsheviks, the military conflict of the civil war, the brutal suppression, murder, torture and imprisonment in the 'Gulag Archipelago' of opposition by the Cheka, Lenin's secret police, and all the other aspects of the subject which involved what one might call defeated alternatives to the Bolshevik vision of the future. Carr's purpose was simply to write about the origins and development of the institutions and policies, principally economic and social, which the Bolsheviks put into effect after they came to power and which he believed held the keys to humanity's future, and so he deliberately ignored everything else.

History was identified in this view with progress, and what was not progressive in Carr's view was largely edited out. 'If Mr Carr's remaining volumes equal this impressive opening,' wrote Sir Isaiah Berlin in a review of *The Bolshevik Revolution*, 'they will constitute the most monumental challenge of our time to that idea of impartiality and objective truth and even-handed justice in the writing of history which is most deeply embedded in the European liberal tradition.'[5] Sir Isaiah saw Carr's volumes as an attempt to rewrite the past in a manner that recalled George Orwell's *1984*. He was echoed in this view by Hugh Trevor-Roper, who thundered:

> What is the most obvious characteristic of *A History of Soviet Russia*? It is the author's unhesitating identification of history with the victorious cause, his ruthless dismissal of its opponents, of its victims, and of all who did not stay on, or steer,

the bandwagon. The 'might-have-beens', the deviationists, the rivals, the critics of Lenin are reduced to insignificance, denied justice, or hearing, or space, because they backed the wrong horse. History proved them wrong, and the historian's essential task is to take the side of History . . . No historian since the crudest ages of clerical bigotry has treated evidence with such dogmatic ruthlessness as this.[6]

Extreme though this invective was, there is some truth in the view that Edward Hallett Carr was essentially a Stalinist, though his insistence on giving coverage to Trotsky as one of the architects of the Soviet system, his criticisms of Stalin as an individual, and other aspects of his *History* caused him to be anathematized by official Soviet historiography as long as he lived. For Carr, history was not about the past in itself nor even about how the past came to be the present, but about how it contributed to the future the historian desired. The propositions advanced in *What is History?* reflected this view of history as progress, as seen from the point of view of the future of the human race in a Soviet-style planned economy: an example, one might say, of the dictum that historians 'remember the future and imagine the past,' though perhaps not quite in the way that the originator of this uncharacteristic witticism, Sir Lewis Namier, intended. In taking this point of view, moreover, Carr was preaching with all the zeal of the convert: for he had spent the earlier part of his academic career writing about those very losers whom he later instructed historians to consign to what Trotsky called the dustheap of history: men such as the anarchist Bakunin, who had failed in almost every political enterprise in which they had engaged.[7]

It is easy to see now the flaws in E. H. Carr's definition of objectivity in history. The sweep of history towards a

Soviet-style planned economy, in the light of which he required historians to judge the past if they were to be deemed objective, came to an abrupt end in 1990. Moreover, those who thought, like the American political writer Francis Fukuyama, that history was now over because liberal-democratic, free-market capitalism had triumphed all along the line – another teleology, with the opposite signs to those of the kind of Marxism E. H. Carr espoused – were also confounded, as religious fundamentalism spread in modernizing states like Iran or prosperous areas such as Israel or the American West.[8] Whatever else it is, historical objectivity is not conformity to an imagined future, not least because, as we saw earlier in this book, historians are no more capable of imagining or predicting the future accurately than anyone else. Carr himself, after all, was a classic example of such a failure.[9]

Well before Carr's vision of objectivity had been falsified by events, it had run into serious criticism not only from philosophers like Sir Isaiah Berlin but also historians such as, most obviously, Sir Geoffrey Elton, whose political conservatism was strongly opposed to the notion of progress that underlay E. H. Carr's approach to historical objectivity. 'One man's better,' he remarked tartly, 'is usually another man's worse.' 'The purpose of history,' Elton declared, 'is to understand the past, and if the past is to be understood it must be given full respect in its own right.' The events of the past occurred, people lived and died, whether or not historians were interested in writing about them. They had an independent reality. The historian's job was to discover and analyse them through the study of the evidential traces they left behind. Establishing what happened, and when, and how, was a major part of historical research, he argued, and differences among historians over these matters often reflected the depth of the historian's knowledge of the sources rather than a contemporary standpoint or opinion. Good historians did not pre-select the evidence according to their point of view. Bias and personal character came into historians' writing simply through impelling them to study one particular subject rather than another. Once they had selected their general topic or area of research, they became the servants of the sources, listening to them, and trawling as widely and as deeply as possible without asking any questions except those posed by the documents themselves.[10] Objectivity was simply a matter of reading the documents without prejudice and using them to reconstruct the past in its own terms.

Elton was surely right to demand openness to the sources, a full and fair dealing with history's losers as well as its winners and the avoidance of the kind of distortion and suppression of evidence which would result if we all followed the prescription for objectivity laid down by Carr. But Elton's own definition of historical objectivity has its problems too. As we have seen, his arguments were influenced at least in part by his strongly held political beliefs and his attraction for the order and strong government that had been so fatally lacking in the Central Europe of his childhood. He was deceiving himself when he supposed that good historians rejected theory and suppressed their present-day concerns when they researched the past. Historians, including Elton himself, do not just listen to the evidence, they engage in a dialogue with it, actively interrogating it and bringing to bear on it theories and ideas formulated in the present. In this process of dialogue we must be conscious of the nature of these theories and concepts; otherwise, if we abandon our self-consciousness and fail to develop the art of self-criticism to the extent that we imagine we are bringing none, then our prejudices and preconceptions will slip in unnoticed and skew our reading of the evidence in the way they did with Elton's reading of Thomas Cromwell's rule in early Tudor England.

If we engage in these conversations with the voices of the past speaking through the documents, will some kind of objective knowledge about the past emerge? Both Carr's and Elton's definitions of objectivity are clearly unsatisfactory as they stand. But does this mean we have to surrender to the hyper-relativism of the postmodernists and admit that in the end no kind of objective knowledge about the past, in the sense of the patterns of interconnectedness that makes it history rather than chronicle, can ever be possible? The fundamental problem with this kind of extreme relativism is, as we have already seen, that it inevitably falls foul of its own principles when they are applied to itself. Why, after all, if all theories are equally valid, should we believe postmodernist theories of history rather than other theories? If all knowledge is relative, if it is impossible to give an accurate summary of a discourse without at the same time projecting one's own reading on to it, then why should we not give to the work of Barthes, or Derrida, or Jenkins, or Ankersmit, or White any significance that we wish to give it? At the most extreme fringes of postmodernism, indeed, an awareness of this problem leads to a self-conscious playfulness and arbitrariness of language, full of puns and metaphors, ambiguities and different concepts linked by the postmodernist oblique stroke, so that the infinite play of significations begins within the text itself. But in practice, even the most extreme deconstructionists do not really accept that their own theories can be applied to their own work. They wish, on the contrary, to retain their own identity as authors, and their own control over the interpretations to which their own texts are subject. Indeed, in their use of technical jargon, as we have seen, they lay implicit claim to the development of a scientific method of analysing texts which they clearly believe has greater validity than other methods. None of this in practice, however, prevents anybody from applying to postmodernist writers the same concepts and methods as they apply to others. Once the intellectual gateway to total relativism has been opened, it cannot be closed again in the interests of one privileged theory or another.

Postmodernists mostly see themselves as situated on the political left. They argue that freeing history from the constricting shackles of objective fact will enable it to become more democratic, more sceptical and more tolerant.[11] In the United States, postmodernist relativism has accompanied multiculturalism (the idea that different, disadvantaged cultural groups in society have equally valid perspectives on historical truth, and that these must be asserted in order to empower these groups in the face of the dominant concept of historical truth held by the ruling white male élite). But if the only grounds we have for preferring one vision or interpretation of the past over another are aesthetic or moral or political, if the persuasiveness of a historical interpretation is simply a matter of the power of its advocates within society and within the historical profession, then it does not follow at all that history should necessarily be a democratic, a tolerant or a sceptical enterprise, or that it should in any way favour the politically or culturally disadvantaged. History can with equal validity as history be a fascist or a Stalinist enterprise, it can portray the past in terms of the struggle of different races for the survival of the fittest, or the inevitable progress towards the Stalinist utopia, as it did in the 1930s, without fear of contradiction except on moral or aesthetic or political grounds.

Historical controversy is here effectively reduced to moral or political debate. Does postmodernism therefore give a licence to anyone who wants to suppress, distort or cover up the past? Where do we draw the line between all this and legitimate reinterpretation?

II

These issues, and some even more serious, were raised in 1987 when a young Belgian scholar discovered that one of the leading postmodernists, Paul de Man, a Professor at Yale University who had been born and grew up in Belgium, emigrated to the USA after the war and died in 1983, had written some 180 articles for a Nazi-controlled newspaper in Brussels during the German occupation from 1940 to 1942. Their focus was cultural, but they included encomia of collaborationist writers in France and – most controversially of all – attacks on the Jewish contribution to European culture in the twentieth century, which de Man decried as mediocre and without great value. At a time when Jews were being rounded up in Belgium and deported to Auschwitz, de Man wrote an article arguing that if the Jews were deported to a Jewish colony outside Europe, European culture would suffer no great loss. After his emigration to the USA, de Man never mentioned this to any of his colleagues or pupils, and indeed always denied any kind of collaborationist involvement in Belgium during the war. Like the Austrian President Kurt Waldheim, he had rewritten his own past without reference to the evidence. On this basis, he built a successful career in American academia, and became an extremely influential literary theorist, leading the 'Yale school' of literary 'deconstructionists' who argued for the irrelevance of authorial intentions and the multiple indeed virtually infinite possibilities of textual interpretation.[12] The point of these revelations about his wartime writings was quickly grasped by deconstruction's critics. Literary criticism, for de Man, seemed to be a way of denying his own past. In his earlier, structuralist phase, he had argued that texts as it were wrote themselves, thus implicitly denying authorial responsibility for them. Deconstructionism could be taken to have similar exculpatory implications. As de Man wrote in his most influential work, *Allegories of Reading*:

> It is always possible to face up to any experience (to excuse any guilt) because the experience always exists simultaneously as fictional discourse and as empirical event, and it is never possible to decide which of the two possibilities is the right one. The indecision makes it possible to excuse the bleakest of crimes because, as a fiction, it escapes from the constraints of guilt and innocence.[13]

It was difficult in the light of the revelations of 1987 to see this as anything but a denial of the 'empirical events' of the author's own wartime past. Still, to leap from this to a blanket condemnation of his entire output of literary theory as no more than a vehicle of personal exculpation was going a long way. In the end, the literary theories developed by de Man had to be confronted on their own terms.

Yet what was striking in the subsequent debate was the use of deconstruction by de Man's defenders to argue away not just the connection between his collaborationism and his literary theories but also the very fact of the collaboration itself. This involved the inevitable stress on the multiple possibilities of interpreting what de Man had written. De Man should not, his friends wrote, be condemned on the basis of a single article; many other European intellectuals had done similar things, and de Man was only being attacked because he was a deconstructionist; and the early essays in any case had nothing to do with deconstructionism at all. The philosopher Richard Rorty defended de Man by arguing that his journalism was unconnected with his literary theory, just as the philosopher Heidegger's phenomenology was unrelated to his Nazi political speeches and his consistent refusal to condemn Hitler after the war. The death of the author and the independent life of each of his texts was used here to counter what Rorty called the condemnation of deconstruction 'on the basis of the young Paul de Man's opportunistic antisemitism'.[14] Moreover, other defenders of de Man argued that the attacks on him were no more than 'a reaction to the genuine threat posed by de Man's work and by that of the so-called deconstructionists generally to a powerful tradition of ideological assumptions about literature, about history, and about the relation of literature to human life'.[15] At the same time, de Man's defenders did not hesitate to make liberal use of the rhetoric of factual objectivity, and more than one of them made the explicit claim to 'set the record straight' about the literary theorist's wartime past, condemning in the process the 'misreadings, distortions and selective slanting of quotations' they believed had been employed by de Man's critics.[16]

For his part, Jacques Derrida claimed that de Man's critique of 'vulgar antisemitism' in his early articles, his insistence that the Jews were mediocrities rather than dangerous and potent racial pollutants, was tantamount to a condemnation of antisemitism itself, because antisemitism was 'always and essentially vulgar'. Thus, as others of his defenders among the deconstructionists argued, de Man was basically engaging in an act of resistance to Nazism when he wrote the article in question. Derrida accused de Man's critics of being Nazis themselves: 'To judge, to condemn the work or the man on the basis of what was a brief episode, to call for closing, that is to say, at least figuratively, for censoring or burning his books, is to reproduce the exterminating gesture which de Man is accused of not having armed himself against sooner with the necessary vigilance.' He convicted de Man's academic critics of 'collaborating' with the mass media in an outburst of journalistic hysteria and vulgarity. Derrida suggested that only deconstructionists were properly equipped to understand de Man's writings, and called his critics 'confused, hurried, and rancorous professor-journalists' whose work was a heap of muck destined for the intellectual compost-heap, and whose views were 'dishonest', 'obscene', 'venomous', 'uneducated', 'indecent', 'grotesque' and 'laughable'.[17]

Like much postmodernist writing, the defence of de Man by the deconstructionists was riddled with contradictions. On the one hand, Derrida and his supporters insisted theoretically on the infinite possibilities of textual interpretation; on the other, they argued in practice that to interpret de Man's early writings as collaborationist or antisemitic was just plain wrong. On the one hand, the author himself theoretically had no control over the meaning of what he wrote; on the other, Derrida denounced in the most polemical terms those he thought were wilfully misunderstanding what he said in de Man's defence. On the one hand, everything, including antisemitism, was a text, and all texts were theoretically subject to the infinite play of significations; on the other, Derrida described antisemitism as 'essentially vulgar'. On the one hand, it was wrong to prioritize élite culture over popular culture, one kind of text over another; on the other, de Man's defenders bitterly resented the involvement of journalists in the debate, and clearly loathed its escape from the élitist discourse of academia. Postmodernists seemed to want to have their cake and eat it. Behind postmodernists' claim, symbolized in their heavy use of jargon and specialized language, to be scientific, there is, in the end, a desire to prioritize a particular way of reading texts that runs completely counter to their own postulate of the essential arbitrariness and openness of textuality.

To equate criticism of a literary theorist with Nazi exterminism was an act of rhetorical hyperbole that went far beyond anything warranted by the evidence. It was, after all, de Man himself who had 'censored' and, 'figuratively speaking', 'burned' his own early work. It was not the case that, as Derrida argued, the circumstances in which de Man had written his articles 'remain unclear to us'. They were easily ascertainable. Nor did the dispute turn on a single article or passage, but on a very large collection of texts, written over two whole years, and also, crucially, on the way de Man had suppressed all mention of them for decades after the war. To read them as an act of resistance to Nazism was completely implausible. If they had been intended as such, why did de Man suppress them? Most significantly of all, perhaps, here was an example of new documents coming to light which materially altered people's perceptions of the past, irrespective of the views they held in the present. As Alan B. Spitzer has commented in his careful dissection of the controversy: 'At a time when there has been considerable emphasis on the way historical writing "constructs" the past, we have a example of the transformation of the present by the unanticipated evidence of past events.'[18] The result was, as another historian commented: 'Although deconstruction should survive the attack of de Man's critics, as a tool for historians it may not survive de Man's defence.'[19] The real issue in the debate, another commentator noted, was 'not what "resistance to theory" the attack on de Man evinces but what "resistance to history" the defence of de Man entails'.[20] Even Dominick LaCapra concluded that the debate indicated how 'deconstruction can be used to justify or rewrite anything'.[21] In the end, as Alan B. Spitzer concludes, the real message of the debate was how both sides, including the postmodernists, appealed to common standards of factuality and evidence and occupied common ground over which they fought – the ground of what inferences or interpretations it was appropriate to derive from a set of documents. 'The people who are indignant over what they take to be misrepresentations of de Man's past are not simply choosing one set of rhetorical conventions over another; they are saying what they think is true and doing what they think is right.'[22]

III

Extreme relativism leaves the door wide open, as Christopher Norris has warned, to far-right historians to create 'a massively falsified consensus, brought about by the misreading or manipulative use of evidence, the suppression of crucial facts and the creation of a certain selective amnesia in those whose memory might otherwise go far back'.[23] To be sure, because White accepts the possibility of proving historical truth at the level of the individual fact, he denies the validity of revisionist attempts to argue away Auschwitz as if it never happened.[24] But in his view this is below the real level of history as such, and here his approach makes it impossible for him (or anyone else, if they accept it) to say that a Nazi or fascist interpretation of Hitler's 'Final Solution' which conceded that it actually happened could be any less valid than any other interpretation. Total relativism provides no objective criteria by which fascist or racist views of history can be falsified. Thus 'Holocaust denial' literature, which declares that six million Jews were never murdered by the Nazis, and that Auschwitz and similar extermination camps are fabrications of a post-war, anti-German, pro-Jewish political lobby, has been given respectability above all in the United States – in Germany it is illegal – by a widespread belief that 'both sides of the picture should be heard', or in other words that both have, at least in principle, equal validity. A leading authority on this literature, Professor Deborah E. Lipstadt of Emory University, Atlanta, Georgia, consistently refuses to take part in public debates with the deniers on the ground that 'to do so would give them a legitimacy and a stature they in no way deserve. It would elevate their antisemitic ideology – which is what Holocaust denial is – to the level of responsible historiography – which it is not.'[25] She reported that radio and television producers repeatedly registered their amazement at her stance, asking her every time why she did not think that their listeners or viewers should hear 'both sides of the story'. A similar attitude was evident on a number of campuses where there had been controversy about the activities of deniers. A commitment to freedom of speech enshrined in the Constitution of the United States led a number of universities protecting the right of 'revisionists' to speak on their premises; but the First Amendment only covers the right of the government to censor free speech, not that of independent institutions like universities. More serious, and more relevant, was the conviction of many that, as an advertisement in one campus newspaper put it, 'Revisionists are . . . reinterpreting history, a practice that occurs constantly, especially on a college campus.'[26]

The history department at the university where this claim was made unanimously rejected this argument. It noted:

> That historians are constantly engaged in historical revision is certainly correct; however, what historians do is very different from this advertisement. Historical revision of major events is not concerned with the actuality of these events; rather it concerns their historical interpretation – their causes and consequences generally.[27]

The Holocaust 'revisionists' *appeared* to be scholarly, with an 'Institute for Historical Review' devoted to their activities, a journal with fully footnoted articles and many other adornments of academic style. But in fact, they were not scholarly, although their style evidently deceived a number of campus newspaper editors into believing that they were. The issue, as Lipstadt puts it, is between prejudice and propaganda on the one hand, and rational arguments and scholarship on the other. Students at one midwestern university, where a history instructor was dismissed for arguing that the Nazi death camps were an anti-German hoax (an argument he put forward, with a dubious sense of relevance, during a class on the Napoleonic Wars), protested that he had been unfairly treated and that his dismissal violated a basic principle of free speech. 'These students,' Lipstadt notes, 'seemed not to grasp that a teacher has a responsibility to maintain some fidelity to the notion of truth.'[28]

The increase in scope and intensity of the Holocaust deniers' activities since the mid-1970s has among other things reflected the postmodernist intellectual climate, above all in the USA, in which scholars have increasingly denied that texts had any fixed meaning, and have argued instead that meaning is supplied by the reader, and in which attacks on the Western rationalist tradition have become fashionable. Coupled with the denial that the notion of truth has any validity at all, this has in Lipstadt's view 'created an atmosphere of permissiveness toward questioning the meaning of historical events' and made it difficult 'to assert that there was anything "off limits" . . . A sentiment had been generated in society – not just on campus – that made it difficult to say: "This has nothing to do with ideas. This is bigotry."' This sentiment, argues Lipstadt, 'fosters deconstructionist history at its worst. No fact, no event and no aspect of history has any fixed meaning or content. Any truth can be retold. Any fact can be recast. There is no ultimate historical reality.' And, she warns:

> Holocaust denial is part of this phenomenon. It is not an assault on the history of one particular group. Though denial of the Holocaust may be an attack on the history of the annihilation of the Jews, at its core it poses a threat to all who believe that knowledge and memory are among the keystones of our civilization . . . (and) to all who believe in the ultimate power of reason.[29]

That this threat is real has been demonstrated recently by the postmodernist historian Diane Purkiss, who has argued that 'most neo-Nazi historians adopt the most conservative possible protocols of discovery, revelation and truth-telling' in their denial of the existence of the death camps. Their use of the scholarly apparatus of footnotes and references, and their insistence that they are telling the objective truth, demonstrates in Purkiss's view the 'dire consequences' of such a scholarly apparatus, the bankruptcy of such a belief in objectivity and truth. But the point is that the *pseudo-scholarship* of the Holocaust deniers is easily unmasked as a sham. If *all* footnotes really were nothing more than a rhetorical device designed solely to produce a spurious 'reality-effect', then we really would *not* be able to tell the difference between genuine scholarship and pseudo-scholarship. But they are not. Relativism and 'the indeterminacy of truth' do not effectively undermine 'the self-proclaimed certitude of deniers' as Purkiss claims, they simply put it on a par with real histories of Auschwitz, and support the claim (which Purkiss endorses) that we can never know the objective truth about either. Purkiss's solution is to tell stories about Auschwitz and not worry too much about whether or not they are based in fact. Yet, while it certainly is the case that stories told by Holocaust survivors, as Purkiss says, are 'moving', does it really not matter whether or not they are true?

In the end, as this suggests, it trivializes Nazism and the Third Reich, as the German history specialist Jane Caplan has argued, to discuss them in terms of 'theories that appear to discount rationality as a mode of explanation, that resist the claims of truth, relativize and disseminate power, cannot assign responsibility clearly, and do not privilege (one) truth or morality over (multiple) interpretation'. She goes on:

> It is one thing to embrace post-structuralism and postmodernism, to disseminate power, to decenter subjects, and all in all let a hundred kinds of meaning contend, when *Bleak House* or philology or even the archaeology of knowledge are the issue. But should the rules of contention be different when it is a question, not simply of History, but of a recent

history of lives, deaths, and suffering, and the concept of a justice that seeks to draw some meaningful relation between these?[30]

Like other new approaches to history, therefore, postmodernist theory would seem to be more applicable to some areas of history than to others. A recognition of this likelihood is the first step in the direction of harnessing its more positive ideas to the research and writing of history in the twenty-first century.

IV

'Postmodern history,' a group of its critics has complained, 'too often seems to consist of denunciations of history as it has been known rather than of new histories for present and hence future time.'[31] But there are plenty of real historical works in which the influence of postmodernist theory, to put it no more strongly, is clearly evident. Postmodernism comes in many guises. If some postmodernists, as we have seen, embrace an extreme scepticism which denies the possibility of historical knowledge altogether, others adopt a more moderate position in which the writing of history is still at least a possibility.[32] They have opened up possibilities of self-renewal for the historical discipline, suggesting a way out of the impasse into which social determinism, above all in its Marxist variants, had run by the beginning of the 1990s. That is not to say that postmodernist history is necessarily always as novel as it frequently takes itself to be; but it has both extended the range of historical writing and breathed new life into some old and rather tired subjects like the history of royalty and the élites, or the study of 'big names' in the history of ideas. Historical writing on that great and problematic phenomenon of the nineteenth and twentieth centuries, nationalism, for example, can only benefit from a shift of focus from the social bases of nationalist movements to the sources and determinants of changing senses and meanings of national identity. A concern with gender and ethnicity, as aspects of social inequality which depend as least as much on discursive constructions of identity as they do on real and identifiable physical characteristics, can only enrich a social history impoverished by a restrictive concentration on class.

Postmodernist history, as one might expect, has rejected the faith in reason and progress which was so central to modernist historiography, and much of its attention has been directed towards the irrational in history, the extraordinary, the transgressive and the magical. It has often thrown over the real for the symbolic. In refusing to prioritize one aspect of history over others, or to construct a central grand narrative and relegate everything else to the margins, it has also in many cases turned to subjects which historians had previously thought trivial or without significance. It has frequently followed the belief that the most interesting animals and plants are to be found in the verges and ditches by the roadside, not on the highway itself. What then does the best postmodernist history look like, what are its advantages and its disadvantages?

One thing which the postmodernist treatment of history as a form of literature has done is to reinstate good writing as legitimate historical practice. In place of the rebarbative social science jargon of the 1970s we can now turn to brilliantly written narratives such as Simon Schama's *Citizens: A Chronicle of the French Revolution*[33] or Orlando Figes's *A People's Tragedy: The Russian Revolution 1891–1921*.[34]

Both these books tackle big, 'traditional' subjects, but both of them interweave small incidents and personal histories, of the famous and the obscure, into the broader narrative, with a constantly shifting focus which is a world away from the smooth factual recounting of more old-fashioned treatments of these themes. Neither pretends to be definitive; and by including detailed sub-plots and biographies whose selection is self-confessedly personal and – though illustrative of larger points – arbitrary, both implicitly admit that the same story could be told in other, equally valid ways. Both of them have an argument, in Schama's case heavily concealed beneath the surface detail; both emphasize, perhaps over-emphasize, the bloody and violent nature of revolution. In *Citizens*, indeed, the French Revolution of 1789–94 becomes almost meaningless in the larger sense, and is reduced to a kind of theatre of the absurd; the social and economic misery of the masses, an essential driving force behind their involvement in the revolutionary events, is barely mentioned; and the lasting significance of the Revolution's many political theories and doctrines for modern European and world history more or less disappears. Both books make utterly compelling reading, in which most effort has gone into structuring the narrative, and rather less into building an interpretation.

At the opposite extreme in terms of scale of events are Natalie Zemon Davis's *The Return of Martin Guerre*[35] and Robert Darnton's *The Great Cat Massacre*.[36] These too are compellingly told narratives, but they build on the obscure and the unknown rather than on the great and the famous. Both books take very small incidents of everyday life and retell them as stories, analysing them as metaphorical and symbolic clues to larger things. In doing so they bring the reader into contact with the fabric and feel of everyday life in a distant and remote mental and physical world, in a manner which the generalizing social-historical projects of the 1970s were quite incapable of doing. Both, however, have been sharply criticized by historians for their allegedly cavalier handling of the evidence, and it is possible that here the influence of postmodernist theory has played a questionable role.

Davis confesses in the preface to her book that 'what I offer you is in part my invention.' She wants to make room in the story, she says, for 'perhapses' and 'may-have-beens'. The documents on which she bases her work tell the story of an impostor who fooled an innocent woman into believing that he was her husband Martin Guerre returning from the wars. The deception was only revealed when the real Martin Guerre turned up, and even so, the wife still defended the impostor at his subsequent trial. Davis reworks this into a narrative of a clever and sensual woman who colluded with the impostor when he was hauled up before the courts on the return of her real husband, because he was better in bed than the inadequate wretch who was the genuine Martin Guerre. In doing this, however, Davis, according to her critics, is indulging in pure speculation. There is nothing in the documents to support any of the major aspects of her reading of the story: not the alleged inadequacy of the real Martin Guerre nor the cleverness and sensuality of the wife nor the supposed virtues of the impostor. Davis's most severe critic, Robert Finlay, commented:

> Speculation, whether founded on intuition or on concepts drawn from anthropology and literary criticism, is supposed to give way before the sovereignty of the sources, the tribunal of the documents. The historian should not make the people of the past say or do things that run counter to the most scrupulous respect for the sources.[37]

On the other hand, Davis countered that her portrayal of Martin Guerre's wife, though not directly based on sources about her or documents from the case itself, was legitimated by everything that we knew about peasant women in that part of France at the time, who appear uniformly in other sources as shrewd, active and enterprising. And indeed indirect and inferential procedures such as these are frequently employed even in the most traditional kinds of history, where the direct source material is inadequate. The question of whether Davis was justified in her interpretation, or whether, as Finlay implied, she was reading into the case of Martin Guerre her present-day feminist belief in the strength and ingenuity of women must remain open. In the end, the element of doubt, and the critical reading it encourages, add to the book's importance and appeal rather than detracting from it.

Robert Darnton, for his part, bases his entire narrative of the 'great cat massacre' on a three-page pamphlet written in 1762, some thirty years after the incident it purported to describe. There is no other evidence to show that the apprentices whom he discusses ever massacred any cats at all. Less still is there any justification for arguing, as Darnton does – and this is the central point of his argument – that the cat massacre was a symbolic prefiguration of the great massacres of the French Revolution another thirty years on, in the 1790s. The symbolism of the cat massacre, if it ever happened, was directed at master artisans, not at the aristocrats or rural seigneurs who were the objects of popular fury in the Revolution; and in any case, the author of the account of 1762 wrote it partly to reassure the authorities that apprentices took out their fury on their employers symbolically rather than through the exercise of real violence. Darnton's essay on the cat massacre does not stand up to even the most cursory scrutiny on Rankean principles, according to his critics. It reveals itself to be a tissue of speculation from start to finish. Yet this is taking too austere a view. We need to understand the violence which accompanied and drove on the French Revolution of 1789, and Darnton's narrative helps us do just that. Full of fascinating detail, it follows the model of 'thick description' pioneered by the anthropologist Clifford Geertz, with whom Darnton has taught at Princeton, and demonstrates many of the strengths of interweaving interpretation into the detail of a narrative.[38]

Postmodernism in its more constructive modes has encouraged historians to look more closely at documents, to take their surface patina more seriously, and to think about texts and narratives in new ways. It has helped open up many new subjects and areas for research, while putting back on the agenda many topics which had previously seemed to be exhausted. It has forced historians to interrogate their own methods and procedures as never before, and in the process has made them more self-critical, which is all to the good. It has led to a greater emphasis on open acknowledgement of the historian's own subjectivity, which can only help the reader engaged in a critical assessment of historical work. It has shifted the emphasis in historical writing – though not in writing about history as a discipline – back from social-scientific to literary models, and in so doing has begun to make it more accessible to the public outside the universities (and indeed to students within them). It has restored individual human beings to history, where social science approaches had more or less written them out. And it has inspired, or at least informed, many outstanding historical works in the last decade or more: works which have been none the worse for continuing in other respects to conform to many of the traditional canons of scholarship which postmodernism in its more radical moments affects to despise.

V

Sir Geoffrey Elton remarked acidly that to the 'disciples of total relativism history matters only insofar as it contributes to their own lives, thoughts and experiences . . . To me, I fear,' he added, 'this is the ultimate heresy. For the historian is in the first place concerned with the people of the past – with *their* experiences, thoughts and actions – and not with the people of the present, least of all with himself.'[39] We rake over the ashes of the past, and only with difficulty can we make out what they once were; only now and then can we stir them into a flicker of life. Yet we should not despair at the difficulty of the goals we have set ourselves. Everyone, even the most diehard deconstructionist, concedes in practice that there is extratextual reality. History is an empirical discipline, and it is concerned with the content of knowledge rather than its nature. Through the sources we use, and the methods with which we handle them, we can, if we are very careful and thorough, approach a reconstruction of past reality that may be partial and provisional, and certainly will not be objective, but is nevertheless true. We know, of course, that we will be guided in selecting materials for the stories we tell, and in the way we put these materials together and interpret them, by literary models, by social science theories, by moral and political beliefs, by an aesthetic sense, even by our own unconscious assumptions and desires. It is an illusion to believe otherwise. But the stories we tell will be true stories, even if the truth they tell is our own, and even if other people can and will tell them differently. Anyone who thinks that the truth about the past does not matter has not, perhaps, lived under a regime like that of the Soviet or Eastern bloc Communists where it is systematically distorted and suppressed. The feeling of liberation, the excitement, the consciousness that justice was at last being done to the victims of Stalin was palpable among Russian historians in the process of opening-up begun by Mikhail Gorbachev.[40] It stood in an exaggerated way for the feelings all historians have when beginning their journey into the past. For as G. M. Trevelyan once wrote:

> The appeal of history to us all is in the last analysis poetic. But the poetry of history does not consist of imagination roaming at large, but of imagination pursuing the fact and fastening upon it. That which compels the historian to 'scorn delights and live laborious days' is the ardour of his own curiosity to know what really happened long ago in that land of mystery which we call the past. To peer into that magic mirror and see fresh figures there every day is a burning desire that consumes and satisfies him all his life, that carries him each morning, eager as a lover, to the library and the muniment room. It haunts him like a passion of terrible potency, because it is poetic. The dead were and are not. Their place knows them no more, and is ours today. Yet they were once as real as we, and we shall tomorrow be shadows like them . . . The poetry of history lies in the quasi-miraculous fact that once, on this earth, once, on this familiar spot of ground, walked other men and women, as actual as we are today, thinking their own thoughts, swayed by their own passions, but now all gone, one generation vanishing into another, gone as utterly as we ourselves shall shortly be gone, like ghosts at cockcrow.[41]

For a long time, Trevelyan's views have seemed deeply unfashionable and out of date. One consequence of the post-modernist incursion into history is to make their emphasis on poetry and imagination seem contemporary once more; but poetry and imagination that are disciplined by fact.

The whole idea of objectivity, concludes Peter Novick in the introduction to several hundred pages of his own writing on the subject, is 'essentially confused'.[42] Yet the book to which he prefaces this remark is objective enough in most normal senses of the word. It does not wilfully distort or manipulate the evidence. And it presents the positions adopted by historians on their professional activities fully and fairly. This does not mean that it has no argument or point of view — far from it. But as Thomas L. Haskell has pointed out, it is important not to confuse objectivity with neutrality, indifference or lack of passion, as Novick himself appears to do. The pursuit of history, Haskell argues,

> requires of its practitioners that vital minimum of ascetic self-discipline that enables a person to do such things as abandon wishful thinking, assimilate bad news, discard pleasing interpretations that cannot pass elementary tests of evidence and logic, and, most important of all, suspend or bracket one's own perceptions long enough to enter sympathetically into the alien and possibly repugnant perspectives of rival thinkers.

All this needs 'detachment', the ability not to put oneself at the centre of a view of the world, as the most narcissistic of the postmodernists do, but to develop what Haskell calls 'a view of the world in which one's own self . . . appears merely as one object among many'. Otherwise, for example, how would we be able to understand phenomena like

Nazism and the Holocaust, or individuals like Stalin and Pol Pot? None of this means that historical judgment has to be neutral. But it does mean that the historian has to develop a detached mode of cognition, a faculty of self-criticism and an ability to understand another person's point of view. This applies as much to politically committed history as it does to a history that believes itself to be politically neutral. Politically committed history only damages itself if it distorts, manipulates or obscures historical fact in the interests of the cause it claims to represent.[43]

As Novick defines it, the idea of objectivity involves a belief in 'the reality of the past, and [to] the truth as correspondence to that reality'.[44] The truth about patterns and linkages of facts in history is in the end discovered not invented, found not made, though, as Haskell adds, 'not without a process of imaginative construction that goes so far beyond the intrinsic properties of the raw materials employed that one can speak of their being "made" as well'.[45] Making such patterns and linkages, causal and otherwise, is by no means the only function of history, which also has a duty to establish the facts and recreate the past in the present, but it is in the end what distinguishes it from chronicle. Trevelyan was right both to point to the importance of the historical imagination in this process, and to insist on the strict limits within which that imagination is bound.

It is right and proper that postmodernist theorists and critics should force historians to rethink the categories and assumptions with which they work, and to justify the manner in which they practise their discipline. But postmodernism is itself one group of theories among many, and as contestable as all the rest. For my own part, I remain optimistic that objective historical knowledge is both desirable and attainable. So when Patrick Joyce tells us that social history is dead, and Elizabeth Deeds Ermarth declares that time is a fictional construct, and Roland Barthes announces that all the world's a text, and Hans Kellner wants historians to stop behaving as if we were researching into things that actually happened, and Diane Purkiss says that we should just tell stories without bothering whether or not they are true, and Frank Ankersmit swears that we can never know anything at all about the past so we might as well confine ourselves to studying other historians, and Keith Jenkins proclaims that all history is just naked ideology designed to get historians power and money in big university institutions run by the bourgeoisie, I will look humbly at the past and say despite them all: it really happened, and we really can, if we are very scrupulous and careful and self-critical, find out how it happened and reach some tenable though always less than final conclusions about what it all meant.

AFTERWORD

I

When it was first published in September 1997, this book aroused far more comment than I had expected. Most of it was favourable, but at the same time a number of reviewers had some critical points to make, and a few of them were downright hostile. The most serious reviewers raised a range of fundamental questions about the book and its arguments; some of them also revealed a variety of misunderstandings about its purpose and thrust. The criticisms came from many different angles. Critics seemed to disagree fundamentally about many of its central theses. Such disagreements raise once more the question of how far readers put meaning into a text, and how far an author is able to limit the variety of meanings people put into it. Thus a response to the book's critics raises yet again some significant issues about meaning, interpretation and evidence in a general sense.[1]

In Defence of History tried to steer a middle course between the extremes of postmodernist hyper-relativism on the one hand, and traditional historicist empiricism on the other. But the weight of the argument was directed against the postmodernists. This was not because I thought, or think, that they are becoming dominant in the historical profession as a whole. On the contrary, their presence is felt amongst working historians in only a relatively few areas, such as European intellectual history, or some kinds of feminist history, for example. The reason why I felt history needed defending was principally because of the dominance of hyper-relativism and scepticism about history's validity as an intellectual enterprise amongst those who write about historiography and history as a discipline in a general, theoretical sense.

In the 1990s increasing numbers of history degree courses, both undergraduate and postgraduate, in Britain and the USA have included a substantial element of historiography in them. It seemed to me that it was at this level that the intellectual validity of history really needed defending in the light of the kind of literature that was, and is still being published on the subject. Beyond this, too, at least some historians, particularly on the left, have been voicing a growing degree of scepticism about the possibility of doing history at all. More broadly still, historians of all persuasions have been talking in increasingly alarmist tones in recent years about the state of crisis they see as overwhelming their profession as a whole. Here too, I wanted to persuade people that it was possible to defend history as an intellectual undertaking by genuinely confronting and arguing with the extreme sceptics rather than by simply ignoring them or covering them with abuse.

These aims, I thought, were clear enough from the book. But a number of critics mistook them and thought the book ought to have done something else. In particular, it was argued in a number of places that the book should have engaged directly with major postmodernist theorists such as Derrida or Baudrillard. The late Anthony Easthope, a well-known cultural critic and theorist, pilloried the book's failure to provide a full-length discussion of Foucault or devote a chapter to Hayden White. The Soviet history specialist Steve Smith demanded 'more philosophical spade-work' to clear up some of the issues at hand. The American historian Joyce Appleby also charged that 'what is lacking in *A Defence of History*' (it is symptomatic of her scholarly stan-dards that she even managed to misquote the book's title) 'is a serious discussion of the way that postmodernists have examined the tools and strategies involved in the production of knowledge.' In similar vein, the Victorian intellectual his-torian Stefan Collini was critical of the fact that the book tackled what he called 'a blend of vulgarised post-structuralist theories of language with self-consciously radical notions about contesting hierarchy, hegemony, and so forth' instead of grappling with the French epistemology which is behind all this 'at the appropriate level of abstraction'. The result, he charged, was a series of 'vulgarised rebuttals of vulgarised ideas'.

If by 'vulgarised' he means 'popularized', then I gladly plead guilty. The book is essentially not about Michel Foucault, Jacques Derrida, Ferdinand de Saussure, or Roland Barthes (though they do get a mention), but much more about Hayden White, Frank Ankersmit, Keith Jenkins, Patrick Joyce, Dominick LaCapra, Beverley Southgate and their likes; it's precisely not an attempt to tackle the com-plex epistemologies of modern French philosophy head-on. This would have resulted in a completely different book. Hayden White is a different matter; his arguments are dis-cussed on twenty-six pages of the book and are in no sense passed over, as Easthope alleged. But Hayden White is a literary theorist, not a philosopher.

Collini's dismissive argument that historians aren't qualified to write about French epistemology, coupled with his view that a vulgarized rebuttal of vulgarized versions of them isn't really worth writing, is to my mind excessively Mandarin. If the only kind of book that's worth writing about postmodernism is a philosophical dissection of the central theories of Foucault, Derrida and other French thinkers at a high ('appropriate') level of abstraction, then the field really will be left open to the Jenkinses and the Ankersmits and the Southgates. Somebody's got to take them on at their level; that's what the book tries to do, and from the point of view of the health of the discipline of history, I remain convinced that this was something worth doing.

Moreover, in my view, it is misguided of Collini to tell historians just to get on with writing history and leave the theorizing to the experts. We all have to make some fundamental decisions about what we're doing nowadays before we do it. History is becoming a more theoretically and epistemologically self-conscious discipline, and that's all to the good. To follow Collini's advice would not only be foolish, it would not really be possible either any more. One feels, somehow, that there's an element of the intellectual historian's 'get off my patch' in his review. To reiterate: *In Defence of History* is not supposed to be a work of philosophy. It's about the influence of post-structuralist and other postmodernist epistemologies on historical theory and practice, not about those epistemologies themselves. It's a book that emerged from, and is intended to be used in, history teaching. It's not a monographic study in the philosophy of history or the history of ideas.

If some reviewers thought that the book was pitched at the wrong level, others thought the book was, in a sense, unnecessary. Writing in the *Times Literary Supplement* for example, Joyce Appleby suggested that the book was only 'defending history from attacks that must surely have vaporized in their own light-headedness'. Its 'destruction of postmodernism may be a little wearying,' Samuel Brittan confessed, 'with chapter after chapter and example after example.' It could easily be done 'in a few lines', he says. Or, to take another tack, the fact that over 40,000 British 'A' level students took history examinations in 1997 and over 15,000 students were reading the subject at university in the same year means, according to the Oxford historian Niall Ferguson, that 'history does not need much defending' anyway.

Ferguson's review displayed considerable confusion on this point. For Ferguson went on to complain that if there was a threat against which history needs defending, it was not postmodernism but 'the expansion of the subject at the universities since the 1960s'. The result of this growth, he thought, had been a dilution of intellectual standards. 'Cosy enclaves such as "gender studies" or "gay history" exist to protect the talentless from serious intellectual challenge.' (It should not be necessary to rebut a statement of such crass prejudice in detail; nowadays, a huge amount of imaginative, pathbreaking and first-rate scholarship is being devoted to these areas.) So Ferguson wraps himself in contradictions. History does not need defending because the numbers of history students are buoyant – rather the large number of history students has resulted in a decline in the subject's intellectual standards; so it does need defending after all.

A more subtle argument was put forward by Daniel Johnson, with implicit support from Michael Burleigh,

Matthew Trinca and Steve Weinberg, and that was that 'it is not history that needs defending, but professional historians', and this is what the book set out to do. History books, both Burleigh and Johnson pointed out, are more popular than ever; but on the whole those that are widely read, they claimed, are written by non-academics, and the popular view of history is stamped not by the Oxbridge professoriate but by cinema and television, and by writers such as Antonia Fraser. Roy Porter, indeed, wished that I had 'looked beyond the walls of academe', just as Daniel Johnson criticized the book's author for giving 'no credit to those who practise his craft outside the university'. In Johnson's view, therefore, the book was written in defence of the academic historical profession, what Matthew Trinca called 'a capital H History that is professional, discretely packaged with neat subspecialisms, and manageable', not in defence of history *per se*. '*In Defence of History* remains the swansong of a golden age of academic supremacy.'

In Defence of History, however, focuses on the issue of how we define and achieve such things as truth and objectivity, whatever kind of history we are practising. These matters are, to my mind, the same whether you are Antonia Fraser, writing for a broad general public outside the academy, or whether you are Joyce Appleby, writing predominantly for a readership of students and other professional historians. It was gratifying, therefore, to see this view confirmed when Antonia Fraser named *In Defence of History* as her book of the year in the Christmas books issue of the *Observer* in 1997. Clearly some popular historians at least *do* think that the book applies to them as well as to their colleagues in academia.

There are two further points worth making in reply to Johnson's criticism. The first is that the book does endorse the writing of popular history by academic historians, and mentions a number of books which provide good examples of this. The more that the gap can be bridged, the better. The second, also mentioned (briefly) in the book, is that it is essentially not true that professional, university-based historians are facing a serious new challenge from popular representations of history in the media. Popular representations of history have always been widespread, whether in folksong and ballad, saga and legend, or broadside and chapbook, and they have always structured the historical perceptions of the majority. Two and a half thousand years ago, the Greek historian Thucydides complained in the preface to his history of the Peloponnesian War that poets and others were purveying false and imaginary accounts of what had happened, and announced his intention of setting the record straight. In the past, only a tiny minority of the literate and the educated were exposed to professional history and historians. Today, with a third to a half of the entire population passing through higher education when they reach the end of their teens in most advanced industrial societies, and a growing proportion of mature and part-time students entering an ever-expanding process of lifelong learning, the number of those who have access to and are influenced by university-based history and historians is probably greater in absolute terms than it has ever been before. So while Johnson is correct to say the book defends history as an academic discipline, principally against its critics within the academy, he is wrong to say it represents in so doing the swansong of a declining élite, and wrong to say that it has no application to non-academic versions of history.

As the above discussion reminds us, the review pages of the daily, weekly and weekend quality press in Britain are still dominated by a generation of young, conservative historians and journalists who came to such intellectual maturity as they have during the long period of Conservative government under Margaret Thatcher and John Major. With the sole exception of John Charmley, writing in the *Daily Telegraph*, they regretted the fact that, as one of them, Michael Burleigh, put it, 'unfortunately Evans keeps a foot in the "progressive" camp'. Like other conservative reviewers, Burleigh thinks the book is unfair to conservative historians.

'Andrew Roberts,' thunders Burleigh, 'is ticked off for his personal sources of income; John Vincent for writing in a tabloid newspaper; Arthur Marwick for being slow with his inaugural lecture. Gossip involving Hugh Trevor-Roper figures more prominently than his major contributions to European history.' Let's look up the passages in question and see what they really say. On page 210, after outlining John Vincent's argument that historians nowadays are all left-liberal because they work for the state, the book says the following of Andrew Roberts:

> If we really believed his somewhat reductionist view, we would only expect robust right-wing opinions from historians who lived off a private income, and while it is certainly true that there are some individuals, such as Andrew Roberts, author of the neo-Thatcherite text *Eminent Churchillians*, who fit into this pattern, there are many more who do not.

No hint of criticism here: Roberts is merely used as an example in an argument.

What about Vincent himself? There are many references to him in the book, a good number of them favourable, including, in the argument just quoted, a mention of the fact that his most original and unconventional historical work was written while he held a university appointment, as indeed he still does, and was not dependent on a private income, which to my knowledge he has never been. But the one to which Burleigh presumably objects is the following, in note 15 to Chapter 4, on page 268:

> Vincent . . . cites with approval A. J. P. Taylor's belief that no new secrets were to be found in unpublished archival sources. Vincent himself advocates paying greater attention than is customary to the newspapers, and declares that newsprint is 'the Venetian archive of tomorrow' . . . Vincent's partiality to newspapers as unbiased sources of information may possibly be coloured by the fact that he himself wrote a column in the *Sun* for a number of years, until student demonstrations at his own university forced him to abandon it – an event which, however deplorable in itself, would scarcely have taken place had the column been a model of impartiality.

This passage also enraged Daniel Johnson, who devoted a whole paragraph to denouncing it and accused the book of unfairness towards Vincent and 'justifying the silencing of a scholar by the mob'. But the passage in question was intended to suggest that newspapers have their biases, not just in columns written by moonlighting dons, but also in their reporting and their general editorial line, whether it be that of the *Sun*, the *Telegraph* or the *Guardian*. The use of the word 'deplorable' gives the lie to Johnson's suggestion that I actually approved of the demonstrations in question. As for Burleigh's objection, nowhere in the passage is there any hint of disapproval of Vincent's work for the *Sun* in itself.

Similarly, on page 299 the reference to Arthur Marwick having delivered his 'inaugural lecture after decades of

occupation of the Chair of History at the Open University'
contains not so much as a hint of criticism for the delay,
however critical the discussion of the lecture is in other
respects. As for Hugh Trevor-Roper (Lord Dacre), it is difficult to work out what Burleigh means by 'gossip', unless it
is perhaps a reference on page 19 to his 'authentication' of
the Hitler diaries, which is not gossip but fact, on the basis of
a cursory examination of the 'diaries' in a Swiss bank vault –
all of which is documented in Robert Harris's excellent book
Selling Hitler. Why *In Defence of History* would have been
improved by mentioning Trevor-Roper's other work on
European history is a mystery.

By contrast, Burleigh finds the book gives 'generous
treatment' to 'the American neo-Marxist David Abrahams'
(Burleigh is not the only reviewer to misspell Abraham's
name) in its account of the controversy over the gross errors
in his book which led to his losing his job as a historian. At
least Stefan Collini finds my book's handling of the Abraham
case 'exemplary'. Given the fact that the book's account
convicts Abraham of subconsciously manipulating evidence
to fit a thesis, inability to tell fact from fiction, failure to
follow basic historical procedures, poor research skills and
excessive haste in research, it is difficult to see how its treatment of him could be fairly be described as 'generous'. I
cannot imagine that Abraham and his friends (including
Peter Novick) are very pleased with the account. Burleigh is
imagining things here again.

Michael Burleigh is not the only young(ish) fogey to be
upset by the book's criticism of admired figures on the right.
Niall Ferguson also convicts the book of 'rudeness' towards
'historians of broadly conservative inclinations'. 'John
Kenyon, for example,' he says in his review of *In Defence of
History*, 'is [found] guilty of "mental insularity and

prejudice".' This remark, which Ferguson quotes correctly from page 179, is a comment on Kenyon's claim, advanced in 1993, that undergraduate courses on the history of West Africa and Indochina were 'hastily cobbled-up' by history departments acting on the dictates of fashion, but soon faded away because the difficulty of finding competent external examiners left students 'at the mercy of their tutor's whims and prejudices'. I have to say that (a) the book's description of this view as reflecting its author's mental insularity and prejudice is no ruder or more insulting than Kenyon's own remarks are to the many distinguished historians of Africa and Indochina teaching and researching in British universities, and (b) it seems to me to be entirely justified to call Kenyon's view insular and prejudiced.

Ferguson goes on to attack the book for describing Hugh Trevor-Roper as 'stubbornly parochial'. This phrase refers not just to Trevor-Roper but to 'a number of stubbornly parochial specialists in European history', among whom he is placed by his remark that Africa has no history, merely 'the unrewarding gyrations of barbarous tribes in picturesque but irrelevant corners of the globe'. Once more, the term used seems to me merely to be accurate rather than rude as a reference to this jibe by Trevor-Roper, who in the course of his long career has proved himself no amateur at invective himself.

Finally, Ferguson took exception to the book's remark that John Vincent's comment that 'History is deeply male . . . History is about the rich and famous, not the poor' shows its author's 'deep ignorance of other kinds of history than the history of British high politics in the nineteenth century which he himself writes'. By omitting the context of the remark and all the words in the quotation except the first two, Ferguson gives the impression that the book is claiming

Vincent suffers from 'deep ignorance' in every respect, which is not true at all, of course. Apart from this, the book's statement seems to me once more to be entirely justified, and no less insulting to Vincent than he is to those many fine historians who have devoted their lives to writing about the female, the poor and the unknown. In a similar way it would not seem unjustified to describe Ferguson's own remarks about gender history as deeply ignorant. It may be rude to say so, but it's also true.

All these points are in the end somewhat trivial ones. More serious by far is the one made, yet again, in the most intelligent of the critical reviews to appear immediately after the book's publication, namely Daniel Johnson's article in *Prospect* magazine. Johnson argues that the book is 'not so much a defence of history as of one school (left, populist, socially conscious) against another school, less fashionable but no less respectable (conservative, élitist, high political)'. But while it argues that history needs defending against the crippling and stultifying influence of narrow and élitist conceptions of what it is, or should be, about, the book does not argue for any one particular conception of history in itself as an alternative. Nor does it say that intellectual history, the history of élites or the history of high politics are in any way wrong in themselves. Its purpose here, as a number of other reviewers, from Ronald Hutton to Roy Porter, have recognized, is to argue for a broad, inclusive conception of history, to celebrate its diversity at the same time as trying in various ways to overcome its fragmentation, and nowhere does it in fact argue that left-wing versions of history are inherently superior as history to those practised on the right. Indeed it has been sharply attacked on the left, for example, by the convenor of the London Socialist Historians' Group, Keith Flett, who thinks that the book needed to be 'more hard-hitting still to repulse the postmodernist challenge', and the Trotskyite writer Chris Harman, who damned it as 'backsliding towards postmodernism'.

II

The blast of criticism that assailed the book from the right was surprising. More predictable, though also slower in being fired off, were the salvoes of disapproval that greeted it from the postmodernists and their sympathizers. The first major argument put forward from this quarter was the view that the book defended an outmoded, indeed indefensible concept of objectivity. Joyce Appleby, writing in the *Times Literary Supplement*, thought that the book was a general assault against postmodernism in all its manifestations, in the name of traditional British historical empiricism. In launching this assault, she charged, the book used the tactic of trying to discredit postmodernism as a whole by attacking its silliest and most extreme manifestations. But in doing so, she succumbed to precisely the kind of dichotomizing thinking of which her review argued postmodernism had taught scholars to be wary. As Appleby surely knows, and as the book makes perfectly clear, 'postmodernism' is a label covering a wide variety of positions, and just because the book rejects some of these, it doesn't follow that it rejects them all. Pursuing this Manichean misreading of the book, Appleby went on to convict it of an outdated belief in the historian's 'impartial and omniscient voice of a reconstructor of events and analyser of developments'. In fact the book uses up a good deal of space trying to demolish such simplistic denials of the historian's subjectivity, and to deny the possibility of historical omniscience.

'Historians,' she continued, 'prefer to think that they reconstruct the past, rather than acknowledge that in the process of doing so they also create texts and construct knowledge.' Contrary to what readers of her review might suppose, however, the book defends the latter position and deploys a range of arguments against those who, like Elton, take the former. On pages 125–6 of the book, far from ignoring Hayden White's ideas on this subject, as Appleby claims, White's most recent account of how historians go about their work of writing and research is endorsed as basically accurate. Thus Appleby's patronizing conclusion that British historians preserve simplistic ideas about truth and objectivity which have long been discarded in the more sophisticated intellectual atmosphere of the United States is based on a superficial misreading of the kind she claims the book is guilty of when it tackles the postmodernists itself.

Appleby's colleague Lynn Hunt thought that the outmoded quality of the book was illustrated by its frequent references to Elton and Carr. But the reason for these references is simply that, as many historians of a variety of different persuasions have conceded, their books still form the basis for much if not most teaching of historical epistemology today. They are still much the most readable and approachable accounts of the nature of historical knowledge written by practising historians. Lynn Hunt found this a 'disappointing . . . flight . . . into "daddyism", the search for fatherly figures that warrant the legitimacy of an approach. Evans,' she declared, 'refers almost obsessively to Carr and Elton as if to reassure himself that he will be their appointed successor; his criticisms of them sound like those of a deferential grandson.' In fact, *In Defence of History* is intended, not to replace their books, but to be read alongside them; hence the chapter headings, adapted from Carr, or the final paragraph, a parody of Carr's final paragraph. Thirty or more years ago there were hardly any books which introduced history students to the conceptual and methodological problems which they faced, so Carr and Elton virtually had the field to themselves. Now there are many such competing texts, and the very idea of any single book achieving the kind of status theirs did is ridiculous.

What all this boils down to is the charge that the book defends an outmoded concept of historical objectivity. Matthew Trinca, for example, ignored the carefully circumscribed definition of objectivity given in the book's final chapter, and, simply assuming that the word could only be used in the absolutist sense intended by traditionalists like Elton, placed the book's central argument squarely in the Eltonian camp. While Trinca obviously disapproved of this, David Gress, advocating a return to military history and the 'rote learning of facts' in school history lessons, saw it as a confirmation of his own conservative approach. Gress enlisted *In Defence of History* in support of his call for a rejection of the 'present-mindedness and political correctness' through which social history, women's history, and other relatively recent new developments in historical scholarship and teaching have created a 'barrier to learning'. Thus Gress found the book's criticisms of Elton to be an 'almost ritualistic' cloak for 'true respect and admiration' on the part of its author (myself). A similar position was taken in the review by the Australian historian Greg Munro, who thought the book did indeed 'embrace wholeheartedly' the 'hard-line concept of historical objectivity espoused by Elton', for all its protestations to the contrary.

In fact, the book rejects Elton's simplistic view that the historian could shake off all present-day beliefs and ideas when studying the documents. It rejects his narrow-minded empiricism and his parochial insistence on the political history of the nation-state as the only real history. It rejects his belief that interpretations spring unaided from the sources. It rejects his whole account of how historians go about the business of research. It explicitly welcomes developments which he found objectionable, such as women's history, social history and so on – all these are, after all, areas of history which have been the subject of much of my own work. On all these points, I side with Carr. On the other hand, the book rejects Carr's account of objectivity and causation, for example, since both of them are tied to his belief in the defining quality of a human future locate inevitably in a Soviet-style planned economy.

Given the fact that the book strongly rejects both Carr and Elton's central ideas about objectivity and many other things, it is difficult to see how it can be understood as using them as ways of legitimating my own approach. More profoundly, as the book makes abundantly clear, obscurantist conservatism of the sort to which Elton too often fell prey, and Stalinist Marxism of the sort which ultimately lay at the root of Carr's work, are both objectionable as well as inadequate bases for historical scholarship and thought.

For Lynn Hunt, the book seems to follow Carr rather than Elton. Thus she considers its account of causation to be merely a 'rehash' of Carr's own views. The conclusion she cites from the book, that 'Carr did not really think his argument through' comes at the end not, contrary to what Hunt maintains, of a mere repetition of his views, but of a lengthy and reasoned criticism of them. This criticism is based principally on my objection to Carr's view that historians should only be interested in understanding the cause of a past event if it could help us change the present and shape the future.

The implication of this latter position is that the

historian should suppress any mention of any causes of a past event, whether accidental or not, if it does not fulfil this purpose. Carr did not mention this (extremely disturbing) implication of his method, however, and that is why I felt justifying in suggesting that he did not really think his argument through. I don't think this is the mere bald assertion Hunt claims it is; no more than is the conclusion of the paragraph-long criticism in the book which is directed at Hunt's own attack on Carr's notion of causation in her (sometimes interesting and often persuasive) book, written with Joyce Appleby and Margaret Jacob (*Telling the Truth About History*) that Hunt's own argument on this point is 'factually incorrect as well as irrelevant'. Perhaps her irritation at this criticism of a part of her book has prompted her irritation with the whole of mine.

At times Hunt's misreading of the book becomes almost comical, as when she objects to the sentence on page 160, in the chapter on causation, where I remark that social and economic history have become the 'principal victims' of 'the new theories'. 'What does this have to do with causation?' she asks rhetorically. The answer is, not a lot, because it's the last sentence in the chapter and is intended to point the way to the next chapter, which is precisely about social and economic history.

Hunt's misrepresentations continue even when she is positive about the book, as in her view that it is at its best when it 'unravels controversies that have nothing to do with epistemological issues, such as the one about David Abraham's reading of sources in his analysis of business interests in Nazi Germany'. The whole point of recounting this controversy, however, as the book makes quite clear in the course of its analysis of the affair, is that it has a direct bearing on central issues of historical epistemology: namely the relationship between fact and interpretation, the possibility of falsifying interpretations by referring to evidence, and the argument of Hayden White that a Marxist historical interpretation such as Abraham's cannot be disproved because what Marxists view as relevant evidence is not so viewed by non-Marxist historians.

Appleby and Hunt were not the only critics to consider that the book was intellectually outmoded. The late Anthony Easthope, too, thought that *In Defence of History* endorsed a 'resoundingly empiricist' notion of objectivity. Let us examine the quotations from the book which he used to support this interpretation. First: 'the past does impose its reality through the sources in a basic way'. The key word here is 'basic', as the following sentence on page 115 of the book makes clear: 'At the most elementary level, one cannot simply read into documents words that are not there.' Second: 'the past does speak through the sources' (p. 126); well, yes, but the whole of the preceding discussion, which includes a lengthy account of the 'Abraham affair', makes it clear that this is not a blanket claim about how historians do their work (merely listening to what the sources say), it is a limited and partial claim; it does not end there; in fact it is only half the argument. What the book actually argues is that the past only speaks through the sources when the historian interrogates them. It's a two-way process, as the book makes clear time and again.

Easthope concluded this part of his argument by citing the book's 'resoundingly empiricist conclusion that, despite it all, "it really happened", we can "find out how" and know "what it all meant".' What this passage in the book actually said, following on a series of references to the theses of various postmodernist writers on history, was as follows: 'I will look humbly at the past and say despite them all: it really happened, and we really can, if we are very scrupulous and careful and self-critical, find out how it happened and reach some tenable though always less than final conclusions about what it all meant.' By removing all the qualifications from this statement, Easthope manipulated it to give it the appearance of a dogmatic confidence in the possibility of absolute knowledge that was a very long way from what was intended. Thus he only managed to support the charge he levels against the book, of mindless empiricism, by giving a deliberately false and distorted version of what it actually says.

Because there seems to be a quite widespread misunderstanding of what I meant by historical objectivity, with numerous reviewers assuming that because I actually dare to use the word it can only have one meaning, that is, a strong and absolute one, rather than, as I intended, a weak and qualified one, I added a sentence to the penultimate paragraph in the American edition: 'Objective history in the last analysis is history that is researched and written within the limits placed on the historical imagination by the facts of history and the sources which reveal them, and bound by the historian's desire to produce a true, fair, and adequate account of the subject under consideration.'

The need for such an addition was further illustrated by the misunderstandings present in the review by the Soviet history specialist Steve Smith, who supposed that *In Defence of History* argued that 'there is a singular truth to be told about the past' and that it can be 'discovered' from the evidence. Of course, the book in fact goes to some lengths to argue that what historians write is the result of a dialogue between their own purposes and ideas and what they find in the sources. Unwilling to recognize this, Smith proceeded to entangle himself in a web of contradictions, as he argued on the one hand that historians' interpretations of past events could not stand or fall by the extent to which they conformed to the historical evidence, and on the other accused the Harvard historian Richard Pipes of providing 'a deeply distorted representation' of the Russian Revolution of 1917.

How can Smith consider Pipes's account to be distorted if not by an appeal to the evidence? Not just the evidence which Pipes himself cited, that is, but more importantly, perhaps, the massive amount of evidence which Pipes omitted from his account. Saying that he, Smith, brings a different narrative perspective to bear on the Revolution doesn't amount to any criticism of Pipes at all, since in this way of thinking there is no criterion by which anyone can decide whether it is Smith's narrative or Pipes's which is distorted; the inescapable conclusion of Smith's *general* argument is that both are equally valid, just as the inescapable conclusion of Smith's *particular* remarks about Pipes is that this general argument is invalid.

Others too, however, seemed to think the book was defending a 'conservative' approach to historiography. Writing in the *London Review of Books*, for example, the Oxford intellectual historian Peter Ghosh claimed that the book was engaged in a 'polemic against history since 1960', that it defended an 'exaggerated empiricism' based on the 'fetishizing of documents' and that I believed that facts and documents 'speak for themselves'. It is hard to believe that Ghosh has read the book properly, or that he is familiar with my other work if he really thinks this. *In Defence of History* actually argues that history has undergone a welcome renaissance since the 1960s, and defends explicitly and at length in Chapter 6 the broadening of the discipline which has taken place in this period against conservative historians who would like to see it return to its old concentration on the politics of the nation-state. My own work on the social history of medicine and disease, the history of ritual, the history of feminism, the history of death, and other topics would not have been possible without all the changes that have taken place in historical studies over the last forty years. The same arguments apply to the criticism raised by Joyce Appleby, who claimed in her review that the book 'certainly will please those who think that pre-1970 history needed no defending'. Leaving aside the mysterious question of what happened in 1970 to make history worth defending in some people's eyes afterwards but not before, it also seems strange that a book explicitly devoted to defending history (both before and after 1970) should please those who think it needs no defending at all.

But such confusions are nothing in comparison to those perpetrated by Ghosh, who elsewhere in his review takes the historicist point of view that 'theory comes from within history', and excoriates the historian's use of theories taken from other disciplines. This is sheer obscurantism. Most advances in historical scholarship since the 1960s and long before have taken place through the use of theories and methods borrowed from elsewhere, whether philology, economics, sociology, anthropology or linguistics.

Ghosh also claims that if any aesthetic impulses go into the structuring of a work of history, that work of history must necessarily be conceptually vacuous. He refers to my book *Death in Hamburg* as an example (because I cite it in *In Defence of History* as an instance of how I used aesthetic criteria to organize historical material, much in the way described by Hayden White for historical work in general). If Ghosh had actually read *Death in Hamburg*, however, he would have discovered that it is structured by a set of Marxist concepts. The point is that conceptual and aesthetic aspects of writing a history book are not mutually exclusive; if they were, all history books would be completely unreadable.

The confusions and contradictions in Ghosh's review were compounded in his subsequent response to the points made above in a letter to the *London Review of Books*, where he went on to declare that a 'Rankean' approach to history as described in my book was an invention of the last thirty years, and asserted roundly that I was a Rankean. 'Rankean' in this sense seems to involve the kind of documentary fetishism that Ghosh accused me of in his review. But what could fetishize the documents more than Ghosh's own apparent belief that interpretations and theories in history can only be legitimate if they spring from history itself, or in other words, from the documents?

Moreover, since Ghosh also argued that it was illegitimate to describe anyone as postmodernist unless they described themselves as such (an example of a concept coming directly from the sources, perhaps), he would presumably have to accept my insistence that I am not a Rankean even though he called me one. Insofar as *In Defence of History* endorses 'Rankeanism', it is only in the very limited sense of insisting that the methods of source-criticism introduced, not in the last few decades, but in the mid-nineteenth century by Leopold von Ranke himself, are still valid for historians today, with modifications, when they are analysing documents in the archive.

Where Ghosh is coming from was indicated by the aggressive 'get off my patch' tone of his letter to the *London Review of Books*, in which he stated that only professional historians of ideas such as himself were qualified to write about historiography, and mere historians of politics, culture and society such as myself should steer well clear. He justified this by claiming that my portrait of the history of ideas as the continual reinterpretation of a limited number of classic texts 'bears no relation to the modern discipline of the history of ideas'. He goes on to note, however, that the 'old version' which I equate with the discipline as a whole 'actually resembles Post-Modernism in the style of Hayden White or Ankersmit'. This is precisely the point made in my book. White is surely, for good or ill, the most influential historian of historical ideas and practices writing today. All his numerous disciples and followers argue that all texts are capable of infinite reinterpretation. White's approach is not old-fashioned; quite the contrary, it is all too fashionable.

What Ghosh seems to be advocating is the method pioneered by Quentin Skinner, of fixing the meaning of a past text by comparing the language it uses with the language used in other, contemporaneous texts: thus we will be able to determine once and for all the meaning of Hobbes's *Leviathan*, for example, by fixing the meaning of the language and concepts it uses through locating them in their contemporary linguistic context. This is a very fruitful and influential approach, but it is not synonymous with the entire 'modern discipline of the history of ideas', and indeed postmodernist writers on historiography regard it as an outdated form of historicism.

It seems to be this approach which leads Ghosh to argue that modern concepts should not be imported into the analysis of past texts. This may be an admirable precept when analysing the meaning of the writings, say, of John Locke, but it will not do when studying, for example, the social structure of a medieval village, or the origins of the First World War. Moreover, if Ghosh believes, as he says in his review, that the 'Great Texts' notion of the history of ideas is now 'defunct', then why is he 'working on a new translation of Max Weber's *Protestant Ethic*', as his biographical notes in the *LRB* reveal? Finally, Ghosh alleged that 'Evans supposes that the modern history of ideas, as practised by Quentin Skinner and Gareth Stedman Jones, for example, and "Post-Modernism" of the White and Ankersmit variety are essentially one and the same.' Nowhere in anything I have written is there the slightest warrant for such an absurd accusation, a further contradiction in what was undoubtedly the most intellectually confused as well as the most aggressive of all the reviews of the book.

Even more beside the point is the lengthy attack on my supposed defence of 'Rankean principles' by Keith Jenkins in his book *Why History?* (London, 1999, pp. 106–12). The arguments Jenkins puts forward are based on an almost comical misunderstanding of what I wrote. On page 19 of *In Defence of History* I argued that Ranke's principles of source-criticism were still useful in historical research today, though obviously they have been much added to in the meantime. Otherwise, as the lengthy critique of other aspects of Ranke's thought in Chapter 1 of the book made clear, I don't think Ranke has much to offer the modern historian. The book rejected for example the historicist notion that the past could be constructed in its own terms. And it made a point of arguing against the empiricist idea that one could build up evidence independently of any guiding hypothesis, until an argument emerged. Jenkins's attacks on it for supposedly defending these allegedly 'Rankean' arguments are therefore misplaced.

Jenkins makes a startling retreat, however, when it comes to dealing with the 'Rankean' point that the authenticity, the provenance and to a considerable extent the meaning of a document can be established by rigorous source-criticism. He sidesteps this point by claiming on page 108 that postmodernists have never argued that there was no 'cognitive element in history' at the level of the individual statement, only that certainty and objectivity were impossible at the level of interpretation (or, as he puts it, 'historical "truth" is not much in dispute at the lower level of the syntactical' (p. 109)). Yet the characteristic postmodernist distancing device of the inverted commas around the word 'truth' suggests that he thinks otherwise, else why would he have put them there?

Moreover, what Jenkins says here goes completely against what he and others have written about the impossibility of inferring past events, situations, beliefs and so on from documentary evidence. Enormous amounts of postmodernist ink have been spilled on trying to prove that documents are so unreliable you can never tell anything from them, that you can never recover the intentions of their authors, and so on. It is a fundamental premise of postmodernist critiques of history that a document is re-invented and re-interpreted every time someone looks at it, so that it can never have any fixed meaning. If this claim doesn't mean that we can never use documents to find out basic historical facts, then it doesn't mean anything at all. Jenkins tries to recover a little of the ground he has conceded here by insisting on the *difficulty* of recovering the past through historical documents; but simply because that recovery may be partial or provisional, may involve argument and interpretation, may be open to criticism from others, or may never be definitive, doesn't mean that it's impossible, as Jenkins previously claimed. Jenkins seems to be undermining his whole larger argument here, and goes much further in the direction of an empiricist defence of 'facts' than I would.

Despite this startling abandonment of his basic theoretical position in favour of a very traditional form of empiricism, Jenkins still tries to portray In Defence of History as part of a conservative, blinkered, hidebound, 'bourgeois' attack on radical, progressive, emancipatory postmodernism. In the course of this, he attributes to me a number of views I do not hold. Often his points are simply speculative. Thus, for example, he writes:

> If one were to ask Richard Evans (as I shall be asking) what 'proper' history is, then he would and does unreflexively reply that, in effect, it's just what he does. It is the craft that he practises. To ask Evans what 'proper' history is to invite him to produce his job description. In this way Evans *et al.* re-enact to the letter that universalizing trait of all ideology, in that a sectional defence is presented as being in the interests of everybody, and that it is not *their* history that is in danger at all but history *per se*.

Jenkins immediately contradicts himself, however, by going on in his very next sentence to assert 'that it really is history *per se* that radical postmodernism threatens with extinction' (p. 9). So he accepts that the book is a broadly-based defence of all approaches to the study of the past, not just a defence of one particular approach. What other kind of history is there anyway, apart from a history that starts from the premise that we can know about the past?

Jenkins indulges in his usual self-dramatization as a radical opponent of bourgeois orthodoxy by presenting the reader with a version of *In Defence of History* that gives the book some kind of would-be official status, laying down the law to everybody as to how history should be studied. He repeatedly alleges that *In Defence of History* was written in defence of 'proper' history and 'proper' historians. Nowhere in fact do I use this term, nowhere do I attempt to define what might be an 'improper' history; on the contrary, I argue repeatedly and at length that there is a huge variety of ways of approaching the past, and that this plurality and diversity are to be welcomed and defended. I would not for one minute wish to say that the kind of history I engage in myself is the only 'proper' kind, and I have never done so. On the contrary, it is Jenkins who is being prescriptive and dogmatic, declaring repeatedly that postmodernity is the *only* proper epistemological, moral and political position to adopt, that history is outmoded, irrelevant, pointless and impossible, and that the *only* option for historians is to join the postmodernists, though of course only if the postmodernists judge them fit to do so. Not much room for plurality and diversity here, then.

Jenkins alleges that I claim to speak for all historians (p. 96). Nowhere does the book make such a claim; it would be wrong as well as presumptuous for me to do so, since I was perfectly well aware that many historians would disagree with many of the views expressed in my book – for example, its criticism of the idea, held by many historians, that the political history of the nation-state should be at the core of the discipline, or its rejection of the assumption that the history of the great mass of people throughout recorded time is of no interest or significance, or its attack on the view that the history of women, or gender, or sexuality, is trivial and not worth pursuing.

Jenkins suggests that what I am defending is simply my own individual practice as a historian ('Evans's history is just him: it's just his', p. 101), and that I present my own work as an ideal example of how history should be done. How can I be a spokesman for historians in general, how can my view be lumped together with those of 'Geoffrey Elton, Gertrude Himmelfarb, John Tosh, J. H. Hexter, C. B. McCullagh, Lawrence Stone' and others (p. 9), how can my arguments indeed be described as 'Evansist/bourgeois' (p. 101), if they are only justifying what I practise as an individual historian?

There are many other instances of Jenkins distorting what I wrote for polemical effect. The book asserts for example that the epistemological issues it discusses are relevant to the problem of how society can obtain the kind of objective certainty about the great issues of our time that can serve as a reliable basis for taking vital decisions for the future. This, says Jenkins, means that I think the fate of history is integral to the fate of civilization itself. But the book does not say that it is integral, only that it is relevant, a far more modest claim.

Jenkins simply cannot accept that anyone can look at a thinker or a body of thought in a critical manner and accept some ideas and reject others; critical and discriminating thought of this kind is condemned on page after page of *Why History?* as 'rigid' and authoritarian 'assimilationism'. In fact, of course, *In Defence of History* goes to some length to point out that postmodernist ideas and trends have not simply been 'assimilated' into the practice of historical writing and research insofar as they have been useful to it, they have actually materially *altered* the way many historians see the past, often for the better.

Jenkins suggests that 'getting one's hands dirty in the archive' is a 'rather precious "artisan" side' to professional history and that my book judges everything by this criterion, declaring history to be a craft that historians have to learn on the job (p. 99). What on earth is so 'precious' about this fundamental aspect of the creation of historical knowledge? As for the training of historians, I don't presume to prescribe how it should be done at all; it depends very much on what kind of history one is pursuing. Some of the more technical kinds of historical research, for example, such as family reconstitution or medieval legal history, cannot be learned on the job, they require extensive previous training. *In Defence of History* also goes out of its way to defend broader-based surveys and interpretations which are not directly based on archival study. Once more, Jenkins is reading into the book things that simply aren't there, and ignoring things that are.

Jenkins describes the book as 'mean-spirited, often rather arrogant and dismissive' (p. 95). But what could be more deserving of epithets such as these than Jenkins's own book? Here, Jenkins repeats several times his by now very familiar assertion that the study of history is about to come to an end if it has not already done so. We can, Jenkins says, now forget history (p. 9). Any defence of it is beside the point because 'the invaders have been and gone', the citadel of 'proper' history, as he calls it, has been destroyed, and the only choice left to 'proper' historians is to join the post-modernists (a term with which, incidentally, Jenkins appears to have no problems, repeatedly identifying himself as a post-modernist), or remain located in an outmoded and increasingly distant past, like, one supposes, the practition-ers of a truly dead discipline like medieval scholasticism. For Jenkins, historians like myself inhabit a mental 'world of the flat-earth variety' (pp. 95–9), and this means that stu-dents in the end should treat 'Richard Evans as "someone to forget"' (p. 201).

Yet what evidence is there to support the view that his-tory is a thing of the past? Jenkins does not cite any, nor, I suppose, given his epistemological premises, would he find it necessary to do so. In fact, of course, there is an over-whelming mass of evidence to the contrary. More history is being written and read than ever before. In what sense, then is all this activity by historians of all kinds, whether conservative or progressive, left-wing or right-wing, élitist or populist, politically neutral or politically engaged, 'bourgeois'? Jenkins repeats his vulgar-Marxist belief that 'Ideological positions . . . are obviously expressive of specific interests' (p. 99), but silently retreats from the crudity with which he put this view in his earlier work. Now, a 'bourgeois' historian (or in other words, a historian of any description in his view) is no longer someone concerned to justify the *status quo* in society, and to propagate a doctrine that prevents social and cultural change. In *Why History?* a bourgeois historian is someone who projects an idealized self-image onto the past – rational, objective, scrupulous and so on (p. 100):

> What Evans is doing here . . . is giving the past the *same* characteristics as he gives himself/the bourgeoisie, on the (unwitting) assumption that if he treats the past in the same way as he (and the bourgeoisie) like to be treated (humbly, scrupulously, with care . . . rationally, objectively, etc.), then the past, he and the bourgeoisie will be cooperative.

To advance such an argument in respect of anyone who works on Nazi Germany, as Jenkins must know I do, is offensive as well as absurd.

Jenkins asks, more interestingly perhaps, at what level we can situate the probable rather than absolute truth that I say is all historians can hope to establish – 'the single statement, medium range inferences, synoptic accounts, etc.'? The answer is, at every level; but in any case, as the philosopher Susan Haack has pointed out, this does no damage at all to the concept of truth as such. Similarly, declaring that my concept of objectivity doesn't meet the objections of Ankersmit is meaningless unless the arguments on both sides are fairly stated and my objections to Ankersmit dealt with, which they aren't in Jenkins's book. Again, Jenkins simply dismisses as 'documentary fetishism' my (I should have thought, fairly obvious) statement that historical knowledge can be generated by the discovery of new documents (such as, for example, the Dead Sea Scrolls). But giving such a statement a disparaging label ('documentarism' is another one, p. 104) doesn't show anything, apart from the fact that Jenkins doesn't like this particular argument. In order to demonstrate his point, he would have to show that the discovery of new documents does *not* generate new historical knowledge, which he doesn't.

In dealing with causation, Jenkins reasonably enough outlines the extreme difficulty of establishing causal hierarchies and relationships for the Industrial Revolution (as he still calls it), but in no sense does he show that such an undertaking is either logically or historically impossible (p. 105). Finally, Jenkins accuses me of 'misreadings' of White and Ankersmit without actually saying what these are (p. 105). Criticism of this kind which refuses to give details, and takes refuge instead in rhetorical overkill, cannot be taken seriously. Where Jenkins does, unusually, supply detail, it is often beside the point. Thus on page 216, note 1, he complains that I have quoted from Tony Bennett's *Outside Literature* a quote which 'is, in fact, taken from my *On What is History?*' But the words quoted were written by Bennett, not by Jenkins, so the criticism is misplaced. True, Jenkins quotes them too. But is he saying he has a monopoly on quoting them? Or that he quoted them wrongly and I have repeated the mistake? Neither seems to be the case. So what is all the fuss about?

Leaving such trivial points aside: the fundamental fact that postmodernist hyper-relativism isn't necessarily radical or emancipatory at all is not addressed in any way by Jenkins, who continues, like other postmodernists, to assume without any justification that it necessarily is. This assumption in turn leads to the belief that everyone who dares to criticize any part of postmodernist theory must be conservative. In fact, as the book points out, extreme relativism opens the door to fascists and racists as well as radicals and progressives by allowing anybody to claim that their view of history, their reading of a document, is as valid as anybody else's, and by making it impossible to refute their arguments on anything but political grounds. Perhaps it is because it challenges this self-designated left-wing radicalism of postmodernists that *In Defence of History* has made so many of them so angry.

III

A more significant criticism of the book advanced by a number of postmodernists related not to its use of the concept of objectivity, but to its version of the concept of a fact. Anthony Easthope, for example, objected to my notion of 'fact' as something that happened or existed in the past irrespective of whether we know about it or not, and dismissed the argument that we *discover* facts as a kind of mindless empiricism. But I use the term 'facts' in this way because I do not want to fall into the trap of supposing, as Hayden White does in a passage quoted in Easthope's review, that what the historian studies are 'events'. Reality of whatever kind does not consist exclusively of events, though Easthope apparently thought it did. A historical fact may be the nature of a field-system under feudalism, the equipment of an army, the structure of a Roman villa, the death-rate from tuberculosis, or any one of a huge range of things which could not be described as events. Thus when White and Easthope use the term 'facts' they are not using it in the way I use it.

Discovering facts in this sense is an important part of the historian's business, but the book argues that the crucial step is when they are used in the service of an argument, and thereby become evidence. Changing White's terminology to mine, that is, his 'events' become my 'facts' and his 'facts' become my 'evidence', I would have nothing to quarrel with in White's statement, endorsed by Easthope, that 'The events have to be taken as given; they are certainly not constructed by the historian.' I suspect that when White goes on, in the passage in question, to say that historians are interested in giving a true account of what really happened in the past, he is really saying that historians are interested in giving a convincing interpretation of what happened in the past. Sticking to political history for the moment, for example, White (and Easthope) might regard an account of the origins of the First World War as a historian's attempt to represent what really happened, whereas my view would be that any account of such a complex and tangled web of facts must of necessity embody an interpretation (distributing responsibility, linking cause and effect, and so on).

We already have, therefore, a real gap between Easthope's view of what I am saying, and my own, and more profoundly, a serious gulf between what he thought history was (the representation of past events) and what I think it is (a subject vastly and rightly far more diverse than this). More seriously, however, Easthope's continual attacks on my qualifiers and modifiers seem to demand a hard-edged piece of logic where statements are made of a bald, extreme and universal kind. If I say, for instance, that historians in general do not work within rigid and constricting paradigms, what I mean by that is that of course a few of the most rigidly dogmatic have done so, and many have worked within a loose and flexible set of theories and assumptions such as Marxism in all its varieties, but that the Kuhnian notion of a strict paradigm which shapes all research in a particular field (e.g. optics) isn't really applicable to what historians do. Easthope slipped the term 'paradigm' in to describe empiricist epistemology, but this isn't what Kuhn meant by a paradigm, as he ought to have known: Kuhn didn't deny the reality of, say, a chemical reaction any more than White now denies the 'given' nature of 'events'.

But Easthope, apparently, did. Of course I am aware of the fact that there is a huge mass of philosophy arguing about whether or not we can prove that we experience reality through our senses, whether we can prove the world exists, what causation is, and so on. In the end, perhaps, no one has proved conclusively and logically that we do exist; but no one has proved that we don't, either. Here again, Easthope got caught in the classic self-contradictions of postmodernism. If he maintained, as he seemed to, that there was a 'radical and irremediable' gap 'between reality and representation', then how could he dare to represent the reality of my text and assume he was being fair or accurate in doing so? Easthope complained that I was lampooning postmodernism. He demanded that the critic must give a 'fair, accurate and detailed account of the arguments he or she intends to attack'. What is the difference between this and demanding that historians must give a fair, accurate and detailed account of the past?

Easthope found fault with my statement that the limits which the language of a text imposes on the possibilities of interpretation were set to a large extent by the original author. There are several points to make here. First, by bringing this sentence on page 106 into immediate proximity to a phrase two pages earlier in the book, Easthope made it look as if I was arguing that the limits referred to were set solely by the *intentions* of the text's author. This is not so: the book went on to argue that the author might include unintentional things in his or her text. And I added what he called the 'dodgy qualifier' ('to a large extent') because it seemed obvious to me that in the case of diplomatic documents (which were the subject under discussion on the pages in question) misinterpretation and ambiguity, whether intended or not, whether the result of an author's intention or the result of a diplomatic compromise, could open the way to further possibilities of interpretation (though these too are limited by the language of the text). Least of all did I mean to argue, as Easthope surely implied, that the intentions of the author alone limit the possibilities of interpretation. There are many other factors involved as well, and the intentions of the author only constitute one of them, though they are far from being as irrelevant as many postmodernists would have us believe. Moreover, if Easthope demanded that an interpretations of a text should be fair, accurate and detailed, then how could he say that such accounts have nothing to do with the language in which the author has written the text?

Finally, when I first read his conclusion ('Though his name is on the cover, Richard J. Evans did not really write *In Defence of History* – rather, the dominant paradigm of the English empiricist tradition wrote it for him, because he made no critical attempt to interfere with its passage through him on to the page'), I thought for a moment that Easthope was indulging in a rare postmodernist moment of self-parody. But no, he really meant it. Easthope tried to defend the polemical tone of this and other remarks by claiming that while he was critical, at least he was not arguing *ad hominem*, and I suppose, strictly speaking, this is true, since how could he be *ad hominem* if he didn't think I wrote the review at all? However, this is more than made up for by his distortion and misrepresentation of the book's contents, his concentration on minor slips and secondary issues in order to avoid confronting the central arguments, and his complete lack of any realization of the self-contradictory nature of his own position, since presumably he would have objected if I had said he did not really write his review, it was written for him by the dogmas of postmodernism which passed unreflected through his blank mind on to the page.

But what is postmodernism? Many reviewers took issue with the book on this account. Thus Lynn Hunt complained that in the book, 'postmodernism . . . is neither clearly defined nor seriously engaged'. She justified this criticism by listing a variety of different positions described as postmodernist in the book and countering them with a single definition of her own: 'For historians,' she wrote, 'postmodernism generally means the view that the historian cannot penetrate the veil of language to historical reality, that is, the historian can only write rhetoric, not truth.' More widely, it involved an attack on modernism and modernity in a general sense.

Hunt complained that the arguments of postmodernism were not seriously engaged in the book. But the problem with Hunt's review is that all she offered in support of this accusation was mere assertion; nowhere did she herself seriously engage with the arguments of the book. Thus she convicted it of 'logical inconsistencies, weakness of philosophical analysis, and failure to grapple with the main tenets of postmodernism', while at the same time failing to identify a single instance of a logical inconsistency or philosophical weakness in the entire book. The single example she provided, namely the book's account of Carr's theory of causation, was based, as we have seen, on misrepresentation and was again a tissue of assertions rather than arguments. Thus she described for example its consideration of post-modernist positions on time as inconclusive, without saying precisely in what way they were inconclusive. She did not mention the fact that the analysis of these positions ended by arguing that time does, contrary to some postmodernist positions, have a forward direction, although historical time moves at different levels and at different speeds in different modes or fields of historical change.

In the end, therefore, Hunt's review was itself 'a mish-mash in which bald assertion substitutes for analysis', to quote her own dismissive verdict on the book. At least it manages to avoid open self-contradiction, however. That distinction belongs to the critique by Peter Ghosh in the *London Review of Books*. Ghosh's comprehensive misreading of *In Defence of History* culminated in the claim that it con-strued 'postmodernism' exclusively as the denial of the possibility of truth and objectivity. If he had read the book with any care, he would have discovered that – to repeat – it treats postmodernism as a convenient label for a variety of positions, and distinguishes at the very least between extreme postmodernist hyper-relativism, which it argues against, and moderate versions of postmodernism, which it (on the whole) defends.

Ghosh declared that it was illegitimate to call anyone a postmodernist unless they described themselves as such or worked on behalf of 'an intellectual cause known as Post-Modernism'. He asserted that there was 'no conscious tradition of Modernism' in history against which people could react, so there could by implication be no such thing as 'Post-Modernism'. If we stuck to such a view, we would never be able to use concepts about people in the past which they did not use themselves. This would make the historian's job completely impossible.

While attempting to argue on the one hand that there was no such thing as postmodernism, Ghosh himself referred in one paragraph of his review to 'the various strains of historical thought grouped under the Post-Modernist label'. In another paragraph he declared: 'Post-Modernism in the historical sphere is a sphinx without a riddle', whatever that meant. While he criticized me for using the label without defining it, he thus did exactly the same thing himself. It is extremely difficult to see any kind of consistency or direction in Ghosh's criticisms in the light of these kinds of contradiction.

Clearly, some of the historical works the book describes as postmodern would probably not be accepted as such by their authors. And yet, something important has happened to history in the last twenty years or so. The great overarching narratives such as Marxism and modernization theory have collapsed. The idea of history as progress has been abandoned. Innovation has come above all from historians writing about the marginal, the bizarre, the individual, the small-scale. It seems reasonable to call these now-defunct metanarratives 'Modernist', as indeed many postmodernist writers on history do; and equally reasonable to call the new development 'postmodern', even if those who have pioneered it and participated in it would not regard themselves as postmodernists in any sense at all.

To put it another way, I know that Orlando Figes would never describe himself as a postmodernist because he has told me so himself. But I also know that his book *A People's Tragedy*, an almost self-consciously literary narrative of the Russian Revolution and Civil War, weaving in the stories of individuals, some of them very obscure, to the larger

picture, and eschewing the kind of socio-economic and statistical analysis commonplace in histories of the Russian
Revolution twenty or thirty years ago, could not have been
written without the theoretical and methodological impact
of postmodernism and the decline and fall of the grand metanarratives, even if this has only had an indirect effect on the
author rather than a direct or personal impact.

The question of the definition of postmodernism certainly isn't one which my book has solved, or indeed set out
to try to solve. Perhaps in the end the charge that my book
fails to deliver such a definition is of rather secondary importance. A far more serious criticism is provided, by contrast,
in Anthony Easthope's review of the book in *Textual Practice*
which charged that the book misrepresents major thinkers
such as Saussure. Unlike, say, Hunt, Easthope actually provided examples of this alleged misrepresentation. Thus for
instance on page 95, where the book says that Saussure's
term 'the signified' meant the thing denoted by a word,
what he actually meant by 'the signified' was the concept or
meaning of a thing. Easthope said roundly: 'This is a howler',
and I'm afraid he was right. Easthope scored another hit
when he complained that no reference was given for the
book's claim on pages 159–60 that Derrida 'rejected the
search for origins and causes as futile'. He was right here
too; I should at least have given a reference, or supported
this assertion with a brief analysis.

Easthope was virtually the only critic to identify real
mistakes in the book in this way. Other points made by
Easthope, however, begin to slip from the identification of
genuine errors or omissions to the partial or in the end complete misrepresentation of what the book actually says. This
started with his complaint that Lyotard is 'dismissed in a
single sentence, and a bizarre one at that, to the effect that

"master-narratives are the hegemonic stories told by those in power".' There are in fact *nine* sentences about Lyotard on the page in question (p. 150), not *one*, and they refer to Lyotard's view that Soviet historiography was a master-narrative which had to be countered by local narratives (or in other words can't be countered by rival metanarratives). This is the context within which the sentence which Easthope thought so bizarre has to be seen. His misrepresentation is compounded by his omission of the qualifying statement that Lyotard '*tended* to' say that 'master-narratives are the hegemonic stories told by those in power' (my italics here). Now perhaps the discussion at this point should have made it clear that Lyotard's definition of metanarrative went way beyond this, including 'the emancipation of the rational or working subject, or the creation of wealth', and so on. Nevertheless, it did not say, as Easthope claimed it did, that *all* Lyotard said was that master-narratives were hegemonic.

This is perhaps a minor distortion. But Easthope was on shakier ground when he went on to assert that the book claimed that Derrida wrote that nothing existed outside language, whereas what he in fact said was that there was nothing extra-textual. However, the previous sentence, not quoted by Easthope, made it clear that Derrida argued that 'everything was "discourse" or "text"'. So the book does after all say that Derrida argued there was nothing extra-textual. It seems a reasonable conclusion to draw from this that Derrida argues that nothing existed outside language. Similarly, Easthope alleged that the book misunderstood what Derrida meant by 'logocentrism'. But in fact it did not attempt a complete account of Derrida's concept, only of one implication or aspect of it, namely his criticism of historians as 'logocentric, that is, they imagined they were rational beings engaged in a process of discovery'. Easthope did not say whether this was part of what Derrida meant by logocentrism or not.

In all these critical points, the book perhaps pays the price of merely mentioning these thinkers tangentially without actually engaging in a full-scale confrontation with their work, something that other critics have done far more effectively and knowledgeably than I could ever hope to do. Tackling them at length would have meant a different book. But I concede that Easthope is at least partially justified in advancing these criticisms, for what they are worth.

Yet we have to go on to ask precisely how all this actually affects the central arguments of my book. Here the answer is clear: it doesn't affect them at all. What Easthope did in his review was to employ a familiar tactic of hostile reviewers: he sought to discredit the book by distracting the reader's attention from its central arguments by pointing to inaccuracies of detail on peripheral points (its brief and marginal allusions to Saussure, Derrida and Lyotard). Rather than engage directly with the book's arguments, he consistently evaded and misrepresented what it had to say. This quickly landed him in a predictably hopeless quagmire of self-contradiction.

Easthope described *In Defence of History* as a 'lampoon' of postmodernist positions, and condemned it for ignoring the basic precept that 'The first obligation of a critic is to give a fair, accurate and detailed account of the arguments he or she intends to attack.' If we read Easthope's review in the light of his own precept, however, what do we find? Take his very first couple of sentences:

> *In Defence of History* aims to defend a mainstream notion of history writing against 'intellectual barbarians' (p. 8), namely 'the invading hordes of semioticians, post-

structuralists, New Historicists, Foucauldians, Lacanians
and the rest' (p. 9). That statement is typical of the tone of
the book . . .

Easthope achieved this impression of blinkered and aggressive prejudice by the simple means of removing the first
three and the last three words of the sentence which he was
quoting. The full version reads as follows, with the following
sentence added:

> Historians should approach the invading hordes of semioti-
> cians, post-structuralists, New Historicists, Foucauldians,
> Lacanians and the rest with more discrimination. Some of
> them might prove more friendly, or more useful, than they
> seem at first sight.

A postmodernist might find nothing wrong in doctoring a
sentence in a text to make it support the argument; I do. It
also stands in crass contradiction to everything Easthope
wrote in his review about the way one should treat texts.

Moreover, the term 'intellectual barbarians' is clearly
meant ironically and was certainly intended to be taken in
this way. It is part of an extended military metaphor actually
started by Patrick Joyce in a reference to the 'commanding
heights' of the academy's walls having 'fallen' to 'skirmishing
bands' of postmodernists in the United States. This has not
prevented Keith Jenkins, however, from going even further
in distorting my use of the term in his book *Why History?*
(London, 1999), where he refers on page 8 to 'various types
of historians and theorists, including postmodern ones ("barbarians" of varying degrees of ferocity, according to Richard
Evans)'. Is Derrida really a barbarian? asks Jenkins rhetorically, in the course of a polemic against my use of the term

that extends over several pages. Of course not! After all, he reads 'several languages' (p. 97)! Jenkins keeps coming back to his point, as if he were proud to have discovered it. After all, he reasons, the fact that I use the term 'barbarians' must show how blinkered and prejudiced I really am.

I must confess that when the book was going through the copy-editing stage, my editor at Granta wanted me to remove this metaphor, since he said some people might take offence at the reference to postmodernists as intellectual barbarians. I told him I didn't believe anyone would be stupid enough to think I genuinely believed that postmodernists really were intellectual barbarians, least of all postmodernists themselves, who were used to reading texts in an ironic mode. He accepted my point and we left it in. How wrong I was.

A somewhat milder foretaste of this kind of response was provided by some of the letters which appeared on 19 and 26 September 1997 criticizing the preview of the book printed in the *Times Higher Education Supplement*. John Arnold, for example, claimed that it was wrong of the book to argue that postmodernism holds that 'there is a multiplicity of equally valid truths'. Rather, he went on, 'it is that truth (as a claim to one dominant and essential position) is untenable . . . all truth (with a small "t") is situational, political and engaged. To claim that something is true is to attempt to place it beyond discussion.' This argument seems to me to be a tissue of contradictions. Is Arnold saying there is no such thing as truth at all? Or is he saying that there is truth with a big 'T' and truth with a small 't'? If the latter, then he is surely saying that there is indeed a multiplicity of equally valid truths. If the former, then how can he believe that what he is saying himself is true?

Secondly, Arnold charges that 'Evans misunderstands

the notions of "text" and "discourse".' He seems to think that I argue that discourse is a false image of reality, whereas in fact in his view it *is* reality 'or at the very least, as close to reality as we are ever going to get'. Already he has introduced a confusion in his argument. I suspect that what he is trying to say is that we can never know reality at all; everything is discourse because everything is mediated through language. I thought that this was the argument I was summarizing in my brief discussion of the postmodernist view that texts are not a window through which we can perceive the reality of the past, but that they in some sense *are* the reality of the past, because the past as such no longer exists. I do not think I gave the impression that discourse is merely a false image of reality; if Arnold took this impression away from what I wrote, then he was under a misapprehension of what I meant to say.

Among a variety of arguments the book deploys against this view is the admittedly rather bald statement that Auschwitz is not a discourse, and it trivializes mass murder to see it as a text. To counter this, Arnold points out that 'the gas chambers were a physical expression and outcome of a particular discourse that presented a "reality" wherein Jews, homosexuals, communists and others were subhuman'. This brings yet more confusions into Arnold's argument. For here he is reintroducing a distinction between Auschwitz and discourse in which the former is the product of the latter; an entirely unexceptionable point made by almost every historian who has ever written about Nazi antisemitism in theory and practice, even if they have used words like 'ideology' rather than 'discourse'. But it is a point that totally undermines Arnold's earlier argument that discourse *is* reality in the sense that Auschwitz itself *is* discourse because we only know about it through language; a position that is far less easy to defend, in my view. We may agree that Jews were beaten, starved and sent to the gas chambers because of the Nazi discourse of antisemitism, but it is quite a different matter when someone tries to tell us that being beaten, starved to death or gassed is also a 'discourse'.

A related argument to that put so confusingly by Arnold was made by David Andress, who suggested that I failed to understand a significant point about the relationship between truth and power. Andress asserted that truth was a moral category rather than something defined by its relation to reality. Thus, E. P Thompson's influence over later historians was greater than that of G. R. Elton, not because Thompson had a better control of fact but because he had a more morally appealing vision of the British past than Elton did. He triumphed, as it were, because his truth was morally superior to Elton's. Andress made this point in response to the argument that the influence of a particular historical work or view of history was not a function of the institutional power of its author, contrary to claims made by writers such as Keith Jenkins. Thus Thompson's *The Making of the English Working Class* had a huge influence despite the fact that its author was never a member of a university history department, while Elton's *Tudor Revolution in Government* was widely disputed and never fully accepted by historians despite the highly influential positions he occupied in academia. Andress argued that it was moral rather than institutional power which made historical arguments influential and caused them to attain the status of 'truth', so that truth was in the end indeed a function of power, contrary to what *In Defence of History* tried to claim.

Andress's point is an interesting and perceptive one, and prompts me to think I should have put my argument a little differently. For if one thinks about it, the central *historical thesis* in Thompson's book – that the English working class was 'made' by 1832 – was even less widely accepted than the central historical thesis in Elton's – that there was a revolution in government and administration under Henry VIII's minister Thomas Cromwell. An examination of subsequent research monographs, articles and textbooks will soon show that very few historians of any kind incorporated Thompson's central thesis into their work, while some at least gave credence to Elton's. The difference in influence lay far more in the *method* and *approach* to history of the two historians, where Thompson was immeasurably more effective. Thompson's book had many imitators, Elton's had few. Elton did not start a wave of studies of administration and government in early modern history; his example was followed only by a handful of his own doctoral students. Thompson inspired a whole generation of social historians to study a whole range of topics in working-class history. When the question is seen from this point of view, Andress is right: Thompson was influential because his vision was more in tune with the spirit of the younger generation of social historians in the 1960s and 1970s.

Yet this has nothing much to do with the truth or otherwise of the interpretations each of the two historians advanced about the historical subjects and events they were investigating. Andress is wrong therefore to say that Thompson's influence was greater because he told a story that was morally appealing enough to be regarded as true. Thompson was influential because even if historians thought he was not giving a true picture of English plebeian and working-class society and politics in the late eighteenth and early nineteenth centuries, they nonetheless thought that the approach he adopted would enable them to give a true picture of the (usually much smaller) historical topics to which they chose to devote their own researches.

The argument which Andress puts forward thus in no way supports the hyper-relativist version of the truth-concept which he is advocating ('history . . . is an exercise in language because that is all it can be'). Andress takes the alarmingly anti-intellectual position that 'the marshalling of facts behind an argument is rendered irrelevant by the reply "I don't believe you, or "I don't care".' The kind of anti-semitism that led to Auschwitz, he says, is dead not because it has been shown to be untrue, but because 'we live in a truth-regime where the values behind those "facts" have been rejected'. If he actually believes that rational argument is so irrelevant, what is he doing teaching in a university? If somebody tells him he or she doesn't accept an argument, why doesn't he challenge him to disprove it rationally? Does he really want to live in a society where the evidence for an argument counts for nothing and the moral (or immoral) force behind its advocacy for everything? Surely the duty of an intellectual or an academic is to fight blind prejudice of the kind Andress so depressingly thinks unanswerable, not to give in to it. Contrary to what he argues, there is plenty of evidence to show that the truth prevails in the end because it is true; that antisemitism is no longer widely accepted because among other things it has been seen to be based on lies. Having reformulated the question of the relationship between power and knowledge in a stimulating way, Andress then delivers an answer that reduces the whole problem to the most basic level of 'might is right'.

While Arnold and Andress attacked particular aspects of my arguments as allegedly based on misunderstandings of postmodernist concepts, William Keenan, also writing in the *Times Higher Educational Supplement*, found my depiction of postmodernism to be a 'caricature'. In a rather polemical letter, Keenan criticized me for my 'apparent unawareness' of the fact that everything I wrote was an assertion or an opinion and not an objective truth. How can we arbitrate between arguments in such a situation? he asked, admitting that his own views were only opinions too. To this he gave no answer, taking refuge in the paranoid assertion that any criticism of postmodernist relativism was evidence of negative stereotyping and a determination on the part of people like me 'to cleanse academic life of views contrary to their own'.

Unfortunately Keenan failed to provide any evidence demonstrating that my account of postmodernist theories was the kind of caricature he said it was. And while he urged 'open discussion' on the topic, he was unable to say how this could take place at all if there was no objective, over-arching principle of evidence or rationality to which we could appeal in order to assess the opposing points of view. In fact the language Keenan uses suggests he does believe it is possible to provide a full, objective and fair description of an argument (the opposite, presumably of caricature), on the basis of which a reasoned debate could actually take place. Otherwise, why is he complaining of an attempt to suppress postmodernism, if he believes it's all about power, and polemicizes so violently himself in order to suppress the modernist views to which he is so vehemently opposed? This position deprives his complaint of any moral force whatsoever.

IV

As well as misunderstanding or misrepresenting postmodernist theory, some critics of *In Defence of History* have attacked the book for what they see as its unfairness to other individuals whose work it criticizes. For example, a number of reviewers, such as John Charmley and Ronald Hutton, not necessarily defenders of postmodernism, have suggested that Keith Jenkins's hostility to conventional history as practised in the universities is ascribed by *In Defence of History* to the fact that he has never had a job in a university himself. But this is not so. The book was *not* saying that Jenkins takes the views he does because he is not teaching in a university. It only says that if he applied his own argument that 'bourgeois' historians take the views they do because they teach in multi-million-pound universities to himself, that is the kind of argument he would end up with. Indeed this is actually put forward as an example of how unfair, how reductionist, postmodernist arguments can be. Furthermore, the book points out that a number of postmodernists have major posts at senior universities.

At least Keith Jenkins does not complain that I have been unfair to him. The complaint of personal unfairness is the speciality of Diane Purkiss, who contributed a two-part defence of her own book *The Witch in History* against the brief remarks made about it in *In Defence of History* to the 'Reviews in History' website of London University's Institute of Historical Research. Purkiss began by accusing me of misquoting from her book and claimed I discussed it without having read it, or alternatively that I read it but did not read it accurately (that these two accusations are mutually contradictory did not seem to occur to her – or is this mere rhetorical hyperbole not intended to be taken seriously?). Purkiss took my allegedly inaccurate reading as evidence for her view that 'reading all the words that are there, just those words and no others, not adding, not taking away, just reading' is a 'nearly impossible task' which 'none of us do . . . most of the time'. Purkiss's critique would certainly provide startling evidence of this point, supposing one was inclined to agree with it.

Let us start with a rather trivial example. On page 4 of *In Defence of History*, she charged, I attribute to her opinions which have been put forward not by her but by unnamed 'conservative defenders of history'. When we look up page 69 of *The Witch in History*, however, which is where the passage in question occurs, what do we find? At the end of a paragraph attacking male historians for their lack of interest in feminist and gender theory, Purkiss concludes that they evade the truth-claims of such theory by dismissing it as of no use to them in their work. There follows the sentence: 'The fact that poststructuralism threatens to throw historians out of work does not make it untrue.' This opinion is not attributed to anyone else and is neither set in quotation marks nor supplied with a footnote referring the reader to someone other than Purkiss herself as its author.

It is, to be sure, followed by another sentence, which reads as follows: 'Though some historinas [*sic*] do offer other refutations, these are usually based on fairly comprehensive misreadings of what they refute, again suggesting a certain interpretive carelessness.' The footnote to this sentence, like the previous footnote in Purkiss's text, refers to Joyce Appleby, Lynn Hunt and Margaret Jacob's *Telling the Truth About History* (a book by three historians, or perhaps we should now call them 'historinas', who can hardly be accused of a conservative approach to the past, or of a lack of interest in feminist and gender theory, or indeed of being male). But the view that poststructuralism threatens to throw historians out of work is not put forward in their book either, nor as far as I know in any other book except *The Witch in History*, apart from Keith Windschuttle's exaggeratedly alarmist *The Killing of History*, which is not cited anywhere in

The Witch in History and which, presumably therefore, Purkiss
had not read at the time when she wrote her book. Purkiss
does not say in her book that conservative defenders of history often sound as if they believe that poststructuralism
will make them unemployed. The sentence in question is
unambiguously her own. Indeed, Purkiss's claim in her website 'Response' that it would be 'hilarious' if she had actually
said that poststructuralism threatened to do historians out of
a job does not prevent her from repeating this view later in
her 'Response', where she remarks: 'Any resemblance
between my work and claims made about it by Evans is
purely coincidental, but of course one simply must have grist
for the conservative argufying machine, otherwise, I suppose, redundancy would truly beckon.'

This leads on to a broader assumption in Purkiss's
'Response', reflecting a more general prejudice in her book,
which is that *In Defence of History* is part of a 'conservative
argufying machine', and, by implication, that I am part of a
wider group of 'conservative defenders of history'. Since
Purkiss never actually explains what she means by 'conservative', this is a charge that it is difficult to refute. However,
if she rereads the book, she will find that it defends, as noted
earlier in this Afterword, a broad approach to history,
including social history, cultural history, feminist history,
and all the other recent innovations condemned by the true
conservative defenders of history like Gertrude Himmelfarb,
Geoffrey Elton, John Kenyon, and indeed all the historians
to whom the young-fogey critics of my book think I have
been so unfair. The book argues that socialist, feminist, black
and other radical histories need a concept of truth and objectivity just as much as any other histories do, but it says
nothing against them in principle, quite the contrary. It also
points out that once you open the relativist door, not only

conservatives but also fascists and neo-Nazis can come in through it too. The US edition of the book provides fresh evidence of the conservative tendencies of at least some postmodernist writers on history (in particular, David Harlan, who calls for a more positive, patriotic approach to the American past and its rescue from over-critical modernists in his book *The Degradation of American History*). It is a travesty to assume that postmodernism or post-structuralism are radical, and anyone who criticizes them is conservative – a view put forward in a particularly unthinking way by Keith Jenkins in his *Why History?*, which has a whole chapter praising Harlan's work.

Purkiss also assumes, to read out the implications of her rhetoric, that I regard feminist and postmodernist historians as a 'rabble'. Where have I ever said such a thing? This is pure invention. Perhaps Purkiss would care to read the books, articles and reviews I wrote on feminist history in the 1970s and early 1980s, or to note the close and repeated attention paid to gender as a social construct in my recent books *Rituals of Retribution* and *Tales from the German Underworld*. Or, indeed, the criticisms advanced in *In Defence of History* of a historian like John Vincent who has declared recently that history is about the rich and powerful, 'history is deeply male'. What I object to is not feminist history – the more of it there is, the better – but crude and blatant sexism of the sort Purkiss displays in her book and her 'Response'. In the latter, she is insistent on referring to me as a 'man', goes out of her way to describe historians of witchcraft as 'gentlemen', says that I think historians should argue in a 'manly fashion', accuses 'academic historians' of 'duffing up a woman historian [i.e. Margaret Murray] for being somehow too close to the figure of the witch', and argues that 'male historians tend to ground rationality in a repudiation of the feminine as problematically inchoate'. She goes on to allege that Keith Thomas and Alan Macfarlane, two influential historians of witchcraft, unconsciously try 'to use the figure of the witch to define history in masculine terms'.

To realize how sexist such remarks are, one only has to reverse the gender designations. If Purkiss thinks it is legitimate to write about male historians in such terms, then what objection could she possibly have to a male historian who insisted on pointing out that someone he disagreed with was a woman and as such part of a school of 'ladies', who accused her of wanting to argue in a 'womanly' fashion, whatever that might be, who objected to her 'duffing up a man historian for being somehow too distant from the figure of the witch', and who raised similar objections about female historians trying to use the figure of the witch to define history in feminine terms? She would rightly find such views sexist and offensive.

Or, to refer again to Purkiss's book, if it is wrong for male historians to 'ground' male identity in a historical myth of women's powerlessness in the past, then why is it not also wrong for female historians to 'ground' female identity in a historical myth of women's articulacy in the past? The point once more is that such arguments cut both ways. If an anti-feminist wants to attack Purkiss's work with sexist political arguments of this sort, if the persuasiveness of historical scholarship depends not on the extent to which its arguments fit the evidence but on the political and moral assumptions behind it, then she has no means of defending herself against her critics. If for example Purkiss objects to the fact that Keith Thomas has used the figure of the witch as the ground for his own academic identity, then what reason has she for objecting to the view that she herself has used the figure of the witch as the ground for her own academic identity?

Purkiss alludes to my description of her as a postmodernist as 'hysterical'. How would she feel if I described her arguments as 'hysterical', or imagined her, as she does Thomas and Macfarlane, writing 'tearfully' and 'with a maniacal cackle'? Once again, I am not using the label 'postmodernist' as a term of condemnation, simply as a useful description, and one to some of whose various manifestations I attribute positive and fruitful intellectual developments; I would be equally happy to call Purkiss a post-structuralist, a designation she appears to approve of, if that was easier for her to accept.

In terms of Purkiss's own work this means that I place it in the context of an approach which makes no distinction between fact and fiction, or to put it another way, different forms of representation. Thus for example where I referred (p. 99) to 'the witches themselves', a phrase to which Purkiss objects, I have to explain that what I meant was the real people in the past – men as well as women – who were accused of witchcraft and who appear in trial and other historical records. I continue to think that there is an important distinction to be made between these people, who really lived, and the figures who appear in literature, poetry and other fictional representations, who did not. I do not say, however, and never have said, that it is wrong to study the latter or even to study both real people and fictional people side by side (indeed I do this in my own book *Tales from the German Underworld*).

This brings us to Keith Thomas and *Religion and the Decline of Magic*. Contrary to what Purkiss claims, I do not accept Thomas's interpretation of early modern English witchcraft in my book, nor do I say anywhere that *Religion and the Decline of Magic* is the 'last word' on the topic (in fact there is now a superb example of an explicitly postmodernist approach to the subject in Stuart Clark's *Thinking with*

Demons, a book which does not manage to avoid the inherent contradictions of post-structuralist theory, but nevertheless provides a stunning illustration of how it can be used to breathe new life into an old subject). Purkiss says Thomas and Macfarlane base their work on a 'misreading of historical materials' and that they 'get it wrong'. This is breathtakingly crude and sweeping. Similarly with the charge that they portray women in the past as weak in order to 'empower' men in the present. Aside from the considerable evidence they marshal for the weak position of elderly widows in early modern society, there is a whole genre of feminist historical writing which portrays women as victims in order to highlight the oppression and injustice under which they have had to suffer through the ages.

Purkiss charges that Thomas uses only printed sources and 'neglects to read these sources scrupulously or carefully' and 'often uses literary sources without distinguishing them carefully from trial materials'. In fact, Thomas's book uses manuscript sources in a variety of archives as well as pamphlet and printed literature. Purkiss charges that I haven't read this literature myself. This is true. I'm not an expert on seventeenth-century English witchcraft. To demand that a critic or commentator on a book has to examine all the evidence on which it rests before being capable of saying anything about it would disqualify anyone from saying anything about any historical work apart from their own. One might indeed legitimately turn the tables and ask how much of the evidence used by Thomas has also been studied by Purkiss. This is not easy to discover since she has not troubled to provide her book with a bibliography. However, a check through Chapter 3 ('The witch in the hands of the historians – a tale of prejudice and fear') reveals references to primary printed sources in seven notes out of eighty, with

a total of seven works listed. There is a handful of manuscript sources cited in the footnotes to other chapters, but
Purkiss's book itself is based overwhelmingly on printed
material. It does not cite more than a tiny fraction of the
source material cited by Thomas. Purkiss says in her book
that she has read more than she cites. Be that as it may, her
book's criticism of Thomas in Chapter 3 is not based on a
comprehensive comparison of what he says with the materials on which it draws, so that her attack on me for not doing
this in my discussion of Thomas's *Religion and the Decline of
Magic* must appear disingenuous, to say the least.

The real quarrel Purkiss has with my discussion of her
work, however, does not relate to the historiography of
witchcraft, but, once more, to postmodernism and
'Holocaust denial'. Purkiss points out quite rightly that
Holocaust deniers claim they are telling the truth, and do
not on the whole use the conceptual apparatus of post-
structuralist relativism. The key passage at issue in her book
The Witch in History is on page 70:

> Historians are fond of pointing out that deconstruction's
> leading American exponent was a Nazi sympathizer and anti-
> Semite during the war, indicating the dire political
> consequences of deconstruction's challenge to conventional
> history. But in that case, traditional empirical history must
> also have dire implications, since most *neo*-Nazi historians
> adopt the most conservative possible protocols of discovery,
> revelation and truth-telling. It might be equally valid to argue
> that notions of the indeterminacy of truth can be used against
> the self-proclaimed certitude of deniers. Deniers' assump-
> tion that the 'truth' about the Holocaust lies around waiting
> to be 'discovered' and encapsulated in a historical text forms
> the greatest possible contrast with the discourse of Holocaust

survivors' testimonies, which affirm the impossibility of representing the ultimate 'truth' of the event.

In her 'Response', Purkiss quotes selectively from this passage in her own book to make it look, once more, as if what she puts forward there as her own views are in fact her summary of other people's. She achieves this by deliberately omitting the second sentence in the passage above. If readers want to look up the passage in my book which discusses this argument, they will find it, not on pages 140-1, where Purkiss directs them (they contain a discussion of postmodernist concepts of time), but on pages 241-2. She does, however, quote the sentence in question correctly, and I accept that I should have put 'dire implications' instead of 'dire consequences'. The meaning and effect are the same, however. The problem with this passage in *The Witch in History* is that it assumes that – at the very least – one cannot distinguish between the methods of real historians and the methods of Holocaust deniers because both present themselves as seekers after historical truth and both use the conventional apparatus of historical scholarship to achieve this effect. Either they both really are seeking after the truth, or they are both putting forward political arguments dressed up as such, but in both cases the effect is the same.

What this argument ignores is the fact that Holocaust deniers are not engaged in a search for truth, but manipulate and falsify the historical record for their own political purposes. Whether or not they really believe they are searching for truth is a question which cannot be answered without recourse to speculation about their own psychology, but the way they treat historical evidence strongly suggests that their falsifications are conscious and deliberate. This is not the case with genuine historians.

Purkiss does not, however, seem to grasp this difference. She goes on to say on pages 70–1 of *The Witch in History* that

> careful reading of texts and especially stories is germane to Holocaust studies. Reading in detail and with due attention to textuality need not imply a fixed or cynical scepticism; such care in reading can signify proper respect for the unique and moving humanity of stories.

Why not proper respect for their truth? Why does it matter that stories are uniquely and movingly humane, but whether or not they are true is a matter of such subordinate importance that it doesn't even warrant a mention? Why should care in reading merely 'signify' respect instead of helping us determine the truth or otherwise of the representations the text contains? Coming after a plea for the validity of 'notions of the indeterminacy of truth' in writing about the Holocaust, these two sentences do indeed warrant the statement in my book (described as 'not even a reasonable inference' in Purkiss's 'Response') that Purkiss is saying that we should tell stories about the Holocaust and not worry too much about whether they are true or not.

What in any case is the truth in such matters, asks Purkiss? 'We can never know the whole or absolute truth' about the Holocaust, she says, 'because it would be more than any of us could bear.' If we cannot know it, how do we know we could not bear it? In pursuing this argument, Purkiss not only gets herself tangled up in contradictions, but also attributes to me a whole series of propositions that I have never advanced. How my book, for example, 'conflates the Holocaust with the witch-trials, ignoring the historical specificity of each', as Purkiss charges, is beyond me; I cannot see any evidence for this absurd charge anywhere in this book.

More importantly, however, to come to the point that really seems to annoy Purkiss, I have never equated her or any postmodernist or post-structuralist either implicitly or explicitly with Holocaust deniers. What I said was – to repeat a point made by Deborah Lipstadt in her book *Denying the Holocaust* – that postmodernist hyper-relativism encourages tolerance of Holocaust denial because it rejects the idea that one can tell truth from fiction and interpretation from falsification. Purkiss's own arguments are themselves evidence of this. But of course they are not responsible for Holocaust denial themselves, just as postmodernism is not responsible for Holocaust denial. Nowhere have I said this; such a claim would be absurd. I am not 'upset' (as Purkiss claims) because postmodernist epistemology is threatening to merge me and my 'party' (I wasn't aware that I had one – perhaps Purkiss would care to supply me with a few names?) with the deniers. Rather, I am arguing that extreme historical relativism, the idea that the truth about history can never be discovered, makes it impossible to refute Holocaust deniers. This does not mean that they would have any truck with such notions themselves, something I have never claimed anywhere. I did not say, and do not think, that Purkiss herself is, as she claims I said, 'part of the threat of Holocaust denial', which is a different thing altogether.

Of course Purkiss is right in saying that 'we can never know the whole or absolute truth' about the Holocaust or indeed about anything else. I tried to express this belief in the much-misunderstood concluding sentence of the book. But just because we can never attain the whole or absolute truth, just because we make mistakes in our search for the truth about the past, just because there will always be something new to say about any historical subject, it does not follow that there is no such thing as the truth at all. In a similar way, as Susan Haack has pointed out (*TLS*, 9 July 1999), just because what is accepted as true isn't necessarily so, does not mean that the concept of the truth itself is merely ideological. Purkiss argues 'against "the truth"' and in favour of 'truths' that are 'local and specific', but it is impossible on the evidence of her 'Response' to see what the difference is. Truth, as Haack points out, is not relative to perspective, though what is accepted as true is; 'a statement is true if and only if things are as it represents them to be'. So there cannot be incompatible truths – and although some postmodernists argue that there can (despite the fact that, as Haack notes, 'incompatible' means 'cannot be jointly true'), I don't see Purkiss taking this position in her 'Response'. So if her 'local and specific truths' fit together with other truths, then they are true, they are aspects of the truth, and Purkiss believes in the truth.

Indeed, as Haack says, 'everyone who believes anything . . . implicitly acknowledges . . . that there is such a thing as truth', and it is encouraging to see Purkiss, along with other critics of my book, acknowledging this by attacking what they see as errors and falsehoods in it, even though for the most part they miss their target. When Purkiss sweepingly condemns a variety of representations of witchcraft as 'wrong because all allow the play of fantasy to replace rigorous reading' she is indeed correct to say that this suggests she believes in truth, even though earlier in the same paragraph she argues 'against "the truth"'. The 'fantasies' she describes, therefore, are not 'local and specific' truths but falsehoods. 'Rigorous reading', one presumes, will deliver the truth rather than fantasies and falsehoods. So far, so good, then; we are in agreement.

And yet Purkiss also describes 'attempts to find out "what really happened" as doomed'. Questions such as why witchcraft persecution in England rose and fell are, she says on page 3 of her book, 'unanswerable', and she goes on: 'I do not try to answer the empirical questions that preoccupy many of my contemporaries' (p. 4). The obvious question to ask is, if questions about why witchcraft persecutions rose and fell are unanswerable, then why aren't questions about the meaning of texts unanswerable? If attempts to find out what really happened are doomed, then why aren't attempts to find out what is really there in texts like *Religion and the Decline of Magic* doomed as well? Purkiss indeed concedes this argument in principle, as I have noted, but I doubt whether she would accept it in practice when applied to the questions asked – and answered – in her own book.

Purkiss argues against 'attempts to squeeze disparate materials into a large and general hypothesis', but her feminist approach itself is based on such a hypothesis about early modern women empowering themselves by fantasizing that they were witches (an interesting idea, let me make clear, and one that deserves further debate and research), and more generally on an even larger and more general set of hypotheses about the power-driven nature of gender relations in past and present. All of this is accompanied by repeated attacks on historians and the historical profession for not reading sources rigorously, failing to note the rhetorical content of documents, and naïvely 'treating each text as a transparent window onto the mind of its writer or the *mentalité* of an entire society' (p. 71). I think these attacks are largely misplaced, but no one could dispute the wisdom of the advice they imply. Once more, it comes down to urging historians to pay more attention to the style and content of the documents they use, the motives, if they can be discovered, of their authors, the audience to which they were addressed, and so on. Who could quarrel with that?

All of these multiple and varied misreadings, misinterpretations and misrepresentations of my book, from Burleigh to Purkiss and beyond, might indeed suggest, as Purkiss notes in her 'Response', that 'all of us have less control over meaning than we might like'. But in accusing me of being unable to read her own work accurately, Purkiss is conceding the point that we can in fact exercise some control over the meaning of the texts we generate, by putting something there that is capable of being read accurately. If this statement does not mean that we mean what we say when we write a sentence, and that readers can discover this if they read accurately what we have written, then it does not mean anything at all.

Purkiss says that 'meanings are generated quite independently of intentions', but this is putting it in too bald and extreme a way; meanings are not generated *entirely* independently of intentions, otherwise Purkiss would have no reason to criticize my reading of the meaning of her work; they do bear *some* relation to them, though it is not necessarily either exclusive or direct (all points made in *In Defence of History*). The truth of these observations is to some extent borne out by this debate. In some cases, I've obviously laid myself open to what I think is misinterpretation, perhaps by failing to make myself entirely clear (e.g. in the definition of objectivity) or by expressing myself poorly. In other cases, I think I have been the victim of a careless reading of my text in which conservative or postmodernist critics have seen what they wanted to see and ignored all the nuances and qualifications I advanced in respect of the argument they have been attacking. In still further cases I have suffered from deliberate distortion or manipulation of what I have said. And in a few instances critics have read into my book things that simply weren't there.

I confess I have been taken aback by the sheer variety and by the utterly contradictory nature of the responses which the book has elicited. I would not have thought it possible for a single book to be read, or misread, in so many different ways. But stimulating debate was one of the book's principal aims; it was never intended to close down discussion (nor would that have been a feasible aim in any case). As those who have attacked the book for failing to confront the major postmodernist thinkers have rightly if somewhat superfluously pointed out, the issues at stake cannot be settled in a couple of hundred pages. So it is important that the debate continues.

NOTES

INTRODUCTION

1 Keith Jenkins, *On 'What is History?'. From Carr and Elton to Rorty and White* (London, 1995), pp. 2–3.

2 John Tosh, for example, in a widely used history primer, still thought in 1991 that the controversy between Carr and Elton was 'the best starting point for the debate about the standing of historical knowledge' (John Tosh, *The Pursuit of History* (London, 1991), p. 236).

3 Dominick LaCapra, *History and Criticism* (Ithaca, New York, 1987), p. 136. However, LaCapra goes on to contradict himself by saying that most introductory history courses in universities end up by providing students with a 'more or less pragmatic and eclectic "synthesis" of the two works' and indeed agrees implicitly with this by saying that 'extreme documentary objectivism and relativistic subjectivism do not constitute genuine alternatives.' (ibid., p. 137.)

4 Jenkins, *On 'What is History?'*, pp. 87–8. Arthur Marwick, *The Nature of History* (3rd edn., London, 1989), p. 412, also describes Elton's *The Practice of History* (London, 1967), as a 'clear statement of the mainstream professional position'.

5 Some postmodernists have attempted to pre-empt criticism of their positions by denying that there is such a thing as postmodernism ('I for one have no idea what a post-modern position would look like,' as one of them put it) or to label the term 'largely unhelpful' because it

IN DEFENCE OF HISTORY

conflates the views of a number of very different contemporary thinkers. But, as others have pointed out, the fact that this label covers a variety of sometimes contradictory and conflicting ideas invites critical investigation rather than silent acceptance of such ideas. Postmodernism is a convenient label; it is not an organized movement, nor does it amount to a coherent ideology, and remarks in the present work about postmodernism should not be taken as generalizations applying to every variant and every practitioner. Another common term, post-structuralism, may be taken as a narrower term denoting certain methods of reading texts. For these claims and counter-claims, see James Vernon, 'Who's afraid of the "linguistic turn"? The politics of social history and its discontents', *Social History*, Vol. 19 (1994), pp. 81–97, here pp. 96–7; and Neville Kirk, 'History, language, ideas and post-modernism: a materialist view', *Social History*, Vol. 20 (1995), pp. 222–40, here p. 222. For a useful survey, see David Harvey, *The Condition of Postmodernism: An Enquiry into the Origins of Cultural Change* (Oxford, 1991).

6 David Harlan, 'Intellectual History and the Return of Literature', *American Historical Review*, Vol. 94 (1989), pp. 581–609, here p. 581.

7 Joyce Appleby, Lynn Hunt and Margaret Jacob, *Telling the Truth about History* (New York, 1995), p. 1.

8 Gabrielle Spiegel, 'History and Post-Modernism', *Past and Present* 135 (May, 1992), pp. 194–208, here p. 195, referring to Nancy Partner, 'Making Up Lost Time: Writing on the Writing of History', *Speculum*, Vol. lxi (1986), pp. 90–117, here p. 95.

9 Lawrence Stone, 'History and Post-Modernism', *Past and Present* 131 (1991), pp. 217–18.

10 Beverley Southgate, *History: What and Why? Ancient, Modern and Postmodern Perspectives* (London, 1996), p. 71. See also Alan Munslow, *Deconstructing History* (London, 1997).

11 Diane Purkiss, *The Witch in History: Early Modern and Twentieth-Century Representations* (London, 1996), p. 69.

12 Allan Megill, 'Recounting the Past: "Description", Explanation, and Narrative in Historiography', *American Historical Review*, Vol. 94 (1989), pp. 627–53, here p. 631.

13 Nancy F. Partner, 'Historicity in an Age of Reality-Fictions', in Frank Ankersmit and Hans Kellner (eds.), *A New Philosophy of History* (London, 1995), pp. 21–39, here p. 22.

14 Vernon, 'Who's afraid of the "linguistic turn"?', p. 81.

15 Patrick Joyce, 'History and Post-Modernism', *Past and Present* 133 (November, 1991), pp. 204–9, here pp. 204–5.

16 Patrick Joyce, 'The imaginary discontents of social history: a note of response to Mayfield and Thorne, and Lawrence and Taylor', *Social History*, Vol. 18 (1993), pp. 81–5, here p. 83; a charge repeated in Patrick Joyce, 'The end of social history?', *Social History*, Vol. 20 (1995), pp. 73–91, here p. 73.

17 Joyce, 'The end of social history?', pp. 80–1.

18 David Mayfield and Susan Thorne, 'Reply to "The poverty of protest" and "The imaginary discontents"', *Social History*, Vol. 18 (1993), pp. 219–33, here p. 221.

19 Geoff Eley and Keith Nield, 'Starting over: the present, the post-modern and the moment of social history', *Social History*, Vol. 20 (1995), pp. 355–64, here p. 364.

20 G. R. Elton, *Return to Essentials. Some Reflections on the Present State of Historical Study* (Cambridge, 1991), pp. 27, 34, 41, 43, 49.

21 Stone, 'History and Post-Modernism'. It is only fair to add that Stone intended this alarmist phrase as a provocation.

22 Raphael Samuel, 'Reading the Signs II', *History Workshop Journal* 33 (1992), pp. 220–51, here pp. 220–1.

23 Arthur Marwick, 'Two Approaches to Historical Study: The Metaphysical (Including "Postmodernism") and the Historical', *Journal of Contemporary History*, Vol. 30 (1995), pp. 5–35, here p. 5.

24 ibid., p. 29.

25 Ellen Somekawa and Elizabeth A. Smith, 'Theorizing the Writing of History, or, "I can't think why it should be so dull, for a great deal of it must be invention"', *Journal of Social History*, Vol. 22 (1988), pp. 149–61, here p. 150.

26 F. R. Ankersmit, 'Historiography and Postmodernism', *History and Theory*, Vol. 28 (1989), pp. 137–53, here p. 149.

27 Jenkins, *On 'What is History?'*, p. 35. For a more wide-ranging account of the postmodernist critique of history, see Pauline Marie Rosenau, *Post-Modernism and the Social Sciences: Insights, Inroads, and Intrusions* (Princeton, 1992), pp. 62–76.

28 Joyce, 'The end of social history?', p. 73. He also says the same for sociology (ibid., p. 83). Add the Foucauldian critique of classifica-tory systems such as psychology, psychiatry, demography, statistics,

economics and criminology, and there is not much left of contemporary systems of knowledge outside the natural sciences.

29 Eley and Nield, 'Starting over', p. 364.

30 Appleby, Hunt and Jacob, *Telling the Truth*, p. 9.

31 Christopher Lloyd, 'For Realism and Against the Inadequacies of Common Sense: A Response to Arthur Marwick', *Journal of Contemporary History*, Vol. 31 (1996), pp. 191–207, here p. 192.

32 Theodore Zeldin, 'Social History and Total History', *Journal of Social History*, Vol. 10 (1976), pp. 237–45, here p. 237.

33 Norman Stone, 'Grim Eminence', *London Review of Books*, 20 January 1983, p. 982.

34 For some considerations on this question, see J. H. Hexter, *Doing History* (London, 1971), pp. 67–71.

35 Ronald F. Atkinson, *Knowledge and Explanation in History. An Introduction to the Philosophy of History* (London, 1978), p. 8.

36 Elton, *Return*, p. 34.

37 Marwick, 'Two Approaches', p. 6; J. H. Hexter, *On Historians. Reappraisals of Some of the Makers of Modern History* (London, 1979), p. 145.

38 Hayden White, 'Response to Arthur Marwick', *Journal of Contemporary History*, Vol. 30 (1995), pp. 233–46, here p. 245.

39 Raymond Martin, 'Objectivity and Meaning in Historical Studies: Toward a Post-Analytic View', *History and Theory*, Vol. 32 (1993), pp. 25–50, here p. 31.

40 Robert William Fogel and G. R. Elton, *Which Road to the Past? Two Views of History* (London, 1983), p. 2.

41 Appleby, Hunt and Jacob, *Telling the Truth*, p. 9.

42 Perez Zagorin, 'Historiography and Postmodernism: Reconsiderations', *History and Theory*, Vol. 29 (1990), pp. 263–74, here p. 264.

43 Joyce, 'The imaginary discontents', p. 84.

44 Jenkins, *On 'What is History?'*, p. 6.

45 ibid., p. 92.

1: THE HISTORY OF HISTORY

1 For an elaboration of these brief introductory remarks, see Ernst Breisach, *Historiography: Ancient, Medieval and Modern* (2nd edn.,

London, 1994). The quotation, often attributed to the eighteenth-century English philosopher Bolingbroke, in fact originated with the ancient rhetorician Dionysius of Halicarnassus (*Oxford Dictionary of Quotations* (3rd edn., Oxford, 1979), p. 184).

2 Fritz Stern (ed.), *The Varieties of History: From Voltaire to the Present* (Cleveland, Ohio, 1956), p. 57.

3 Peter Novick, *That Noble Dream. The 'Objectivity Question' and the American Historical Profession* (Cambridge, 1988), pp. 27–9; Leopold von Ranke, *The Secret of World History: Selected Writings on the Art and Science of History* (ed. Roger Wines, New York, 1981), p. 21; see also Stephen Bann, *The Clothing of Clio: A study of the representation of history in nineteenth-century Britain and France* (Cambridge, 1984), pp. 8–10.

4 Stern (ed.), *The Varieties of History*, p. 55.

5 Leopold von Ranke, *The Theory and Practice of History* (eds. Georg G. Iggers and Konrad von Moltke, Indianapolis, 1973), p. 119.

6 Novick, *That Noble Dream*, p. 36.

7 Robert Harris, *Selling Hitler: The Story of the Hitler Diaries* (London, 1986), pp. 23, 354. For forgeries and falsifications relating to the origins of the First World War, see for example J. C. G. Röhl, 'Admiral von Müller and the Approach of War', *Historical Journal*, Vol. XII (1969), pp. 651–73; and Fritz Fischer, *Juli 1914: Wir sind nicht hineingeschlittert: Das Staatsgeheimnis um die Riezler-Tagebücher. Ein Streitschrift* (Reinbek, 1983), pp. 49–54, 75–82.

8 Novick, *That Noble Dream*, p. 33.

9 Stern (ed.), *The Varieties of History*, p. 179.

10 All quoted in Novick, *That Noble Dream*, pp. 37–9.

11 Lytton Strachey, *Eminent Victorians: Cardinal Manning – Florence Nightingale – Dr Arnold – General Gordon* (London, 1925), p. vii.

12 John Kenyon, *The History Men. The Historical Profession in England since the Renaissance* (2nd edn., London, 1993), p. 212.

13 Peter Gay, *Style in History* (London, 1975), ch. 2.

14 John Pemble, *Venice Rediscovered* (Oxford, 1995), pp. 82–3.

15 J. B. Bury, *An Inaugural Lecture, delivered in the Divinity School, Cambridge, on January 26, 1903* (Cambridge, 1903); see also Stern (ed.), *The Varieties of History*, pp. 209–26.

16 For other, similar reactions to Bury's lecture, and other, similar echoes of Bury's argument among Edwardian historians, see Kenyon, *The History Men*, pp. 183–6.

17 Stern (ed.), *The Varieties of History*, pp. 227–45.

18 G. M. Trevelyan, *England under Queen Anne* (3 vols, London, 1930–34).

19 Stern (ed.), *The Varieties of History*, pp. 229–33.

20 Droysen quoted in Stern (ed.), *The Varieties of History*, p. 138. More generally, see Georg G. Iggers, *The German Conception of History. The National Tradition of Historical Thought from Herder to the Present* (Middletown, Conn., 1968).

21 Novick, *That Noble Dream*, pp. 116–32, 206–24; Christopher Parker, *The English Historical Tradition since 1850* (Edinburgh, 1990), pp. 104–17.

22 Klaus Schwabe, *Wissenschaft und Kriegsmoral* (Göttingen, 1969); Stuart Wallace, *War and the Image of Germany. British Academics 1914–1918* (Edinburgh, 1988), pp. 29–42, 58–73.

23 Quoted in Wallace, *War and the Image of Germany*, p. 37, quoting L. P. Jacks, Principal of Manchester College, Oxford.

24 David Cannadine, *G. M. Trevelyan: A Life in History* (London, 1992), pp. 213–15.

25 Novick, *That Noble Dream*, pp. 131–2.

26 H. A. L. Fisher, *A History of Europe* (3 vols., London, 1935), p. vii. For a particularly savage attack on Fisher's views see Christopher Hill, 'A Whig Historian', *The Modern Quarterly*, Vol. 3 (1938), pp. 276–84.

27 Benedetto Croce, *History as the Story of Liberty* (London, 1941), p. 19.

28 R. G. Collingwood, *The Idea of History* (Oxford, 1946), Part V, Sections 4–5.

29 E. H. Carr, *What is History?* (2nd edn., London, 1987), p. 21.

30 All quotes on Namier in Ved Mehta, *Fly and the Fly-Bottle. Encounters with British Intellectuals* (London, 1963), pp. 179, 183.

31 Even in 1995, however, Professor John Vincent thought that 'the great historians of the twentieth century in England were two: Namier and Butterfield. Both stood out the more,' he added, 'because of the surrounding dullness.' They were great, he said, not because they wrote great historical masterpieces, but because they destroyed the dominant 'Whig interpretation' of history based on the supposed rise of parliamentarism, and so affected the wider political culture of the country (John Vincent, *An Intelligent Person's Guide to History* (London, 1995), pp. 58–62).

32 Linda Colley, *Lewis Namier* (London, 1989), p. 63.

33 (Anon.), 'The Namier View of History', *Times Literary Supplement*, 28 August 1953.

34 See L. B. Namier, *The Structure of Politics at the Accession of George III* (London, 1927, 2nd edn. 1957); idem, *England in the Age of the American Revolution* (London, 1930). More generally, see Frank O'Gorman, *The Rise of Party in England: the Rockingham Whigs 1760–82* (London, 1975); John Cannon, *The Fox–North Coalition: Crisis of the Constitution 1782–4* (London, 1969); and John Brewer, *Party Ideology and Popular Politics at the Accession of George III* (London, 1976). Namier's obsession with the *History of Parliament* led to a critical comment from E. H. Carr: 'Bricks are important, but a pile of bricks is not a house. And should the master-builder spend his time in a brick field?' (E. H. Carr, 'English History's Towering Outsider', *Times Literary Supplement*, 21 May 1957).

35 ibid., pp. 91–3. The attacks mounted from the left on the Whig interpretation by Marxist historians such as Christopher Hill and E. P. Thompson, who argued that there was a good deal of self-interest behind the middle-class advocacy of parliamentarism in the seventeenth and eighteenth centuries, were just as effective as the assault launched by Namier from the right.

36 Karl Popper, *The Poverty of Historicism* (London, 1957).

37 For elaborations of these points, and numerous examples, see Richard J. Evans, *Rereading German History: From Unification to Reunification 1800–1996* (London, 1997).

38 Peter Burke, *Sociology and History* (London, 1980), is a good, if rather belated, example of this genre.

39 Lawrence Stone, 'History and the Social Sciences in the Twentieth Century', in idem, *The Past and the Present* (London, 1981), pp. 3–44.

40 Emmanuel Le Roy Ladurie, *The Territory of the Historian* (Chicago, 1979), pp. 15, 6.

41 Oscar Handlin *et al.*, *Harvard Guide to American History* (Cambridge, Mass., 1954), pp. 24–5.

42 Fogel, '"Scientific" and Traditional History', in Fogel and Elton, *Which Road?*, pp. 7–70.

43 The ambitions of American quantifiers like J. Morgan Kousser can be traced in the early issues of the journal *Social Science History*. It is worth noting that in Britain, grants for postgraduate research in economic and social history are administered by the government-funded

Economic and Social Research Council, which will not issue them for university institutions unless they have a training programme in place that includes statistical and 'cliometric' techniques. And the bulk of the large-scale faculty research grants given to historians by the Council now goes mainly to teams of researchers working on the computer-assisted compilation and analysis of serial quantitative data and publishing their results in specialized articles rather than general books. At the end of the line, historical epistemology thus translates into hard cash.

44 Georg Iggers, introduction to the *International Handbook of Historical Studies. Contemporary Research and Theory* (eds. idem and Harold Parker, Westport, Conn., 1979).

45 Elton, 'Two Kinds of History', in Fogel and Elton, *Which Road*, pp. 71–122, esp. pp. 83, 106; also Stone, 'History and the Social Sciences in the Twentieth Century', pp. 32–5.

46 Robert W. Fogel and Stanley L. Engerman, *Time on the Cross* (Boston, 1974).

47 Paul A. David *et al.*, *Reckoning with Slavery: A Critical Study in the Quantitative History of American Negro Slavery* (New York, 1976), p. 339; for further critiques, see Herbert Gutman, *Slavery and the Numbers Game: A Critique of 'Time on the Cross'* (Urbana, 1975) and Peter Kolchin, 'Toward a Reinterpretation of Slavery', *Journal of Social History*, Vol. 9 (1975), pp. 99–111.

48 Thomas Kuhn, *The Structure of Scientific Revolutions* (2nd edn., Chicago, 1970), pp. 164–5.

2: HISTORY, SCIENCE AND MORALITY

1 Carr, *What is History?*, p. 56.

2 However, in Britain at the beginning of the 1980s, the Education Secretary in Mrs Thatcher's Conservative Government, Sir Keith Joseph, forced the government-funded Social Science Research Council to change its name to the Economic and Social Research Council, because he did not believe that there was such a thing as social science.

3 See the sensible discussion in Novick, *That Noble Dream*, pp. 24–5.

4 Carr, *What is History?*, pp. 72–3.

5 Elton, *Return*, p. 51.

6 ibid., pp. 62–3.

7 ibid., pp. 49, 66.

8 Jenkins, *On 'What is History?'*, p. 70.

9 Carr, *What is History?*, p. 162.

10 David Knowles, *The Historian and Character* (Cambridge, 1955), p. 19.

11 W. C. Sellar and R. J. Yeatman, *1066 and All That. A memorable history of England: comprising all the parts you can remember . . .*, (London, 1930).

12 Carr, *What is History?*, pp. 78–9.

13 ibid., pp. 80–6.

14 David Knowles, *The Religious Orders in England* (Vol. III, Cambridge, 1959), p. 468.

15 ibid., pp. 121, 126.

16 Robert Conquest, *The Harvest of Sorrow* (New York, 1985); Alec Nove, *Was Stalin Really Necessary?* (London, 1965).

17 For an excellent example of the effectiveness of these techniques, see the work of Michael Burleigh, especially *Death and Deliverance. 'Euthanasia' in Germany 1900–1945* (Cambridge, 1994).

18 Elton, *Return*, pp. 62–3.

19 J. A. Froude, *Short Studies on Great Subjects* (London, 1963, first published 1867), p. 21.

20 Pieter Geyl, *Debates with Historians* (London, 1955), pp. 176–82, 201–3, 210. Geyl's comprehensive demolition of Toynbee stretches across several chapters of the book, from p. 112 to p. 210. See also idem, *Encounters in History* (London, 1963), pp. 276–306, for Geyl's riposte to Toynbee's answer to his critics, which occupied 674 pages of an additional volume of *A Study of History*.

21 H. T. Buckle, *History of Civilization in England* (2 vols., London, 1856 and 1861).

22 Carr, *What is History?*, p. 63.

23 ibid., p. 69.

24 Vincent, *Intelligent Person's Guide*, p. 19.

25 Allan Megill, 'Recounting the Past: "Description", Explanation, and Narrative in Historiography', *American Historical Review*, Vol. 94 (1989), pp. 627–53, here p. 633. The German philosopher Wilhelm Windelband's distinction between 'nomothetic' sciences concerned with general laws and 'idiographic' sciences concerned with particular

entities did not rule out the one or the other as a science. Both, as far as he was concerned, were sciences. But this meant the German term *Wissenschaft*, organized knowledge, and so had little relevance to the debate as it was proceeding in English-speaking lands. (Wilhelm Windelband, 'History and Natural Science', *History and Theory*, Vol. 19 (1980), pp. 169–85 (translation of work originally published in 1894, with an introduction by Guy Oakes).)

26 For a particularly striking example of this failure, see Richard J. Evans, *In Hitler's Shadow. West German Historians and the Attempt to Escape from the Nazi Past* (New York, 1989), pp. 105–6.

27 Paul Kennedy, *The Rise and Fall of the Great Powers. Economic Change and Military Conflict from 1500 to 2000* (London, 1987), p. 513.

28 Elton, *Return*, pp. 56–8.

29 Quoted in Kenyon, *The History Men*, p. 198.

30 Quoted in Stern (ed.), *The Varieties of History*, p. 193.

31 Somekawa and Smith, 'Theorizing', p. 152.

32 Theodore Zeldin, 'Social History and Total History', *Journal of Social History*, Vol. 10 (1976/7), pp. 237–45, here p. 237.

33 White, 'Response', p. 243.

34 Elton, *Practice*, p. 148.

35 Lawrence Stone, 'History and Post-Modernism II', *Past and Present* 135 (May, 1992), pp. 189–94, here p. 189.

36 ibid., p. 99.

37 LaCapra, *History and Criticism*, p. 36. LaCapra unfortunately fails to give any examples of this use of language. Russell Jacoby, 'A New Intellectual History?', *American Historical Review*, Vol. 97 (April 1992), pp. 405–24, here p. 416, similarly notes that LaCapra 'rarely tells us which historians or what histories are guilty' of the 'sins' he so trenchantly criticizes. See also Anthony Pagden, 'Rethinking the Linguistic Turn: Current Anxieties in Intellectual History', *Journal of the History of Ideas*, Vol. 49 (1988), pp. 519–29.

38 LaCapra, *History and Criticism*, p. 42.

39 Alan Knight, reviewing Marjorie Becker, *Setting the Virgin on Fire. Lázaro Cárdenas, Michoacán peasants and the redemption of the Mexican revolution* (Berkeley, 1995), in *Times Literary Supplement*, 21 June 1996, p. 31

40 Note the wonderfully double-edged testimony on the cover of *Historical Culture* by Professor Mark Poster: 'No historian who reads and comprehends this book will ever write in the same way again.' See

Sande Cohen, *Historical Culture. On the Recoding of an Academic Discipline* (Berkeley, 1988).

41 Jacoby, 'A New Intellectual History?', pp. 413, 419.

42 Appleby, Hunt and Jacob, *Telling the Truth about History*, p. 229. See also Zagorin, 'Reconsiderations', p. 264, and the special *Beiheft* 19 (1980) of *History and Theory* devoted to White's *Metahistory: Six Critiques*.

43 Hayden White, *Metahistory: The Historical Imagination in Nineteenth-Century Europe* (Baltimore, 1973); White's subsequent work contains almost no references at all to history as it has been researched and written in the twentieth century. See also Stephen Bann, *The Clothing of Clio* (Cambridge, 1984); idem, *The Inventions of History: Essays on the Representations of the Past* (Manchester, 1990); Linda Orr, *Jules Michelet: Nature, History and Language* (Ithaca, 1990); eadem, *Headless History: Nineteenth-Century French Historiography of the Revolution* (on Michelet, Blanc, Quinet and Tocqueville); Ann Rigney, *The Rhetoric of Historical Representation* (Cambridge, 1990), also on nineteenth-century histories of the revolution; Frank Ankersmit, 'Tocqueville and the Sublimity of Democracy', *Tocqueville Review*, Vols. 14 (1993), pp. 173–201 and 15 (1994), pp. 193–218; L. Shiner, *The Secret Mirror: Literary Form and History in Tocqueville's Recollections* (Ithaca, New York, 1988).

44 Marwick, 'Two Approaches', p. 29.

45 Arthur Marwick, *Culture in Britain since 1945* (Oxford, 1991), p. 5.

46 Arthur Marwick, *Beauty in History: Society, Politics and Personal Appearance c. 1500 – the Present* (London, 1988), pp. 365, 47.

47 Arthur Marwick, *British Society since 1945* (London, 1982), pp. 63, 75.

48 Isaiah Berlin, *Historical Inevitability* (London, 1954), p. 5, n. 1. For a comparable view of the hybrid nature of history, see Michel de Certeau, *Heterologies: Discourse on the Other* (Manchester, 1980), pp. 199–224, and Bann, *The Clothing of Clio*, pp. 164–77.

49 Marc Bloch, *The Historian's Craft* (with a preface by Peter Burke, Manchester, 1992).

3: HISTORIANS AND THEIR FACTS

1 Elton, *Return*, pp. 27, 65.

2 ibid., p. 68.

3 Carr, *What is History?*, p. 12, echoed by Gareth Stedman Jones, 'History: the poverty of empiricism', in Robin Blackburn (ed.), *Ideology in Social Science* (London, 1972), p. 113.

4 See for example Anthony Easthope, 'Romancing the Stone: history-writing and rhetoric', *Social History*, Vol. 18 (1993), pp. 235–49, here p. 236; and Marwick, *The Nature of History*, pp. 194–6.

5 George Kitson Clark, *The Making of Victorian England* (Cambridge, 1962), pp. 61–2, citing Lord George Sanger, *Seventy Years a Showman* (2nd edn., London, 1926), pp. 188–9. Here the crowd is identified as a group of miners wearing iron-tipped clogs. For contemporary reports, see *Manchester Guardian*, 17 July 1850, p. 7, col. 3; 27 July 1850, p. 9, col. 6; *Manchester Examiner and Times*, 17 July 1850, p. 7, col. 6; 20 July 1850, p. 7, col. 3; *Manchester Courier and Lancashire General Advertiser*, 20 July 1850, p. 8, col. 1; 27 July 1850, p. 8, col. 2; *Manchester Spectator and Commercial Gazette*, 20 July 1850, p. 8, col. 3; 27 July 1850, p. 8, col. 4. In 1850 Stalybridge, which was in Lancashire (it is now in Cheshire), had no local newspaper of its own, nor did Ashton-under-Lyme, which was the nearest fair-sized town. The Manchester papers therefore carried Stalybridge news under the rubric 'Stalybridge' or 'Ashton-under-Lyme'. There were no reports of disturbances at the Wakes in 1851 or 1852 either, ruling out the possibility that Sanger had got the year wrong.

6 For a discussion of this general point, see Partner, 'Making Up Lost Time', p. 105.

7 White, 'Response', pp. 233–46.

8 ibid., p. 239.

9 Beverley Southgate, *History: What and Why? Ancient, Modern and Postmodern Perspectives* (London, 1996), pp. 26–7.

10 Partner, 'History in an Age of Reality-Fictions', here p. 23. For an elaboration of this kind of argument, see also Munslow, *Deconstructing History*.

11 Somekawa and Smith, 'Theorizing', p. 151.

12 LaCapra, *History and Criticism*, p. 11.

13 ibid., pp. 11, 17.

14 ibid., p. 38.

15 ibid., p. 47.

16 Partner, 'History in an Age of Reality-Fictions', p. 21.

17 Catriona Kelly, 'History and Post-Modernism', *Past and Present* 133 (November, 1991), pp. 209–13.

18 Stone, 'History and Post-Modernism II', pp. 189–90.

19 Raphael Samuel, 'Reading the Signs', *History Workshop Journal* 32 (1991), pp. 88–109, and 33 (1992), pp. 220–51; quote on p. 233.

20 Keith Thomas, *Religion and the Decline of Magic. Studies in Popular Beliefs in Sixteenth- and Seventeenth-Century England* (London, 1977).

21 E. P. Thompson, *The Making of the English Working Class* (London, 1963).

22 Emmanuel Le Roy Ladurie, *Montaillou. Village occitan de 1294 à 1324* (Paris, 1978).

23 Elton, *Return*, p. 55.

24 H. Stuart Hughes, 'Contemporary Historiography: Progress, Paradigms, and the Regression toward Positivism', in Gabriel Almond, Marvin Chodorow and Roy Harvey (eds.), *Progress and its Discontents* (Berkeley, 1982), p. 245.

25 William H. McNeill, 'Mythistory, or Truth, Myth, History, and Historians', *American Historical Review*, Vol. 91 (1986), pp. 8–9.

26 Elton, *Return*, p. 53.

27 Spitzer, *Historical Truth*, p. 61.

28 Richard J. Evans (ed.), *Kneipengespräche im Kaiserreich. Die Stimmungsberichte der Hamburger Politischen Polizei 1892–1914* (Reinbek, 1989).

29 Otto Brunner *et al.* (eds.), *Geschichtliche Grundbegriffe. Historisches Lexicon zur Politisch-Sozialen Sprache in Deutschland* (Stuttgart, 1972–94).

30 Jenkins, *Re-thinking*, pp. 40–1, and George Steiner, *After Babel* (Oxford, 1975), p. 18.

31 Carr, *What is History?*, p. 16.

32 Peter Burke, 'Overture: The New History', in idem (ed.), *New Perspectives on Historical Writing* (Oxford, 1991), pp. 1–23, here p. 5.

33 Somekawa and Smith, 'Theorizing', p. 153.

34 Carr, *What is History?*, p. 52.

35 Quoted in Kenyon, *The History Men*, pp. 8–9. See also Marwick, *The Nature of History*, pp. 198–200, including a discussion of the uncertain status of autobiography, which is an eyewitness account, but not contemporary with the events it attests.

36 See the useful summary account in David Lehman, *Signs of the Times. Deconstruction and the Fall of Paul de Man* (London, 1991), pp. 28–37,

106–9. Among voluminous writings, see Roland Barthes, *Image, Music, Text* (New York, 1977), and Jacques Derrida, *Of Grammatology* (Baltimore, 1976), *Writing and Difference* (Chicago, 1978), *Positions* (Chicago, 1981), and *Dissemination* (Chicago, 1983).

37 Stone, 'History and Post-Modernism II'. See also the same author's 'Dry Heat, Cool Reason: Historians under Siege in England and France', *Times Literary Supplement*, 31 January 1992.

38 Spiegel, 'History and Post-Modernism', p. 197, and eadem, 'History, Historicism, and the Social Logic of the Text in the Middle Ages', *Speculum*, Vol. 65 (1990), pp. 59–96.

39 Joyce, 'History and Post-Modernism', p. 208.

40 Hans Kellner, 'Introduction: Describing Redescriptions', in Frank Ankersmit and Hans Kellner (eds.), *A New Philosophy of History*, pp. 2–30, here p. 10.

41 Jenkins, *Re-thinking*, pp. 47–8.

42 ibid., p. 47.

43 Ankersmit, 'History and Post-Modernism', pp. 152, 144.

44 Jenkins, *Re-thinking*, p. 34.

45 Diane Purkiss, *The Witch in History*, pp. 2–4, 59–63.

46 White, *Metahistory*, pp. xi–xii, 5–7.

47 Somekawa and Smith, 'Theorizing', p. 50.

48 White, *The Content of the Form*, pp. 44–7.

4: SOURCES AND DISCOURSES

1 Harlan, 'Intellectual History', p. 585.

2 Paul Ricoeur, *Hermeneutics and the Human Sciences* (Cambridge, 1981), p. 146, quoted in Harlan, 'Intellectual History', p. 587. For Ricoeur's critique of White, see his *The Reality of the Historical Past* (Milwaukee, 1984), pp. 33–4.

3 LaCapra, *Rethinking Intellectual History*, pp. 34–6, 40.

4 Quoted in Roy Porter, *Gibbon: Making History* (London, 1988), p. 163.

5 Appleby, Hunt and Jacob, *Telling the Truth*, pp. 245–6.

6 Quoted in Porter, *Gibbon*, p. 163.

7 Southgate, *History*, p. 8.

8 Joyce, 'History and Post-Modernism', p. 208.

9 Patrick Joyce, *Visions of the People: Industrial England and the Question of Class, 1848–1914* (Cambridge, 1991), pp. 17, 330, 338, quoted in Spiegel, 'History and Post-Modernism', p. 202.

10 Joyce, *Visions*, p. 338, quoted in Joyce, 'The imaginary discontents of social history', p. 81. Joyce subsequently came to criticize his own book's 'nostalgia for collective social subjects and bedrock "experience"' and to adopt a more hard-line version of discursive determinism: see Patrick Joyce, *Democratic Subjects. The Self and the Social in Nineteenth-Century England* (Cambridge, 1994), pp. 11–12. See also Joan W. Scott, 'The evidence of experience', *Critical Inquiry*, Vol. 17 (1991), pp. 773–97, and David Mayfield and Susan Thorne, 'Reply to "The poverty of protest" and "The imaginary discontents"', p. 221.

11 Jenkins, *Re-thinking*, p. 42. However, in recent years the use of original documents in transcript or excerpt has become more important in history teaching at all levels, a development that is very welcome.

12 Hayden White, 'New Historicism: A Comment', in H. A. Veeser (ed.), *The New Historicism* (London, 1989), pp. 293–302, here p. 297. But when White describes the phrase 'history is a text' as a metaphor here, he clearly means history as a written representation of the past, not the past itself; the issue of whether or not the representation can be true is entirely separate.

13 Spiegel, 'History, Historicism, and the Social Logic of the Text in the Middle Ages', p. 76.

14 Spiegel, 'History and Post-Modernism', p. 207, n. 31.

15 Vincent, *Intelligent Person's Guide*, p. 8. Vincent has himself been critical of 'documentary fetishism', however. He cites with approval A. J. P. Taylor's belief that no new secrets were to be found in unpublished archival sources. Vincent himself advocates paying greater attention than is customary to the newspapers, and declares that newsprint is 'the Venetian archive of tomorrow'. Yet Taylor's reluctance to use manuscript sources and his excessive reliance on printed material was in fact one of his greatest weaknesses as a historian; while Vincent's partiality to newspapers as unbiased sources of information may possibly be coloured by the fact that he himself wrote a column in the *Sun* for a number of years, until student demonstrations at his own university forced him to abandon it – an

event which, however deplorable in itself, would scarcely have taken place had the column been a model of impartiality (Vincent, *Intelligent Person's Guide*, pp. 9–10).

16 Mark Monmonier, *How to Lie with Maps* (Chicago, 1991).

17 Jenkins, *On 'What is History?'*, p. 30.

18 Hayden White, 'The Problem of Change in Literary History', *New Literary History*, Vol. 7 (1975), p. 109.

19 Zagorin, 'Reconsiderations', p. 171.

20 Henry VIII to Ann Boleyn, Letter No. 2, in C. H. Williams (ed.), *English Historical Documents 1785–1558* (London, 1971), p. 700.

21 Spiegel, 'History and Post-Modernism', p. 195.

22 Jenkins, *Re-thinking*, p. 19.

23 Appleby, Hunt and Jacob, *Telling the Truth*, pp. 254–6. For the same view, see Somekawa and Smith, 'Theorizing', pp. 156–7.

24 Henry Abelove *et al.* (eds.), *Visions of History* (New York, 1978), p. 14.

25 Richard J. Evans, 'From Hitler to Bismarck: Third Reich and *Kaiserreich* in Recent Historiography', *Historical Journal*, Vol. 26 (1983), pp. 485–97 and 999–1020, reprinted in idem, *Rethinking German History: Nineteenth-Century Germany and the Origins of the Third Reich* (London, 1987), pp. 55–92, here pp. 77–9.

26 Henry Ashby Turner, review of Abraham in *Political Science Quarterly*, Vol. 97 (1982–30), pp. 739–41, and letter in the *American Historical Review*, Vol. 88 (1983), pp. 1143–9, with Abraham's response.

27 This mass of material finally emerged into print in a controversy between Feldman and Abraham in *Central European History*, Vol. 17 (1984), pp. 159–293, where Abraham in particular paraded many of the behind-the-scenes manoeuvres of the previous two years before the readership, somewhat to the embarrassment of the journal's editor.

28 White, *Metahistory*, p. 284.

29 Tim Mason, letter in the *American Historical Review*, Vol. 88 (1983), p. 1146.

30 Gerald D. Feldman, 'A Collapse in Weimar Scholarship', *Central European History*, Vol. 17 (1984), pp. 159–77, here p. 176. See also Ulrich Nocken, 'Weimarer Geschichte(n)', *Vierteljahrschrift für Sozial- undWirtschaftsgeschichte*, Vol. 71 (1984), pp. 505–27, which, however, lists a large number of trivial errors and fails to distinguish them satisfactorily from the major ones which caused the controversy.

31 David Abraham, *The Collapse of the Weimar Republic* (2nd edn., New York, 1986). This edition still contains numerous errors, however, because Abraham was unable to go back to the archives in Communist East Germany where he had gathered a substantial amount of documents and so repeats the mistakes made in his original transcriptions and notes on them.

32 Feldman, 'A Collapse', p. 165.

33 David Abraham, 'A Reply to Gerald Feldman', *Central European History*, Vol. 17 (1984), pp. 178–245, here p. 184.

34 Feldman, 'A Collapse', p. 169.

35 Abraham, 'A Reply', p. 186.

36 Hexter, *On Historians*, pp. 243, 250–1, quoting Christopher Hill, *Intellectual Origins of the English Revolution* (Oxford, 1965), p. vii. However, Hexter was arguably doing the same in combing Hill's work for evidence in favour of his own critique of it. Hexter criticized Hill for 'lumping' diverse historical groups together into a small number of crudely over-simplified categories, but then 'lumped' all historians into the two even cruder categories of 'lumpers' like Hill supposedly was, and 'splitters' like himself, who had an allegedly more differentiated and therefore more accurate view of the past. For these points, see William G. Palmer, 'The Burden of Proof: J. H. Hexter and Christopher Hill', *Journal of British Studies*, Vol. 19 (1979), pp. 121–9.

37 Novick, *That Noble Dream*, pp. 612–21; Novick was honest enough to admit that Abraham 'was my student, and is my good friend' and that, therefore, by implication, his own account of the affair was inevitably partisan.

38 Quoted in Novick, *That Noble Dream*, p. 620.

39 Lawrence Stone, 'The Anatomy of the Elizabethan Aristocracy', *Economic History Review*, Vol. 18 (1948), pp. 1–53; Hugh Trevor-Roper, 'The Elizabethan Aristocracy: An Anatomy Anatomized', *Economic History Review*, 2nd series, Vol. 3 (1951), pp. 279–98; Lawrence Stone, 'The Elizabethan Aristocracy – A Restatement', *Economic History Review*, 2nd series, Vol. 4 (1952), pp. 302–21; J. P. Cooper, 'The Counting of Manors', *Economic History Review*, 2nd series, Vol. 8 (1956), pp. 377–89; J. H. Hexter, *Reappraisals in History* (London, 1961), pp. 117–62 ('Storm over the Gentry'), esp. p. 138; Kenyon, *The History Men*, p. 258.

40 Hayden White, 'Historical Emplotment and the Problem of Truth', in Saul Friedländer (ed.), *Probing the Limits of Representation: Nazism and the "Final Solution"* (Cambridge, Mass., 1992), pp. 37–53. White's citation of a comic-book version of Auschwitz, Art Spiegelman's *Maus: A Survivor's Tale* (2 vols., London 1989–91), in which the characters are portrayed as various types of animal, does not amount to a statement that Auschwitz can be emplotted as a comedy: Spiegelman's comic strip is undeniably cast in the tragic mode.

41 White, 'Response', p. 241.

42 Jacoby, 'A New Intellectual History?' p. 418.

43 Stone, 'History and Post-Modernism', p. 190.

44 Jenkins, *Re-thinking*, p. 15.

45 ibid., p. 32.

46 Somekawa and Smith, 'Theorizing', p. 153.

5: CAUSATION IN HISTORY

1 E. H. Carr, *What is History?*, p. 87.

2 ibid., pp. 86–104.

3 ibid., pp. 104–5.

4 Appleby, Hunt and Jacob, *Telling the Truth*, p. 304.

5 A. J. P. Taylor, *War by Timetable* (London, 1976).

6 Idem, *A Personal History* (London, 1985).

7 The spelling *antisemitism* is used throughout this book in preference to the conventional *anti-Semitism*. The latter is itself an antisemitic formulation; there was, and is, no such thing as 'Semitism', except in the minds of antisemites.

8 Carr, *What is History?*, p. 108.

9 ibid., p. 120.

10 Martin, 'Objectivity and Meaning ', pp. 48–9.

11 Megill, 'Recounting the Past', p. 627.

12 Geoffrey Barraclough, *History and the Common Man* (London, 1967), pp. 3–15.

13 Vincent, *Intelligent Person's Guide*, pp. 45–9.

14 Zeldin, 'Social History and Total History', p. 243. The word 'links' is misquoted, amusingly, and no doubt due to mere carelessness, by

Gertrude Himmelfarb as 'lines' in her book *On Looking into the Abyss: Untimely Thoughts on Culture and Society* (New York, 1995), p. 138.

15 Zeldin, 'Social History and Total History', p. 243.

16 Theodore Zeldin, *France 1848–1945*, Vol. I: *Ambition, Love and Politics* (Oxford, 1973), Vol. II: *Intellect, Taste and Anxiety* (Oxford, 1977).

17 Christopher Lloyd, 'For Realism and Against the Inadequacies of Common Sense: A Response to Arthur Marwick', *Journal of Contemporary History*, Vol. 31 (1996), pp. 191–207, here p. 192.

18 Hayden White, 'The Burden of History', in idem, *Tropics of Discourse* (Baltimore, 1978), pp. 27–50; see also Hans Kellner, 'White's Linguistic Humanism', *History and Theory*, Supplement 19 (1980), pp. 1–29. It is just worth noting that White's work, above all in *Metahistory*, is clearly structuralist rather than post-structuralist, in other words modernist rather than postmodernist. However, many of his ideas have been taken up with enthusiasm by postmodernists, so that while the structuralist aspects of his approach were a dead end, their relativist implications for history were not.

19 White, 'The Politics of Historical Interpretation: Discipline and Sublimation', in idem, *The Content of the Form*, pp. 58–82.

20 Hayden White, *Metahistory*, pp. xi–xii.

21 Jenkins, *Re-thinking*, pp. 32–3.

22 Frank Ankersmit, *History and Tropology: The Rise and Fall of Metaphor* (Berkeley, 1994), pp. 33–4.

23 Rosenau, *Post-Modernism*, pp. 67–8.

24 Elizabeth Deeds Ermarth, *Sequel to History: Postmodernism and the Crisis of Historical Time* (Princeton, 1992), pp. 22, 212; Appleby, Hunt and Jacob, *Telling the Truth*, pp. 205, 211, 235; see also Robert Young, *White Mythologies: Writing History and the West* (London, 1990), where history *tout court* is seen as 'colonialist'.

25 David Carr, review of Ermarth, *Sequel to History*, in *History and Theory*, Vol. 32 (1993), pp. 179–87, here pp. xi, 14, 29, 25.

26 ibid., p. 184, here p. 191.

27 White, *The Content of the Form*, p. 27.

28 LaCapra, *History and Criticism*, p. 119.

29 Possibly LaCapra has only consulted the English abridgement of the book, from which most of the anthropological analysis of the original French edition has been omitted.

30 Richard J. Evans, *Death in Hamburg. Society and Politics in the Cholera Years 1830–1910* (Oxford, 1987).

31 Hayden White, *Tropics of Discourse* (Baltimore, 1978), p. 50.

32 Richard Hofstadter, *The Progressive Historians: Turner, Beard, Parrington* (New York, 1968), pp. 463–6.

33 Sande Cohen, *Historical Culture. On the Recoding of an Academic Discipline* (Berkeley, 1986), pp. 19–21, 171, 174, 228, 326.

34 See Geoff Bennington, *Lyotard: Writing the Event* (Manchester, 1988); and Jean-François Lyotard, *Dérive à partir de Marx et Freud* (Paris, 1973), and *Instructions païennes* (Paris, 1977).

35 Jean-François Lyotard, *The Postmodern Condition: A Report on Knowledge* (Minneapolis, 1984), pp. xxiii–xxiv.

36 Elton, *Return*, p. 44.

37 ibid., p. 45.

38 Zeldin, 'Social History and Total History', p. 245.

39 Namier, *Structure*; Eugene D. Genovese, *Roll, Jordan, Roll: The World the Slaves Made* (New York, 1974); Hans-Ulrich Wehler, *Das Deutsche Kaiserreich 1871–1918* (Göttingen, 1973).

40 F. W. Maitland, *Domesday Book and Beyond. Three Essays in the Early History of England* (Cambridge, 1897); Hellmut Diwald, *Geschichte der Deutschen* (Frankfurt am Main, 1978).

41 Quoted in Peter Burke, 'Preface' to Marc Bloch, *The Historian's Craft* (Manchester, 1992), p. xvi.

42 For an example of this ignorance, see Somekawa and Smith, 'Theorizing', pp. 155–6.

43 Southgate, *History*, p. 114.

44 Quoted in Peter Burke, *The French Historical Revolution. The Annales School 1929–1989* (Oxford, 1990), p. 39.

45 ibid., p. 35.

46 Fernand Braudel, *The Mediterranean and the Mediterranean World in the Age of Philip II* (2 vols., London, 1972–73). Sceptically inclined post-modernist critics have labelled Braudel's *The Mediterranean* as 'narrative history' anyway because the view that it is not depends on a simplistic understanding of narrative as a description of events sequential in time, whereas a more sophisticated view would have it combining action, happening, character and setting, and of the last-named, there certainly is plenty in Braudel's great work. But while it is at least welcome that someone has actually sought to define

narrative instead of simply assuming we all know what it is, this definition is really far too all-encompassing to be really useful, and flies in
the face not only of common usage among historians but also of the
concept employed by Braudel himself, namely '*histoire évenementielle*',
an event-based history.

47 Jean Delumeau, *La peur en Occident (XIVe − XVIIIe siècles), une cité assiegée*
(Paris, 1978); *La péché et la peur. La culpabilisation en Occident (XIIIe −
XVIIIe siècles)* (Paris, 1983).

48 Confusingly, perhaps, Ermarth dates the beginnings of postmodernism
to the beginning of the twentieth century, thus excluding modernist
art, music and architecture from the modern.

49 Kenyon, *The History Men*, pp. 195–6.

50 Zagorin, 'Reconsiderations', pp. 269–70.

51 Kirk, 'History, language, ideas', *Social History*, p. 227.

52 Appleby, Hunt and Jacob, *Telling the Truth*, pp. 223–5.

6: SOCIETY AND THE INDIVIDUAL

1 Joan W. Scott ticks off unnamed American colleagues for ascribing it
to Herbert Baxter Adams, only to ascribe it wrongly herself to
Edward Freeman (Joan Wallach Scott, 'History in Crisis? The Other
Side of the Story', *American Historical Review*, Vol. 94 (1989), pp.
680–92, here p. 680). For the correct attribution, in Seeley's *The
Growth of British Policy* (London, 1895), see the *Oxford Dictionary of
Quotations* (3rd edn., Oxford, 1979), p. 419.

2 Gertrude Himmelfarb, 'Some Reflections on the New History',
American Historical Review, Vol. 94 (1989), pp. 661–70, here p. 663.

3 Quoted in Richard Cobb, *The Police and the People* (Oxford, 1970), p.
81.

4 Mehta, *Fly and the Fly-Bottle*, pp. 187–9.

5 Cannadine, *G. M. Trevelyan*.

6 See Lawrence W. Levine, 'The Unpredictable Past: Reflections on
Recent American Historiography', *American Historical Review*, Vol. 94
(1989), pp. 671–9, here p. 674.

7 He subsequently brought it out with another publisher, defiantly reti-
tled *An Intelligent Person's Guide to History* (London, 1995).

8 Carr, *What is History?*, p. 149.

9 Vincent, *Intelligent Person's Guide*, pp. 1–8.

10 E. P. Thompson, *The Making of the English Working Class*, p. 12.

11 G. M. Trevelyan, *English Social History* (revised edn., London, 1978).

12 Quoted in Kenyon, *The History Men*, p. 167.

13 Eric Hobsbawm, 'From Social History to the History of Society', *Daedalus*, No. 100 (1971), pp. 20–45.

14 Appleby, Hunt and Jacob, *Telling the Truth*, pp. 202, 216.

15 Peter N. Stearns, 'Coming of Age', *Journal of Social History*, Vol. 10 (1976), pp. 246–55. This article is also notable for the unintentionally hilarious consequences of the author's confusion of Lord Acton the historian with Dr William Acton the Victorian expert on prostitution and female sexuality (p. 249).

16 John Breuilly, 'What is Social History?', in Juliet Gardiner (ed.), *What is History Today?* (London, 1988), pp. 49–51, here p. 51.

17 Geoff Eley, 'Some Recent Tendencies in Social History', in Georg G. Iggers and Harold T. Parker (eds.), *International Handbook of Historical Studies* (London, 1980), pp. 55–70.

18 Ankersmit, *History and Tropology*, p. 175.

19 Zeldin, 'Social History and Total History', pp. 240, 242.

20 Jon Lawrence and Miles Taylor, 'The poverty of protest: Gareth Stedman Jones and the politics of language – a reply', *Social History*, Vol. 18 (1993), pp. 1–15, here p. 12.

21 Gardiner (ed.), *What is History Today?*, pp. 1–2.

22 Carr, *What is History?*, p. 15.

23 Zagorin, 'Reconsiderations', p. 273.

24 Laurence Veysey, quoted in Novick, *That Noble Dream*, p. 592.

25 See Jim Sharpe, 'History from Below', in Peter Burke (ed.), *New Perspectives on Historical Writing* (Oxford, 1991), pp. 24–41, here p. 37.

26 Thomas Nipperdey, *Deutsche Geschichte 1800–1866: Bürgerwelt und starker Staat* (Munich, 1983); *Deutsche Geschichte 1866–1918*, I: *Arbeitswelt und Bürgergeist* (Munich, 1990); II: *Machtstaat vor der Demokratie* (Munich, 1992); Hans-Ulrich Wehler, *Deutsche Gesellschaftsgeschichte*, I: *Vom Feudalismus des Alten Reiches bis zur Defensiven Modernisierung der Reformära 1700–1815* (Munich, 1987); II: *Von der Reformära bis zur industriellen und politischen 'Deutschen Doppelrevolution' 1815–1845/49* (Munich, 1987); III: *Von der 'Deutschen Doppelrevolution' bis zum Beginn des Ersten Weltkrieges 1849–1914*

(Munich, 1995). Philippe Ariès and Georges Duby (eds.), *A History of Private Life* (5 vols., Cambridge, Mass., 1989–92); Georges Duby and Michelle Perrot (eds.), *A History of Women in the West* (5 vols., Cambridge, Mass., 1993–5).

27 Mark Kishlansky, *A Monarchy Transformed: Britain 1603–1714* (London, 1996); Peter Clarke, *Hope and Glory: Britain 1900–1990* (London, 1996), both volumes in the *Penguin History of Britain*, edited by David Cannadine; the publisher's claim is taken from the dust-jacket.

28 Norman Davies, *Europe: A History* (Oxford, 1996); a book whose imaginative sweep is seriously compromised by its factual inaccuracy.

29 Novick, *That Noble Dream*, p. 628.

30 Vincent, *Intelligent Person's Guide* , p. 103.

31 ibid., p. 107.

32 Hugh Trevor-Roper, *The Rise of Christian Europe* (London, 1965), p. 9.

33 ibid., p. 104. 'We' presumably means the British historians and history students to whom Vincent is addressing his book.

34 Kenyon, *The History Men*, pp. 297, viii.

35 Carr, *What is History?* , pp. 150–2.

36 Elton, *Return*, pp. 101–26.

37 Juliet Gardner (ed.), *The History Debate* (London, 1990).

38 Elie Halévy, *A History of the English People in the Nineteenth Century* (5 vols., London, 1924–32); François Bédarida, *A Social History of England, 1851–1975* (London, 1979).

39 See for example note 26 above; or Philippe Ariès, *The Hour of Our Death* (London, 1971).

40 Jonathan D. Spence, *The Search for Modern China* (New York, 1990).

41 See Lawrence W. Levine, 'The Unpredictable Past: Reflections on Recent American Historiography', *American Historical Review*, Vol. 94 (1989), pp. 671–9, here p. 674.

42 David Mayfield and Susan Thorne, 'Social history and its discontents: Gareth Stedman Jones and the politics of language', *Social History*, Vol. 17 (1992), pp. 165–88, here pp. 165–7.

43 Mayfield and Thorne, 'Social history', p. 179.

44 Eley and Nield, 'Starting over: the present, the post-modern and the moment of social history', pp. 355–64.

45 David Carr, review of Ermarth, *Sequel to History*, p. 185, here pp. 56, 60, 62, 147, 177.

46 Wendy Lesser, *Pictures at an Execution. An Enquiry into the Subject of Murder* (Cambridge, Mass., 1994).

47 Lest this be thought unfair, it may be noted that Joyce, *Democratic Subjects*, pp. 12–15, explicitly embraces a linguistic determinism in which society, poverty and so on are determined by language, culture and imagination, not by experience; or in other words, people are not really poor, they only imagine they are.

48 Carr, *What is History?* , p. 34.

49 J. Arch Getty, *Origins of the Great Purges. The Soviet Communist Party Reconsidered, 1933–1938* (Cambridge, 1985).

50 E. H. Carr, *Socialism in One Country*, Vol. I (London, 1958), p. 151.

51 Carr, *What is History?*, pp. 169–70.

52 Carlo Ginzburg, *The Cheese and the Worms: The Cosmos of a Sixteenth-Century Miller* (Baltimore, 1980). More generally, see Edward Muir and Guido Ruggiero (eds), *Microhistory and the Lost Peoples of Europe* (Baltimore, 1991).

53 For a particularly crass example of this kind of approach, see Robert Conquest, *Stalin: Breaker of Nations* (London, 1991).

7: KNOWLEDGE AND POWER

1 Brenda Marshall, *Teaching the Postmodern* (London, 1992), p. 4.

2 Carr, *What is History?*, p. 26.

3 Elton, *Return to Essentials*, p. 8.

4 Braudel, *The Mediterranean*, Vol. I, pp. 19–21 and Vol. II, pp. 32, 67, 71; idem, *The Identity of France*, Vol. I (London, 1988), pp. 15, 19–21.

5 Pierre Chaunu, 'Le fils de la morte', in Pierre Nora (ed.), *Essais d'ego-histoire* (Paris, 1987), pp. 61–107, here p. 93.

6 Quoted in Kenyon, *The History Men*, p. 223.

7 Lawrence Stone, *The Past and the Present* (London, 1981), pp. 109–11.

8 Sheila Rowbotham, *Hidden from History: 300 Years of Women's Oppression and the Fight Against It* (London, 1973); Renate Bridenthal and Claudia Koonz (eds), *Becoming Visible: Women in European History* (Boston, 1977).

9 For this general point, see Vernon, 'Who's afraid of the "linguistic turn"?', p. 83, n. 8.

10 For this argument, see Mayfield and Thorne, 'Social history', p. 173.

11 Michel Foucault, *Language, Counter-Memory, Practice: Selected Essays and Interviews,* transl. Donald F. Bouchard and Sherry Simon (Ithaca, New York, 1977), p. 153.

12 Purkiss, *The Witch in History*, pp. 1–4, 59.

13 Rudy Koshar, 'Playing the Cerebral Savage: Notes on Writing German History before the Linguistic Turn', *Central European History*, Vol. 22 (1989), pp. 343–59.

14 Newton to Robert Hooke, 5 February 1675/6 (*Oxford Dictionary of Quotations* (3rd edn., Oxford, 1979)), p. 362.

15 See the note on 'postmodernism's replication of the eternally recurring pretension of absolute originality characteristic of intellectual debate since the Enlightenment' in William Reddy, 'Postmodernism and the public sphere: implications for an historical ethnography', *Cultural Anthropology*, Vol. 7 (1992), pp. 135–68.

16 Peter N. Stearns, 'Some Comments on Social History', *Journal of Social History*, Vol. 1 (1967), pp. 3–6.

17 Stearns, 'Coming of Age', pp. 246–55. What can happen to a newly created sub-discipline over the long term is shown by the case of economic history, which emerged in the 1880s. The first university chair in the subject was created in 1892, at Harvard. In Britain, the Economic History Society was founded in 1926, and by 1975 its membership had reached 2,500. But in the mid-1980s the economic historian Martin Daunton declared that while separate departments of economic history had originally emerged in order to escape from the narrow concentration on high political and diplomatic history which had characterized mainstream history departments in the earlier part of the century, 'a separate identity is no longer required to protect a neglected area of enquiry and, on the contrary, it is now departments of economic history which have become introverted and narrow.' By 1993, the membership of the British Economic History Society had declined to 1,750. The next year, the Economic History Section of the British Academy was abolished and its members migrated either to the Economics Section or to one or other of the various History Sections. In their 1996 Research Assessment Exercise, the Higher Education Funding Councils rolled-up history and economic history into a single Unit of Assessment, in contrast to their previous practice. All these were signs of the demise of economic history as a

separate discipline a mere century or so after its original emergence. See M. J. Daunton, 'What is Economic History?', in Gardiner (ed.), *What is History Today?*, pp. 37–8, and Vincent, *Intelligent Person's Guide*, p. 97.

18 George Melly, *Revolt into Style. The Pop Arts in Britain* (London, 1970).

19 Jenkins, *Re-thinking*, p. 19.

20 ibid., pp. 20–1.

21 Southgate, *History*, p. 24.

22 ibid., p. 8.

23 Somekawa and Smith, 'Theorizing', p. 157.

24 Tony Bennett, *Outside Literature* (London, 1991), pp. 16–30.

25 Wulf Kansteiner, 'Searching for an Audience: The Historical Profession in the Media Age – A Comment on Arthur Marwick and Hayden White', *Journal of Contemporary History*, Vol. 31 (1996), pp. 215–19.

26 Jenkins, *On 'What is History?'*, p. 22.

27 E. P. Thompson, *Warwick University Limited. Industry, Management and the Universities* (Harmondsworth, 1970); idem, *The Making of the English Working Class*. Thompson was only elected a Fellow of the British Academy, an accolade accorded to many historians much his junior in age and reputation, near the end of his life.

28 Penry Williams and G. L. Harriss, 'A Revolution in Tudor History?', *Past and Present* 25 (1963), pp. 3–58.

29 G. R. Elton, *The Tudor Revolution in Government: Administrative Changes in the Reign of Henry VII* (Cambridge, 1953); Stone, *The Past and the Present*, p. 107. Elton's pupils and admirers sometimes take a different view: see the largely uncritical account by Kenyon, *The History Men*, pp. 219–24.

30 Vincent, *Intelligent Person's Guide* , p. 53.

31 ibid., pp. 52, 54.

32 John Vincent, *The Formation of the Victorian Liberal Party 1857–1868* (London, 1966).

33 Laura Lee Downs, 'If "Woman" is Just an Empty Category, Then Why Am I Afraid to Walk Alone at Night? Identity Politics Meets the Postmodern Subject', *Comparative Studies in Society and History*, Vol. 35 (1993), pp. 414–37, here p. 416.

34 Vincent, *Intelligent Person's Guide*, pp. 12, 15.

35 ibid., pp. 40–2.

36 Southgate, *History*, p. 116.

37 Carl Bridenbaugh, 'The Great Mutation', *American Historical Review*, Vol. 68 (1963), pp 322–3.

38 Fernand Braudel, *The Identity of France*, Vol. I, pp. 15, 19–21.

39 J. F. C. Fuller, *The Decisive Battles of the Western World, and their Influence upon History* (3 vols., London, 1954–6); idem, *The Conduct of War, 1789–1961. A Study of the Impact of the French, Industrial and Russian Revolutions on War and its Conduct* (London, 1961).

40 Paul Boghossian, 'What the Sokal hoax ought to teach us: the pernicious consequences and internal contradictions of "postmodernist" relativism', *Times Literary Supplement*, 13 December 1996, pp. 14–15.

41 Joanna Bourke, *Dismembering the Male. Men's Bodies, Britain and the Great War* (London, 1996); Ute Frevert, *Ehrenmänner. Das Duell in der bürgerlichen Gesellschaft* (Munich, 1991).

42 Andreas Hillgruber, *Zweierlei Untergang. Die Zerschlagung des Deutschen Reiches und das Ende des europäischen Judentums* (Berlin, 1986).

43 ibid., pp. 414–15.

44 ibid., pp. 423–4.

45 Joan Scott, '"The Tip of the Volcano"', *Comparative Studies in Society and History*, Vol. 35 (1993), pp. 438–43; see also Laura Lee Downs, 'Reply to Joan Scott', *Comparative Studies in Society and History*, Vol. 35 (1993), pp. 444–51.

46 Ragnhild Hatton, *George I, Elector and King* (London, 1978); Olive Anderson, *Suicide in Victorian and Edwardian England* (Oxford, 1987); Annie Kriegel, *Aux Origines du Communisme Français 1914–1920* (2 vols., Paris, 1964). These are three more or less arbitrarily chosen examples from a list that could be extended almost indefinitely.

47 Purkiss, *The Witch in History*, pp. 66–8.

48 Southgate, *History*, p. 9.

49 Ann Wordsworth, 'Derrida and Foucault: Writing the History of Historicity', in D. Attridge *et al.* (eds), *Post-structuralism and the Question of History* (Cambridge, 1987), p. 116.

50 Somekawa and Smith, 'Theorizing', p. 154.

51 ibid., p. 153.

52 Boghossian, 'What the Sokal hoax ought to teach us', p. 15.

53 Martin Bernal, *Black Athena* (2 vols., London, 1987 and 1991); Mary R. Lefkowitz and Guy Mclean Rogers (eds), *Black Athena Revisited*

(Chapel Hill, 1996); and Mary R. Lefkowitz, *Not Out of Africa* (New York, 1996).

54 John Boswell, *Christianity, Social Tolerance, and Homosexuality. Gay People in Western Europe from the Beginning of the Christian Era to the 19th Century* (Chicago, 1980); idem, *The Marriage of Likeness. Same-Sex Unions in Pre-Modern Europe* (New York, 1994); Jeffrey Weeks, *Sex, Politics and Society. The Regulation of Sexuality since 1800* (London, 1981), esp. ch. 6; Richard Davenport-Hines, *Sex, Death and Punishment. Attitudes to Sex and Sexuality in Britain since the Renaissance* (London, 1990).

8: OBJECTIVITY AND ITS LIMITS

1 Carr, *What is History?*, p. 30.

2 ibid., ch. 5.

3 Carr, *What is History?*, p. 6.

4 E. H. Carr, *The Bolshevik Revolution*, Vol. I (London, 1950), pp. 5–6.

5 Quoted in Mehta, *Fly and the Fly-Bottle*, p. 117.

6 H. R. Trevor-Roper, reviewing *What is History?* in *Encounter*, quoted in Mehta, *Fly and the Fly-Bottle*, p. 117.

7 E. H. Carr, *Michael Bakunin* (London, 1937); idem, *The Romantic Exiles. A Nineteenth-Century Portrait Gallery* (London, 1933).

8 Francis Fukuyama, *The End of History and the Last Man* (London, 1992).

9 It is on grounds such as these that Carr's work on Soviet history can legitimately be criticized, rather than on the supposed personal failings catalogued in Norman Stone's vitriolic attack on Carr in 1983 ('Grim Eminence', p. 982).

10 Elton, *Practice*, pp. 4–7.

11 Thus Appleby, Hunt and Jacob, *Telling the Truth*; Jenkins, *Re-thinking*; Southgate, *History*; and many others.

12 For a readable and intelligent account of de Man's career, see Lehman, *Signs of the Times*. Virtually all the relevant material by and about de Man is usefully collected in Werner Hamacher, Neil Hertz and Thomas Keenan (eds), *Responses: On Paul de Man's Wartime Journalism* (Lincoln, Nebraska, 1989) and the same editors' *Wartime Journalism 1939–1943, by Paul de Man* (Lincoln, Nebraska, 1988).

13 Cited in Lehman, *Signs of the Times*, p. 209.

14 Richard Rorty, 'Taking Philosophy Seriously', *The New Republic*, 11 April 1988, quoted in Lehman, *Signs of the Times*, p. 229.

15 J. Hillis Miller, 'An Open Letter to Professor Jon Wiener', in Hamacher *et al.* (eds), *Responses*, p. 342.

16 As pointed out by Alan B. Spitzer, *Historical Truth and Lies about the Past* (Chapel Hill, 1996), pp. 68–71, here quoting Hillis Miller, who elsewhere had stated that every interpretation of everything was always necessarily false (see Rosenau, *Post-Modernism*, p. 119).

17 All cited in Lehman, *Signs of the Times*, pp. 214, 216, 323–9.

18 Spitzer, *Historical Truth*, p. 11.

19 James T. Kloppenberg, 'Objectivity and Historicism: A Century of American Historical Writing', *American Historical Review*, Vol. 94 (1989), p. 1030.

20 Paul Morrison, 'Paul de Man: Resistance and Collaboration', *Representations*, Vol. 32 (1990), p. 71, quoted in Spitzer, *Historical Truth*, p. 94.

21 Dominick LaCapra, 'The Personal, The Political and the Textual: Paul de Man as Object of Transference', *History and Memory*, Vol. 4 (1992), p. 30, in an article devoted mainly to an utterly implausible psycho-analytical account of the behaviour of Derrida and other defenders of de Man.

22 Spitzer, *Historical Truth*, pp. 95–6.

23 Christopher Norris, *Deconstruction and the Interests of Theory* (Norman, Oklahoma, 1989), p. 16.

24 White, *The Content of the Form*, pp. 78–80.

25 Deborah E. Lipstadt, *Denying the Holocaust. The Growing Assault on Truth and Memory* (New York, 1993), p. 1.

26 The *Duke Chronicle,* justifying a decision to print an advertisement by Holocaust deniers, quoted in Lipstadt, *Denying the Holocaust,* p. 198.

27 Cited in Lipstadt, *Denying the Holocaust,* p. 198.

28 ibid., pp. 3, 137–56, 183–208.

29 ibid., pp. 19–20.

30 Jane Caplan, 'Postmodernism, Poststructuralism, and Deconstruction: Notes for Historians', *Central European History*, Vol. 22 (1989), pp. 274, 278. In quoting these passages, Gertrude Himmelfarb, *On Looking Into the Abyss*, p. 143, convicts Caplan of being unable to decide these issues. But the questions are clearly rhetorical.

31 Appleby, Hunt and Jacob, *Telling the Truth*, p. 236.

32 See the useful distinctions made in Pauline Marie Rosenau, *Post-Modernism and the Social Sciences*.

33 Simon Schama, *Citizens: A Chronicle of the French Revolution* (New York, 1989).

34 Orland Figes, *A People's Tragedy: The Russian Revolution 1891–1921* (London, 1996).

35 Natalie Zemon Davis, *The Return of Martin Guerre* (Cambridge, Mass., 1983).

36 Robert Darnton, *The Great Cat Massacre* (London, 1983).

37 Robert Finlay, 'The Refashioning of Martin Guerre', *American Historical Review*, Vol. 93 (1988), pp. 553–71; see also Natalie Zemon Davis, 'On the Lame', ibid., pp. 572–603.

38 Harold Mah, 'Suppressing the Text: The Metaphysics of Ethnographic History in Darnton's Great Cat Massacre', *History Workshop Journal*, 31 (1991), pp. 1–20.

39 Elton, *Return*, p. 43.

40 R. W. Davies, *Soviet History in the Gorbachev Revolution* (London, 1989); Gerd Meyer (ed.), *Wir brauchen die Wahrheit. Geschichtsdiskussion in der Sowjetunion* (2nd edn., Cologne, 1989).

41 Quoted in Cannadine, *G. M. Trevelyan*, pp. 75, 196.

42 Novick, *That Noble Dream*, p. 6.

43 Thomas L. Haskell, 'Objectivity is not Neutrality: Rhetoric and Practice in Peter Novick's *That Noble Dream*', *History and Theory*, Vol. 29 (1990), pp. 129–57; quotations on p. 132.

44 Novick, *That Noble Dream*, pp. 1–2.

45 Haskell, 'Objectivity', p. 141.

AFTERWORD

1 The reviews and comments considered in the Afterword are as follows: Michael Burleigh, 'Making History or Making-up History?', *Sunday Telegraph*, 14 September 1997, review section, p. 13; Roy Porter, 'Defending History', BBC Radio 3 *Book of the Week*, 15 September 1997; Bernard Crick, 'The Truth, the Whole Truth – and Nothing But', *Independent* Saturday Magazine, 20 September 1997, p. 14; Niall Ferguson, 'History is Dead. Long Live History!', *Sunday Times*, 21

September 1997; Ronald Hutton, 'What Is History Really About?', *Times Educational Supplement*, 26 September 1997; Samuel Brittan, 'The Many Failings of Post-modernism', *Spectator*, 27 September 1997; John Charmley, 'Time to Move Past Postmodernism?', *Daily Telegraph*, 27 September 1997, p. A4; Steven Kassem, 'In Defence of History', *Epigram*, 16 October 1997; Keith Thomas, 'A Good Kicking', *New Statesman and Society*, 17 October 1997, p. 46; A. C. Grayling, 'Historical Truth Put on the Line', *Financial Times*, Weekend Supplement, 25/26 October 1997, p. vi; Joyce Appleby, 'Does It Really Need Defending?' *Times Literary Supplement*, 31 October 1997, p. 10; Steve Smith, 'Truth in an Age of Challenge', *Times Higher Educational Supplement*, 28 November 1997, p. 26; Stefan Collini, 'The Truth-vandals', *Guardian*, 18 December 1997, p. 15; Daniel Johnson, 'The History Man', *Prospect*, November 1997, pp. 64–5; Matthew Trinca, 'History's Impossible Dream', *Australian*, 3 December 1997; Chris Harman, 'Subjects and Objects', *Socialist Review* 215 (January 1998), p. 27; Peter Ghosh, 'Laid Down by Ranke', in *London Review of Books*, 19 October 1998 (and subsequent correspondence in the *LRB*); Lynn Hunt, 'Does History Need Defending?', in *History Workshop Journal*, Issue 46, December 1998; Anthony Easthope, in *Textual Practice*, Winter 1998, pp. 563–6; Roy Porter, 'The Untrustworthy', in *The New Republic*, 14 December 1998; Steve Weinberg, 'Not All Ways of Recalling the Past are Equal', in *Christian Science Monitor*, Boston, 21 January 1999; David Gress, 'The "End" of History?', in *Orbis: A Journal of World Affairs*, Spring 1999, pp. 314–36; Doug Munro, in *Journal of Social History*, Vol. 32, Summer 1999, pp. 941–2; Diane Purkiss, 'Response to Professor Richard Evans', Internet <reviews-list@ihr.sas.ac.uk>; Keith Jenkins, *Why History? Ethics and Postmodernity* (London, 1999), Chapter 4, 'On Richard Evans', and elsewhere in the same book; Diane Purkiss, 'Richard Evans, Yet Once More', Internet <reviews-list@ihr.sas.ac.uk>.

In addition, this reply also considers some of the points raised in letters published in the *Times Higher Educational Supplement* on 19 and 26 September 1997 in response to my article 'Truth Lost in Vain Views', published in the same periodical on 12 September 1997 (p. 18). A longer and earlier version of this Afterword is published on the website of the Institute of Historical Research, University of London. It includes responses to the German edition, omitted here.

FURTHER READING

The classic starting-point for thinking about problems such as objectivity, causation and the role of the individual in history, E. H. Carr's *What is History?* (London, 1961), was reprinted posthumously in 1987 with a new chapter added by his collaborator the Soviet specialist R. W. Davies, giving some of Carr's reconsiderations based on notes for a second, revised edition. Carr completed the preface to this planned second edition before he died in 1982, and it is also reprinted by Professor Davies, along with Davies's commentary on Carr's notes. The new material makes interesting reading. Carr evidently intended, for example, to deal with the challenge to history posed by structuralist linguistics; it is a pity that death prevented him from grappling with this problem. Carr's own historical work *A History of Soviet Russia* (14 vols, London, 1950–78), is worth consulting to see how he put his views into practice; his book *The Russian Revolution from Lenin to Stalin 1917–1929* (London, 1979), is a handy one-volume summary. Norman Stone, 'Grim Eminence', *London Review of Books*, 20 January 1983, p. 982, is a notorious demolition job on Carr the man as well as Carr the historian.

Carr's principal conservative critic, G. R. Elton, put his views most cogently in *The Practice of History* (Sydney, 1967). This not only offers a trenchant defence of the neo-Rankean view of history as grounded essentially in the sources rather than in the theories and ideas of the historian, but also provides many hints on the practicalities of researching, writing and teaching. Elton's own qualities as a practising historian are still best sampled through his first book *The Tudor Revolution in Government: Administrative Changes in the Reign of Henry VIII* (Cambridge, 1953). His views are cogently criticized both in Lawrence Stone, *The Past and the Present* (London, 1981, subsequently republished with new material as *The Past and the Present Revisited*, and containing a splendidly readable collection of review essays mostly on major works of social history), and in Penry Williams and G. L. Harriss, 'A Revolution in Tudor History?', *Past and Present* 25 (1963), pp. 3–58.

For those who wish to know more about the history of history as a discipline, which features (mostly in passing) in both Carr and Elton's work, the best introduction is the collection of extracts from historians' manifestos through the ages published by Fritz Stern, *The Varieties of History: From Voltaire to the Present* (Cleveland, Ohio, 1956). For those seeking an outline history of history, Ernst Breisach, *Historiography: Ancient, Medieval and Modern* (2nd edn., Chicago, 1994), provides a serviceable if inevitably brief and selective introduction. In Georg G. Iggers, *New Directions in European Historiography* (London, 1985), the coverage of German social history is particularly useful. For critical accounts of recent German historiography, see Richard J. Evans, *Rereading German History* (London, 1997). The Italian 'microhistorians' are best approached through Edward Muir and Guido Ruggiero (eds), *Microhistory and the Lost Peoples of Europe* (Baltimore, 1991).

The changing aspirations and fortunes of social history in America can be traced in three editorials by Peter N. Stearns: 'Some Comments on Social History', *Journal of Social History*, Vol. 1 (1966–67), pp. 3–6; 'Coming of Age', *Journal of Social History*, Vol. 10 (1976/7), pp. 246–55; and 'Social History Update: Encountering Postmodernism', *Journal of Social History*, Vol. 23 (1989/9), pp. 176–87.

Harvey J. Kaye, *The British Marxist Historians* (Cambridge, 1984), is a useful and sympathetic introduction to a notable group of practitioners including E. P. Thompson, Eric Hobsbawm and Christopher Hill. There is also an illuminating collection of interviews with these and other left-wing historians edited by Henry Abelove and others, *Visions of History* (New York, 1978), made by the quaintly-named Mid-Atlantic Radical Historians' Organization and originally published in its journal *Radical History*. The coming of modern, largely non-Marxist social history in Britain was heralded by a special issue of the *Times Literary Supplement* on 7 April 1966, in which the contribution by Keith Thomas is perhaps the most notable. Eric Hobsbawm, 'From Social History to the History of Society', *Daedalus*, No. 100 (1971), pp. 20–45, is a classic statement of the optimism which social historians felt around this time. Theodore Zeldin, 'Social History and Total History', *Journal of Social History*, Vol. 10 (1976), pp. 237–45, was an early expression of scepticism by a historian more influenced, perhaps, by the *Annales* school.

On the *Annales* school itself, Peter Burke, *The French Historical Revolution: The Annales School 1929–89* (Oxford, 1990), is disappointingly basic and descriptive, and written in almost complete ignorance of the wider intellectual history of France in the period it covers. Peter Burke (ed.), *New Perspectives on Historical Writing* (Oxford, 1991), is also disappointing, arbitrarily thrown together, with contributions of variable quality, some of them extremely obscurely written. Jim Sharpe's chapter on 'History from Below', pp. 24–41, is perhaps the most perceptive. The best approach to the *Annales* school is still the wonderful essay by J. H. Hexter in his *On Historians* (London, 1979), written as a parody of the style of Fernand Braudel. Braudel's own musings can be found in his *On History* (Chicago, 1980); those of a leading figure in the third generation of *Annalistes* in Emmanuel Le Roy Ladurie, *The Territory of the Historian* (Brighton, 1979).

John Kenyon, *The History Men: The Historical Profession in England since the Renaissance* (2nd edn., London, 1993), is an entertaining and well-informed survey of its chosen subject, full of excellent detail; on the other hand, it is also a monument to the inveterate parochialism and conservatism of so many native specialists in English history. This applies even more to John Vincent, *An Intelligent Person's Guide to History* (London, 1995), a brief and sometimes thought-provoking introduction to the discipline which was originally commissioned by Oxford University Press but rejected because of a distinct (and, in truth, absolutely predictable) lack of political correctness. Vincent's slim volume takes much the same point of view as Kenyon, but narrows it down still further, and has some remarkably blinkered and prejudiced passages that demonstrate considerable ignorance about the world of historical scholarship outside the narrow confines of the history of Victorian high politics. As an antidote to Kenyon, Christopher Parker, *The English Historical Tradition since 1850* (Edinburgh, 1990), launches a sustained attack on the traditional empiricism of the profession.

Ved Mehta, *Fly and the Fly-Bottle. Encounters with British Intellectuals* (London, 1963), reprints a series of four lengthy articles originally published in the *New Yorker* magazine. The first two deal with philosophers; the third and fourth are about historians. They include a number of revealing and often hilarious interviews with notable scholars of the day such as Hugh Trevor-Roper, A. J. P. Taylor and the eccentric Namierite John Brooke, and offer an entertaining, intelligent and highly enjoyable introduction to some of the major historical controversies of the 1950s and early 1960s, including the row caused by E. H. Carr's *What is History?*. The fragmentation of the discipline a quarter of a century later can be observed in Juliet Gardiner (ed.), *What is History Today?* (London, 1988), which brings together a large number of very brief essays on the nature of political history, religious history, military history, and so on, by British practitioners of these various genres, some of whom pursue their own hobby-horses, others of whom occasionally have something of wider interest to say.

Among older works, Pieter Geyl, *Debates with Historians*

(London, 1955), is still worth reading for its discussions of historians from Macaulay and Michelet onwards, and above all for its demolition of Arnold Toynbee's *A Study of History* in Chapters 5 to 8. Geyl's *Napoleon: For and Against* (London, 1954) is a classic study of how historians' judgments have varied and clashed over time, according to the context in which the historians have written: the book concludes with Geyl's famous statement that history is 'argument without end'.

The conservative American historian Gertrude Himmelfarb, a specialist in the history of Victorian England, has been one of the most trenchant and articulate critics of all forms of historical scholarship which displace politics and events from the centre of the picture. Her two collections of essays, *The New History and the Old: Critical Essays and Reappraisals* (Cambridge, Mass., 1987), and *On Looking into the Abyss* (New York, 1994), are essential: highly readable and thought-provoking, but marred by a polemical technique which simply states her own position without arguing it, and tries to dispose of alternatives mainly by innuendo about the motives of those who advocate them. Himmelfarb invents something called 'the new history' out of very diverse forms of historical scholarship and then castigates it for failing to achieve unity or synthesis such as the (equally imaginary) 'old history' of politics supposedly did. Nevertheless, while her overall argument does not really convince, she manages to make a number of vitally important points along the way.

Peter Novick, *That Noble Dream: The 'Objectivity Question' and the American Historical Profession* (Cambridge, 1988), is a major historical survey of the American scene, far wider in scope than its title implies. Brilliantly written and profoundly researched, it is full of fascinating material and acutely perceptive analysis: not only essential reading but enjoyable too. Novick's strongly relativist position has attracted a predictable chorus of criticism. The lengthiest and most persuasive is perhaps by Thomas L. Haskell, 'Objectivity is not Neutrality: Rhetoric vs. Practice in Peter Novick's *That Noble Dream*', *History and Theory*, Vol. 29 (1990), pp. 129–59; another perceptive critique is James T. Kloppenberg, 'Objectivity and Historicism: A Century of American Historical Writing', *American Historical Review*, Vol. 94 (1989), pp. 1011–30. Theodore Hamerow, *Reflections on History and Historians* (Madison, Wisconsin, 1987), offers an alternative, often rather gloomy view of the American historical profession from a conservative point of view.

Although he wrote little original history himself, the Yale historian J. H. Hexter published a considerable quantity of well-informed, perceptive and often entertaining analyses of other historians' work. Some of these were collected in his *Reappraisals in History* (London, 1961). See also his *Doing History* (London, 1971), with a useful chapter on E. H. Carr. Hexter's *On Historians* (London, 1979), contains a famous attack on Christopher Hill, worth looking at as a basis for a discussion of perils of some historical methods led by ideology and for the question of whether similar things can be said about all methods. William G. Palmer, 'The Burden of Proof: J. H. Hexter and Christopher Hill', *Journal of British Studies*, Vol. 19 (1979), pp. 121–9, is a rather self-consciously literary account of the debate that nevertheless manages to make some good critical points. Hexter's attack originally appeared under the title 'The Burden of Proof', in the *Times Literary Supplement*, 24 October 1975; for Hill's 'Reply to Hexter', see the issue of 7 November 1975; Hexter wrote a 'Reply to Hill' in the issue of 28 November 1975.

Writings by philosophers on the nature of history are generally concerned with a narrow range of questions which are approached at a high level of abstraction, far above the level of real works of history. One of the most highly praised of such works, W. H. Walsh, *An Introduction to Philosophy of History* (3rd edn., London, 1967) is disappointingly laboured, and now seems seriously out of date. Michael Stanford, *The Nature of Historical Knowledge* (Oxford, 1986) is even more laboured, and mainly tries to develop a systematic description of what historians do, in terms acceptable to a reader trained in philosophy. Stanford's *Companion to the Study of*

History (Oxford, 1994), is a pedestrian survey of some of the major theoretical problems, relentlessly didactic in tone. R. G. Collingwood, *The Idea of History* (Oxford, 1946), is a difficult but rewarding classic.

The best starting-point for postmodernist theories of history is probably the work of the Dutch philosopher Frank Ankersmit: *Narrative Logic: A Semantic Analysis of the Historian's Language* (The Hague, 1983); 'Historiography and post-modernism', *History and Theory*, Vol. 28 (1989), pp. 137–53; and *History and Tropology: The Rise and Fall of Metaphor* (Berkeley, 1994). Ankersmit and his American colleague Hans Kellner have edited a varied collection of essays on *A New Philosophy of History* (London, 1995), of which the contribution by the medievalist Nancy F. Partner is the most intelligible. The nature of the turn to postmodernism by radical American historians is clearly expressed by Ellen Somekawa and Elizabeth A. Smith, 'Theorizing the Writing of History, or "I can't think why it should be so dull, for a great deal of it must be invention"', *Journal of Social History*, Vol. 22 (1988), pp. 149–61. D. Attridge *et al.* (eds.), *Post-structuralism and the Question of History* (Cambridge, 1987), is another collection of essays championing the 'linguistic turn'.

The most influential single figure in all this has probably been Hayden White, whose much-discussed but little-imitated *Metahistory: The Historical Imagination in Nineteenth-Century Europe* (Baltimore, 1987), was followed by a string of essays, collected in *Tropics of Discourse* (Baltimore, 1978), and *The Content of the Form* (Baltimore, 1987). These texts, for those who care about such things, were structuralist rather than post-structuralist in inspiration: but their use of literary theory to study historical works, and their relativistic relegation of the empirical content of history writing to a side-issue or an irrelevancy, opened the way to more radical postmodernist attacks on the ideas of truth and objectivity in historical research in texts such as Linda Hutcheon's *A Poetics of Postmodernism: History, Theory, Fiction* (London, 1988).

Elizabeth Deeds Ermarth, *Sequel to History: Postmodernism and the Crisis of Representational Time* (Princeton, 1992), is one of the most radical of postmodernist texts on history, arguing for the abolition of historical concepts of time. For an acute critique, see the review by David Carr in *History and Theory*, Vol. 32 (1993), pp. 179–87. Sande Cohen, *Historical Culture: On the Recoding of an Academic Discipline* (Berkeley, 1986), is perhaps the most extreme of all, worth looking at mainly to get an idea of the extent to which an author will go to invent jargon in order to advertise his 'scientific' approach to the subject.

There have been some notable attempts recently to popularize postmodernist ideas of history. One of the more accessible is Beverley Southgate, *History: What and Why? Ancient, Modern and Postmodern Perspectives* (London, 1996). The heavy weighting given to the discussion of ancient historians does not help the book's championing of the postmodernist approach. Alun Munslow, *Deconstructing History* (London, 1997) is another postmodernist history primer arguing along broadly similar lines. Keith Jenkins, *Re-thinking History* (London, 1991), an irritating mixture of condescending didacticism and wilful obscurity, still provides a useful summary – and sometimes vulgarization – of some of the main postmodernist positions. The same author's *On 'What is History'? From Carr and Elton to Rorty and White* (London, 1995), goes over the same ground at greater length and takes up some of the points made by both sides in the growing controversy over postmodernist approaches to history since the beginning of the 1990s; nearly half the book is devoted to a laboured exposition of the ideas of Richard Rorty and Hayden White. Geoff Eley, 'Is all the world a text? From social history to the history of society two decades later', in T. McDonald (ed.), *The Historical Turn in the Human Sciences* (Ann Arbor, 1992), is a largely uncritical account of the 'linguistic turn', whose precepts Eley has so far done little to incorporate into his own historical writing.

Among the many replies to and criticisms of the postmodernist attack on history and the 'linguistic turn' in historical studies, the best have so far appeared in article form. Perez Zagorin,

'Historiography and Postmodernism: Reconsiderations', *History and Theory*, Vol. 29 (1990), pp. 263–74, is a good place to start, offering a point-by-point reply from an American specialist in seventeenth-century English history to the earlier article in the same journal by Frank Ankersmit referred to above; Ankersmit's 'Reply to Professor Zagorin', *History and Theory*, Vol. 29 (1990), pp. 275–96, is characteristically arrogant and unconvincing. Hayden White's *Metahistory* was the subject of the *Beiheft* No. 19 of *History and Theory* issued in 1980 under the title *Metahistory: Six Critiques*. Among the most cogent critiques of White's work is an essay by the great historian of Ancient Rome, Arnaldo Momigliano, in his paper 'The Rhetoric of History and the History of Rhetoric: On Hayden White's Tropes', *Comparative Criticism: A Yearbook* (ed. Elinor Shaffer, Cambridge, 1981), pp. 259–68. White's ideas have also been taken up, and intelligently criticized, in a number of articles by the American intellectual historian Dominick LaCapra. His *History and Criticism*, (Ithaca, New York, 1985), is a brief collection of essays, of which the first, 'Rhetoric and History', is particularly relevant. Lloyd S. Kramer, 'Literature, Criticism, and Historical Imagination: The Literary Challenge of Hayden White and Dominick LaCapra', in Lynn Hunt (ed.), *The New Cultural History* (Berkeley, 1989), pp. 97–128, offers a critical perspective on both writers.

Among recent book-length defences of history against extreme postmodernist critiques, Joyce Appleby, Lynn Hunt and Margaret Jacob, *Telling the Truth About History* (New York, 1994), is mainly devoted to the specialist field of the history of science; the last three chapters, however, are worth reading as an attempt to refute the more subversive implications of the postmodernist critique of historical scholarship. Alan B. Spitzer, *Historical Truth and Lies about the Past* (Chapel Hill, 1996), argues that all political debates about the past, including those in which postmodernists are involved, ultimately appeal to criteria of objective truth and historical accuracy. His account of the de Man affair is particularly illuminating in this respect.

David Lehman, *Signs of the Times. Deconstruction and the Fall of Paul de Man* (London, 1991), is a lucid, witty and persuasive account of the furore surrounding the discovery of de Man's wartime activities and its implications for some aspects of postmodernist theory. Two volumes edited by Werner Hamacher, Neil Hertz and Thomas Keenan, *Wartime Journalism 1939–1943, by Paul de Man* (Lincoln, Nebraska, 1988), and *Responses: On Paul de Man's Wartime Journalism* (Lincoln, Nebraska, 1989), conveniently present virtually all the relevant material. Taking its cue from another, far less weighty scandal, Paul Boghossian, 'What the Sokal hoax ought to teach us', *Times Literary Supplement*, 13 December 1996, pp. 14–15, is a cogent and forceful attack on key postmodernist positions, taking as its starting-point the uproar occasioned by the acceptance by the postmodernist magazine *Social Text* of an article its author subsequently admitted was a parody of postmodernism, signalling its identity as a spoof by including numerous deliberate mistakes which were not spotted by the editors.

The most balanced and informed critique of postmodernist views on history from the left came from Raphael Samuel, in his two-part article 'Reading the Signs', *History Workshop Journal* 32 and 33 (1992), pp. 220–51. Like much of Samuel's work, it remained unfinished, and the promised third part, containing a direct critique of postmodernist hyper-relativism, never appeared. Bryan D. Palmer, *Descent into Discourse: The Reification of Language and the Writing of History* (Philadelphia, 1990), is a crude attack on the 'linguistic turn', reflecting the vulgar-Marxist position of its author. Another Marxist attack, on a more general front, Terry Eagleton's self-indulgent and overwritten tract *The Illusions of Postmodernism* (Oxford, 1996), does not even begin to address the challenge postmodernism poses to history. Equally disappointing, though coming at the problem from a completely different angle, is G. R. Elton's *Return to Essentials. Some Reflections on the Present State of Historical Study* (Cambridge, 1991), which contains three lectures on postmodernism and history, delivered in Michigan in 1990. The product of Elton's dotage, they mix prejudice and pomposity in equal measure and are useful mainly as a quarry for alarmist quotes. The two earlier lectures which make up the rest of this rather thin volume are not much better.

Pauline Marie Rosenau, *Post-Modernism and the Social Sciences: Insights, Inroads, and Intrusions* (Princeton, 1992), is a level-headed and wide-ranging survey of the state of play at the beginning of the 1990s. It usefully distinguishes between ultra-sceptical variants of postmodernism, which are deeply subversive of the social sciences, including history, and more constructive ones, which can be helpful and stimulating to self-reflection and disciplinary renewal. Another useful survey is provided by David Harvey, *The Condition of Postmodernism: An Enquiry into the Origins of Cultural Change* (Oxford, 1991).

Joan W. Scott, *Gender and the Politics of History* (New York, 1988), offers some postmodernist arguments in favour of the 'linguistic turn' from a feminist perspective. Catherine Hall, 'Politics, Post-structuralism and Feminist History', *Gender and History*, Vol. 3 (1991), pp. 204–10, voices some mild doubts. The Michigan-based historical anthropology journal *Comparative Studies in Society and History* ran an interesting and important exchange at the feminist end of the postmodernist spectrum in 1993. Laura Lee Downs, 'If "Woman" is Just an Empty Category, Then Why Am I Afraid to Walk Alone at Night? Identity Politics Meets the Postmodern Subject', *Comparative Studies in Society and History*, Vol. 35 (1993), pp. 414–37, begins with a perceptive critique of Scott's approach, but follows it up by a lengthy and not very plausible account of some psychohistorical work as a possible alternative. Scott's angry and dismissive reply, accusing Downs of 'ignorance and misrepresentation', a 'glib . . . superficial . . . and schematic' approach and 'an abdication of professional responsibility', and concluding that the article 'cannot be the basis for a serious discussion of the issues raised by post-structuralist and psychoanalytic theories for history,' appeared as '"The Tip of the Volcano"', *Comparative Studies in Society and History*, Vol. 35 (1993), pp. 438–43, and seems to me to be itself largely a tissue of misunderstandings, misrepresentations and indeed in part sheer invention. It was followed by Downs's 'Reply to Joan Scott', *Comparative Studies in Society and History*, Vol. 35 (1993), pp. 444–51, which does not add much, mainly because of its understandable refusal to pay back Scott in the same linguistic coinage.

Outside the specialized pages of *History and Theory*, the debate about history and postmodernism in the journals was slow to get started. The *American Historical Review* was first in the field, with an article by John E. Toews, 'Intellectual History After the Linguistic Turn', *American Historical Review*, 92 (1987), 879–908, followed by a double symposium on postmodernism in its 1989 issue. The opening article, by David Harlan, 'Intellectual History and the Return of Literature', *American Historical Review*, Vol. 94 (1989), pp. 581–609, puts the postmodernist case that intellectual history which tried to recover the meanings intended by authors like Thomas Hobbes or John Locke by relating them to their historical context was simply a 'trick'; the response by David Hollinger, 'The Return of the Prodigal? The Persistence of Historical Knowing', *American Historical Review*, Vol. 94 (1989), pp. 610–21, fails to grapple with the central theoretical points at issue. David Harlan's 'Reply to David Hollinger', *American Historical Review*, Vol. 94 (1989), pp. 622–6, repays him in the same coin. A second piece, by Allan Megill, 'Recounting the Past: "Description", Explanation, and Narrative in Historiography', *American Historical Review*, Vol. 94 (1989), pp. 627–53, says little of interest beyond attempting to rehabilitate description and narrative in the face of criticisms by *Annales* and other 'structural' historians who dismissed them as mere fact-grubbing. It was followed by a diverse set of articles in a forum on 'The Old History and the New', by Theodore S. Hamerow, 'The Bureaucratization of History', *American Historical Review*, Vol. 94 (1989), pp. 654–60, Gertrude Himmelfarb, 'Some Reflections on the New History', *American Historical Review*, Vol. 94 (1989), pp. 655–70, Lawrence W. Levine, 'The Unpredictable Past: Reflections on Recent American Historiography', *American Historical Review*, Vol. 94 (1989), pp.

671–9, Joan W. Scott, 'History in Crisis? The Other Side of the Story', *American Historical Review*, Vol. 94 (1989), pp. 680–92, and a judicious summing-up by John E. Toews, 'Perspectives on "The Old History and the New": A Comment', *American Historical Review*, Vol. 94 (1989), pp. 693–8, which managed to place Hamerow and Scott in one camp and Himmelfarb and Levine in the other, thus neatly reversing the polarities intended by the other four contributors. The forum spawned a further set of contributions, including Joyce Appleby, 'One Good Turn Deserves Another: Moving Beyond the Linguistic: A Response to David Harlan', *American Historical Review*, Vol. 94 (1989), pp. 1326–32. It continued in the *American Historical Review*, Vol. 97 (April 1992), in the form of an entertainingly critical article by Russell Jacoby, 'A New Intellectual History?', pp. 405–24, and a rather pompous and vapid reply by Dominick LaCapra, 'Intellectual History and Its Ways', pp. 425–39.

The debate in *Central European History*, though focusing on the implications of postmodernism and the 'linguistic turn' specifically for historians of Germany, was also wide-ranging. A number of articles were published in a special double issue of Vol. 22 (1989), Nos. 53–54, on 'German Histories: Challenges in Theory, Practice, Technique', resulting from a conference held in October 1989 on postmodern challenges to German history. The seeming promptness of publication was deceptive: at that time, the journal, produced in Atlanta, Georgia, was running years behind schedule: hence the seemingly incongruous remark of the editors of the special 1989 issue that the conference was held 'ages ago' (p. 229) when the volume would actually seem to the uninitiated to have been published before the conference had taken place. Among the most relevant contributions are Michael Geyer and Konrad H. Jarausch, 'The Future of the German Past: Transatlantic Reflections for the 1990s', pp. 229–59, Isabel V. Hull, 'Feminist and Gender History Through the Literary Looking-Glass: German Historiography in Postmodern Times', pp. 279–300, Rudy Koshar, 'Playing the Cerebral Savage: Notes on Writing German History Before the Linguistic Turn', pp. 343–59, and Konrad H. Jarausch, 'Toward a Social History of Experience: Postmodern Predicaments in Theory and Interdisciplinarity', pp. 427–43, all of which are written from an explicitly postmodernist perspective. Jane Caplan, 'Postmodernism, Poststructuralism, and Deconstruction: Notes for Historians', pp. 260–78, offers an intelligently-argued corrective. It is worth noting that while the actual historical work of one of the two editors, Michael Geyer, never easy to understand at the best of times, has now descended into complete incomprehensibility, the work of the other, Konrad H. Jarausch, remains resolutely empirical and has been seemingly completely uninfluenced by the postmodernist principles he appeared to embrace in 1989 (see for example Konrad H. Jarausch, *The Rush to German Unity* (New York, 1994)).

The debate in the British journals was generally less illuminating. The controversy in *Social History* centred on a book of (mostly previously published) essays by the Cambridge historian Gareth Stedman Jones, *Languages of Class: Studies in English Working-Class History 1832–1982* (New York, 1983), which registered its author's early enthusiasm for the 'linguistic turn'. Reflecting Stedman Jones's position as an influential figure in the rather restricted field of the left-wing, broadly Marxist historiography of the nineteenth-century British labour movement, the controversy had a decidedly parochial feel to it, which became stronger as it developed. It began with an article by David Mayfield, 'Language and social history', in *Social History*, Vol. 16 (1991), pp. 353–8, and was followed up by David Mayfield and Susan Thorne, 'Social history and its discontents: Gareth Stedman Jones and the politics of language', *Social History*, Vol. 17 (1992), pp. 165–88. This was followed by an angry and rather opaque riposte from two of Stedman Jones's Cambridge pupils, Jon Lawrence and Miles Taylor, 'The poverty of protest: Gareth Stedman Jones and the politics of language – a reply', *Social History*, Vol. 18 (1993), pp. 1–15, and another, even more irritated reply from the ubiquitous Patrick

Joyce, in 'The imaginary discontents of social history: a note of response to Mayfield and Thorne, and Lawrence and Taylor', *Social History*, Vol. 18 (1993), pp. 81–5. The controversy rumbled on, with an increasing tendency to generate more heat than light, and accusations of 'reductionism' flying around on all sides, in David Mayfield and Susan Thorne, 'Reply to "The poverty of protest" and "The imaginary discontents"', *Social History*, Vol. 18 (1993), pp. 219–33, James Vernon, 'Who's afraid of the "linguistic turn"? The politics of social history and its discontents', *Social History*, Vol. 19 (1994), pp. 81–97, Neville Kirk, 'History, language, ideas and post-modernism: a materialist view', *Social History*, Vol. 19 (1994), pp. 221–40, Patrick Joyce, 'The end of social history?', *Social History*, Vol. 20 (1995), pp. 73–91, and Geoff Eley and Keith Nield, 'Starting over: the present, the post-modern and the moment of social history', *Social History*, Vol. 20 (1995), pp. 355–64, the last-named being confined mainly to an attempt to rescue the concept of 'class' in a Marxist sense, misreading Patrick Joyce's position and largely avoiding the substantive issues, as Joyce points out in his rejoinder, 'The end of social history? A brief reply to Eley and Nield', *Social History*, Vol. 21 (1996), pp. 96–8. The whole debate is predicated on a narrow understanding of social history as a fundamentally Marxist project; it is, of course, far wider and more diverse than that.

Somewhat tangential to this debate, but well worth reading, is Anthony Easthope, 'Romancing the Stone: history-writing and rhetoric', *Social History*, Vol. 18 (1993), pp. 235–49, combining a brief exposition of some postmodernist ideas on history with an interesting analysis of the rather tired metaphors used by Lawrence Stone in an article of 1958; the theoretical consequences of the not altogether new discovery that Stone is prone to use cliché-ridden language are not immediately clear. Easthope does establish that the article in question assumes people bought titles for material rather than cultural reasons, but this is only an article, after all, and a familiarity with *The Crisis of the Aristocracy* would have shown Easthope that Stone was aware of other aspects of the aspirations of the upper classes in sixteenth- and seventeenth-century England as well. Nevertheless, this is one of a relatively small number of texts based on a linguistic analysis of a practising historian's published work, and important for that reason if for no other

Easthope's analysis was a discussion point when the debate exploded in the *Journal of Contemporary History* with an article by one of the journal's editorial board, Arthur Marwick, 'Two Approaches to Historical Study: The Metaphysical (Including "Postmodernism") and the Historical', *Journal of Contemporary History*, Vol. 30 (1995) pp. 5–35, an intemperate and sometimes ill-informed attack on a variety of targets, first delivered as Professor Marwick's inaugural lecture (after decades of occupation of the Chair of History at the Open University) under the title: 'Metahistory is Bunk – History is Essential'. It should be read in conjunction with the measured and surprisingly readable 'Response to Arthur Marwick' by Hayden White in the same journal, Vol. 30 (1995), pp. 233–46. The exchange prompted a series of articles in the *Journal of Contemporary History*, Vol. 31 (1996), in which the noise of grinding axes is sometimes difficult to ignore. They included Christopher Lloyd, 'For Realism and Against the Inadequacies of Common Sense: A Response to Arthur Marwick', pp. 191–207; Beverley Southgate, 'History and Metahistory: Marwick versus White', pp. 209–14; Wulf Kansteiner, 'Searching for an Audience: The Historical Profession in the Media Age – A Comment on Arthur Marwick and Hayden White', pp. 215–19; and Geoffrey Roberts, 'Narrative History as a Way of Life', pp. 221–8.

Briefer, but more to the point than much of this, was the exchange in *Past and Present* sparked by Lawrence Stone's opening warning shot, 'History and Post-Modernism', *Past and Present* 131 (1991), pp. 217–18, and followed by Patrick Joyce, 'History and Post-Modernism', *Past and Present* 133 (1991), pp. 204–9, Gabrielle Spiegel, 'History and Post-Modernism', *Past and Present* 135 (1992), pp. 194–208, Catriona Kelly, 'History and Post-Modernism', *Past and Present* 133 (1991), pp. 209–13, and a further exchange between

Stone and Joyce under the same title in issue 133, pp. 204–1, and 135, pp. 189–94. Gabrielle Spiegel, 'History, Historicism, and the Social Logic of the Text in the Middle Ages', *Speculum*, Vol. 65 (1990), pp. 59–96, is also relevant here.

What a postmodernist history might look like can be sampled in Patrick Joyce, *Democratic Subjects: The Self and the Social in Nineteenth-Century England* (London, 1994), Diane Purkiss, *The Witch in History: Early Modern and Twentieth-Century Representations* (London, 1996), Natalie Zemon Davis, *The Return of Martin Guerre* (Cambridge, Mass., 1983) and Robert Darnton, *The Great Cat Massacre* (London, 1983). Two important critiques of the latter two books, raising many wider issues, are Robert Finlay, 'The Refashioning of Martin Guerre', *American Historical Review*, Vol. 93 (1988), pp. 553–71, with a reply from Davis ('On the Lame'), ibid., pp. 572–603; and Harold Mah, 'Suppressing the Text: The Metaphysics of Ethnographic History in Darnton's Great Cat Massacre', *History Workshop Journal*, 31 (1991), pp. 1–20. Simon Schama, *Citizens: A Chronicle of the French Revolution* (New York, 1989), and Orlando Figes, *A People's Tragedy: The Russian Revolution 1891–1921* (London, 1996), exemplify the best aspects of postmodernism's influence on mainstream history, Simon Schama, *Dead Certainties* (London, 1991) the worst.

Some of the most problematical aspects of the impact of hyper-relativism are laid bare in Deborah E. Lipstadt, *Denying the Holocaust. The Growing Assault on Truth and Memory* (New York, 1993) a sober and well-informed account of the history of attempts to deny the reality of Hitler's death camps and the policies that led to them. Saul Friedländer (ed.), *Probing the Limits of Representation: Nazism and the 'Final Solution'* (Cambridge, Mass., 1992), provides a crucial collection of conference papers including a rethinking by Hayden White of his earlier positions ('Historical Emplotment and the Problem of Truth', pp. 37–53). The 'Abraham controversy', in which issues central to the debate over objectivity and partisanship in historical research were raised, is best approached through the special issue of the journal *Central European History* devoted to it (Vol. 17 (1984)), beginning with a lengthy critique of Abraham's work by Gerald D. Feldman, 'A Collapse in Weimar Scholarship', on pp. 159–77.

Since the first edition of this book was published, Keith Jenkins has produced a useful anthology of texts in *The Postmodern History Reader* (London, 1997), and a further dose of his own views in *Why History? Ethics and Postmodernity* (London, 1999). Joyce Appleby *et al.* (eds), *Knowledge and Postmodernism in Historical Perspective* (London, 1996) provides another anthology of texts. David Harlan, *The Degradation of American History* (Chicago, 1997) includes lengthy accounts of the ideas of White, Rorty and Foucault. John Arnold, *History: A Very Short Introduction* (Oxford, 2000) tries engagingly to work through some postmodernist ideas by examining some specific historical examples. By far the best and most thoughtful defence of postmodernist approaches to historical epistemology yet written is Robert E. Berkhofer, Jr., *Beyond the Great Story: History as Text and Discourse* (Cambridge, Mass., 1995).

Among recent critiques of postmodernist theories of history, the most comprehensive is C. Behan McCullagh, *The Truth of History* (London, 1998). McCullagh puts forward a reasoned defence of weak but meaningful concepts of truth and objectivity. Keith Windschuttle's alarmist *The Killing of History: How a Discipline is Being Murdered by Literary Critics and Social Theorists* (Paddington, New South Wales, 1994) is a collection of polemical critiques of postmodernist historians, entertaining but over the top.

Useful recent anthologies of theoretical texts include Robert M. Burns and Hugh Rayment-Pickard (eds), *Philosophies of History from Enlightenment to Postmodernity* (Oxford, 2000), and Anna Green and Kathleen Troup (eds), *The Houses of History: A Critical Reader in Twentieth-Century History and Theory* (Manchester, 1999). Michael Bentley's *Modern Historiography: An Introduction* (London, 1999) does what the title promises readably and concisely; Eric Hobsbawm, *On History* (London, 1997) is a collection of magisterial essays.

INDEX

*For further information about Granta Books
and a full list of titles, please write to us at*

Granta Books

2/3 HANOVER YARD

NOEL ROAD

LONDON

N1 8BE

enclosing a stamped, addressed envelope

———————————

You can visit our website at

http://www.granta.com

Dear mouse friends,
welcome to the world of

Geronimo Stilton